The Surviving Solo Series

Moving On
By Staying Still

Mary Hadow

Other Titles by Mary Hadow:

Surviving Solo Vol 1: Dare B&B
Surviving Solo Vol 2: Back On The Shelf
Snow Way

CONTENTS

To Mum

The WOW Factor
24/05/2015

"WOW!" breathes Faye. Four times. Trying not to, because she knows that's what I want her to say.

'Haldon Brake' is the fifth house that she has been forced to look at this afternoon.

Being thirteen years old, what impresses my daughter most about my proposed utopian love nest, are some metallic modern kitchen light fittings, and a sunken trampoline in the garden.

We're here because I have decided that finally I really must Move On – as all the post-divorce self-help books tell you to - after my marriage collapsed nearly six years ago.

I am braced to Start A New Life. To Begin All Over Again. To Put The Past Behind Me.

New home, new friends, new job, new bloke – to look ahead instead of backwards.

To close my B&B and become rich and famous through being a successful writer.

And, finally, to find myself a lifelong Soul Mate.

I've done childhood and marriage. Now I'm all ready for Chapter Three: Loving Partnership Through The Twilight Years.

Online dating's proved a disaster area. I really must meet some real men through real life. But to do that, I need to be near some. Which, at the moment, with me still stuck in our dilapidated family home, 'Wydemeet', in the middle of remotest Dartmoor, twenty minutes from a pint of milk, is not really happening.

If I move nearer to civilisation, perhaps I'll meet some there. Or, if I make myself famous, maybe they'll actually come to me!

So here we are. Operation 'Move On'.

There aren't that many houses in the small triangle southwest of Exeter where I want to be, so even fewer are available to buy. We've done well to find so many to look at - any one of which I would be happy to live in.

But this one - a Scandinavian wooden single storey chalet - really does have the 'wow' factor, as it looks thirty miles across the entire Exe valley towards Ottery St Mary.

It would be like buying a two-seater open-top sports car. A mid-life crisis, mad, impractical thing to do.

I think all three of us - Faye, my 18 yr old son Will, and myself - would be intensely proud to bring friends back to it.

I immediately put through a call to my estate agent, to ask him to check it out, but it's Bank Holiday Monday and his office is empty.

So for now I am forced to play the waiting game. I am trembling with excitement and apprehension. What will he say?

Oo-er
30/05/2015

"I loved the house and can see why you love it. It's very different and the views are awesome," charming Charles emails, three days later.

"It's a unique property, but one that I think will always fetch more than expected for the right buyer."

The green light.

I immediately contact the owner, an ageing rockstar from Tangerine Dream, telling him that I want to pay the asking price for his house, exchanging straight away (I can cash in a pension I'd forgotten about, thanks to the new government, and to my being so old) with a delayed completion for when I've sold my existing home; and then Faye and I head off to the health club for a swim, while my heart is pounding.

"Twist and Shout!!" Faye and I sing along to my truck, the Golden Monster's stereo system, as we sit in a traffic jam on our journey home.

"Could you just check my emails?" I yell at her, over The Beatles.

3G leaps into action.

"Time is not an issue," reads Faye.

"WHAT???????????!!!!!!!!!!!!!!!!!" I scream at her. "Read that again!"

"Time is not an issue," she repeats.

Mr Rockstar is prepared to wait for a delayed completion!

WOW! WOW! WOW!

So I'm buying it.

This is scary. Nearly as life-changing as finding a new partner. The one difference being that once you've found the house you want, it doesn't have to like you back.

So we're off. I'm buying the first house I've looked at, before mine is even properly on the market, let alone sold. This could prove quite a roller coaster! But it feels perfect! I am so very happy!

We're On
12/06/2015

We've gone live!

Wydemeet is now officially for sale. Not just listed on eBay anymore, but being sold through proper estate agents!

Two hundred full colour brochures have been printed, and we are listed on 'RightMove'.

And we have already had two viewings which came via the agents. The first one was an ex-Lloyds-Boy, with a pretty, delicate-looking Asian wife, who recognised me from my wilder London days (circa 1985); and the second was a couple who drove a Mitsubishi Shogun. This wife was wearing sparkly flip-flops and loads of make-up. No feedback since, from either of them. I'm wondering how either of the two ladies would cope with living an hour away from the nearest department store.

However, I won't be able to comment on further potential buyers coming to see round my house, as I am banned from being present.

"First time viewers feel much more comfortable if the vendor isn't there," said Charles. I am still unsure whether to take this personally or not.

Meanwhile, the little family who came to stay at my B&B a few weeks ago, has offered me a £10,000 deposit in order for me to reserve Wydemeet for them, while they wait for their own house to sell.

I said "I'd be nuts to go along with that in my current position - Wydemeet's only been officially on the market for a week!"

Everywhere I look I appear to be selling something. Myself on the 'Encounters' online dating site, my B&B on TripAdvisor, my holiday rental via the 'Owners Direct' site, and Wydemeet itself through Knight Frank. Sell, sell, sell. It's really hard work. I am exhausted. That's a lot of 'no's to experience every day.

Oh well. Chin up.

And what's worse, I can't keep the stupid moles, which are wrecking my 'lawn', at bay, so soon no one will want to buy, or even stay at Wydemeet anyway. I have stuffed all those odd socks you get left with after a wash, soaked in petrol, down the many, many mole holes, but this doesn't seem to have helped at all. Every time it rains - up pops another small mound of top-soil. Usually directly beneath the solar-powered mole scarers as the beasts' special little joke. And now there is an entire line of mounds winding its way right across the whole of my grassed area.

What Do Other People Think?
13/06/2015

"Crazy house! Hope it hasn't got woodworm," emailed back my sister, when I sent her details of my exciting new home. She likes trying to be funnier than I am.

So I'm sort of laughing now, and sort of worrying a bit too - what if it has? Well - I guess I could just burn it down and buy another flat pack, and ask Faye to knock up a new wooden chalet out of it for me. She's good at that sort of thing.

"Hi Mum - would you like to lend me £50,000 to exchange on a little wooden house I like? I'll complete once I sell Wydemeet," I enquire casually of my sensible 84 year old mother, over the phone, hoping to avoid cashing in my pension and incurring income tax on three-quarters of it.

"I think I'm a bit too old for that kind of thing," she replies. Damn. She thinks I'm mad, taking the risk of not selling my house in time to complete on the new one.

Time to garner some more opinions.

An old school friend who plays in a very successful folk music band and is a multi-millionaire as a result of the advertising agency he set up thirty years ago, just happens to live 2 1/2 miles down the road from my potential new lodgings. He is 6'4" tall, retains loads of thick red hair, sports a great big grey beard, and has a very loud, low, posh voice.

Anyhow - I ask him whether, as a new neighbour, he might like to visit my potential new home and see what he thinks.

"Why don't you go out with the owner?" is the first comment of his gorgeous wife, post-viewing.

I then send my sister-in-law over to take a look.

"It will be the most brilliant hang-out place for Brad (her son, my nephew) when he starts at Exeter University," I say. "The bus comes from central Exeter right past the drive!"

"I love it! Why don't you go out with the owner?" is her verdict, when I meet up with her later at my club, which I joined because it's directly opposite the Exeter Chiefs rugby club.

Half A Million Quid No Problem
28/06/2015

I am so excited about buying Haldon Brake that my digestion has been all funny for a week. I spend hours at a time day-dreaming about what it's going to be like living in the middle of Haldon Forest with my endless view, surrounded by youths from Exeter University drinking beer, lounging on the sun terrace by its little pool.

All that needs to happen now, before I hand the deposit over to my rockstar, is to have the thing surveyed to double-check that my sister's joke has not hit the mark, and it's not riddled with woodworm.

I speak to two surveyors from Exeter, and both want to do something called a 'Home Owners Report'. It costs over £500 plus VAT!!! I don't think so. A builder is what I need.

Renaldo, Issie's dad from school, is a developer, and over a barbequed burger at Issie's 13th birthday party he recommends Peter to me.

"Peter's a buddhist - gave me back half my money from the last job because he said I'd paid too much," explains Renaldo.

Peter and I start haggling almost immediately. "That'll be £45 for three hours' work," says Peter.

"That's far too little!" I complain.

"OK - just pay me what your conscience tells you," suggests Peter, and we leave it at that.

I draw up in the Golden Monster after Peter and Mr Rockstar have already spent half-an-hour going over the place.

Peter is jumping up and down with excitement. The beauty! The potential!

"I think, because it's all wood, we could turn it from the advertised four small bedroom, two titchy bathroom chalet, into a six largish bedroom, three big bathroom house, with stabling and a paddock, for £50,000, don't you?" I gabble.

And now I just can't sit still!

Five Years ... That's All It Takes
28/06/2015

David Bowie was wrong.

It takes more than five years to put a bust-up behind you, and restart with a clean slate.

In fact, if you've got children, I suspect it never quite happens at all.

But I've just had a brainwave.

I had been worrying that Mr Rockstar's little piece of Heaven was going to be a problem, as in where would I put all my furniture?

And then it dawned on me. I've hardly got any furniture! All the nice stuff belongs to Ex!

It's suited us both up until now for most of Ex's possessions to remain stored here at Wydemeet. These include about a million tiny porcelain tea and coffee sets, several large pieces of walnut inlaid furniture, hundreds of hand-cut glasses, huge old books that nobody has ever read, bookcases, flower vases, every single bedside table, about ten faded rugs, innumerable pictures, silver objects, china ornaments... all providing continuity for the children, a house with furniture in it for our B&B guests, and somewhere to live for all Ex's bits and pieces.

But now the time has come for me finally to have a place that is entirely my own, without reminders of Ex everywhere that I (as well as any potential new partner) look.

It's been nearly six years now, David, and counting! Watch this space Rendells Auction House!

Exchange and Completion - Simples
28/06/2015

I'd forgotten about a couple more pensions I've got. They're worth fifty thousand each! Handy! One's meant to be dedicated to covering Beloved Daughter's school fees, but what the Hell.

Thank you government, for allowing me to cash them in now I'm 55. I'm rich! Hurray!

To get my hands on the first one, they insist I appoint a financial adviser. He's called Tom and sounds terribly nice. Answers the phone immediately, on a Sunday!

For the second, I need to prove that I was married and have changed my surname. But I've lost the Decree Absolute and my marriage certificate. I don't think the court ever sent them back, actually. What a pain. I will need duplicates.

Anyhow. So £55,000 for exchange is no problem! I needn't lean on Mum or the family or anyone else after all! We can worry about the rest later!

Or can we.

My new solicitor's blurb about buying Haldon Brake has pages and pages in it about where the finance for completion is to come from.

I research buy-to-let-mortgages, bridging loans, and family trust money.

Oh no. Oh dear. Oh no, no, no.

This is not going to happen. I am sitting on around £850,000 if the estate agents' valuations of Wydemeet are correct, but I cannot extract the money. I can't believe we're talking about such a catastrophic, life-changing, cash-flow problem. Nobody is going to lend me half a million quid, not knowing when or if I am ever going to sell my home.

The cheapest loan would be a buy-to-let mortgage, and that would incur a fee of £18,000 at the very least to cover just six months. What if I don't sell Wydemeet this summer? What if I don't sell it next summer? It would be utterly mad to go ahead and sign on the dotted line.

I cannot buy Haldon Brake.

Could you please excuse me for a second?

I've got to have a little sob.

Angus, Thongs and Full Frontal Snogging
29/06/2015

I am feeling a little more upbeat about my potential new career as a writer today. Well - at least my scribblings might appeal to 13 year olds.

Because, having purloined Faye's copy of "Angus, Thongs and Full-Frontal Snogging", to my surprise and glee I'm finding that its author, Louise Rennison, and I appear to share a similar sort of approach to this writing thing.

One difference being, of course, that my diary is true, whereas that of Georgia Nicolson, the 14 year old heroine of AT&F-FS, is made up. The same going for, fairly obviously, those other well-known diarists: Adrian Mole and Bridget Jones.

I am absolutely loving AT&F-FS though. This, and something by Sophie Kinsella that I've just finished, are the only books I've read for years that have actually made me laugh out loud.

I googled "Funniest British Female Authors" to see if I was missing something, and it would appear that I'm not. Ms Kinsella occupies almost every slot in the top 40; Jill Mansell, Jilly Cooper and Helen Fielding come up once or twice, and there doesn't seem to be anybody else much. No wonder I can never find anything good to read at the airport.

I think that every mother of a teenager should read Ms Rennison's Georgia Nicolson books.

AT&F-FS, for instance, has explained and excused Faye's apparent current obsession with boys. In the book, Georgia dreams 24/7 about a boy who is much older than she is, who clearly sees her as an irritating child. It would appear that Georgia lives in total fantasy land regarding this little chap. I don't know what happens next in the book, because I haven't finished it yet, but I do know that in real life, almost every passing male teenager appears to turn into the temporary target of Beloved Daughter's dreams. She's almost worse than me!

Four Blobs!
01/07/2015

They've driven into a rock and got a puncture. They call me up and I go and collect them from Huccaby Bridge. Their Hertz hire car doesn't come with a spare. I spend four hours on the phone, working out how to get the thing fixed. I have upgraded them and put them in my Hexworthy Room without charging extra - a saving of £60. The sun shines and all is beautiful for their three day stay.

Today I have discovered that they've only given my B&B four blobs out of five on TripAdvisor. The full five for service, but only four for 'room' and for 'cleanliness'. Wydemeet's ranking under 'Best B&Bs on Dartmoor' zooms downwards, from No 4 to No 10.

How could they do this to me? 57 reviewers out of 57 giving me the full monty can't be wrong! Hexworthy represents fantastic value at Dartmeet's price of £110pn! I know I don't clean the bath out every day, but surely they haven't noticed?

And then it dawns on me. They were helping themselves to the very expensive home-made lemon curd I'd bought as a special treat for them, from down the road in Ponsworthy, and they found it had gone a bit mouldy around the top of the jar. I am never serving lemon curd again.

Crusty the Clown
01/07/2015

One of my daughter's posh school leavers' rituals is to get their ears pierced.

Apparently I promised Faye that she could get hers done if she won a scholarship to Big School.

Well I forgot all about that, but I was very aware of the school custom, and badgered by Faye, booked an appointment at Tavistock's beauty salon for her. It was just before her sax lesson.

They do it with a gun that goes blip, as it pushes out a blob of skin and replaces it with a gold-plated stud. Enough to make any loving mother feel sick.

Driving back to school after the lesson it was all too apparent that Faye was far more excited about her pierced ears (£20), than her new sax (£250).

A few days later, all the school leavers went camping and surfing for a few days.

Faye returned with a rash, burns and blistering all over her neck so bad that the minute I'd picked her up, we went to the local hospital, where they supplied her with antibiotics and steroid cream.

Today, the bubble of skin in the middle of her chest is 3/4" inch high, and full of puss. Her entire neck is nothing but orangey green hard scales hanging off. I have to rub the cream on. It makes my mouth water with a sort of feeling of nausea and general repugnance. To cheer ourselves up we make ourselves laugh about how she resembles Crusty the Clown and Fungus The Bogeyman. Sashka, my partner in crime, right arm, left arm and both legs when it comes to running the B&B and looking after my horses, remarks that I should be reported to the NSPCC. But if we didn't laugh, we'd cry.

We think the condition has been caused by chemical burning of the skin, through over-use of liquid undiluted antiseptic in the sunshine, wind and salty sea air. Funny that - as it's supposed to be used to cure burns, not cause them!

This morning Faye went to school in a scarf.

If You Snooze You Lose
01/07/2015

'If You Snooze You Lose' has become my life's mantra, as of last Saturday.

I was wondering whether to make myself go to Widdifest again this year - the party down the road that, in the end, I loved so much last time. When the other day Sashka suggested that we go together, instead of each of us having to walk in alone, I was touched to my core.

Astonishingly, scarf, scabs and all, Faye proved determined to come with us too.

Sashka and I began the evening at our hamlet's mansion where she was house-sitting, with a bottle of Pink Cava, while Faye watched a re-run of Harry Potter, and then the three of us ambled over to the by now swinging party.

Well. When I say swinging. There was a lot of jolly barn dancing going on, the fiddle amplified to a level where it was very difficult to hear anything else.

I felt, as usual, that if I were to conduct a shouted conversation with any of the assembled local throng, it would have to be me that started it.

There they all sat or stood around. Complacent, happy, smug marrieds. Each wretched loving partner negating that fear in the other, of finding themselves left all alone in a corner, Billy No Mates, like me. All chatting away to other jolly couples, dads to dads discussing the latest crop yields, mums to mums comparing teachers at the local comprehensive.

Never does it cross any of their un-empathetic minds how horrid and difficult it is to be at these things on your own. Never do any of them come over to me, to help make things easier for me.

Not kind. Not considerate. Not thoughtful. Not fair.

Bet none of them would even dare come through the door of this party if they were on their own. There is not one person, male or female, in this entire local so-called community, who is living alone like me. A pariah.

Other mums daily driving backwards and forwards past my gate. In all these years, not one of them has ever dropped by for a coffee, or to check if I'm coping OK on my own, in my great big lonely isolated house.

I've nothing in common with any of them, except, say, well, where do we start: horses, children, mutual acquaintances, location, the changing seasons, the National Parks, tourists, twenty minutes to a pint of milk, etc etc

If they'd been left all alone like I have, I bet they would have scuttled off back to their Mums and to civilisation, rather than sticking it out, rattling around in the old family home, in order to provide some stability to their children, where the only single males within a ten mile radius have four legs and are covered in wool.

What did I ever do to deserve this? Why do I force myself to be sociable, over and over and over again? I must be crazy, banging my head against a brick wall in order to achieve what, exactly? What sort of a community is this?

Maybe it's me? In my darker moments I wonder whether none of them likes Mad Mary, Lady Muck of the Moor, and they only answer my jolly chat out of courtesy. But somehow I do have loads of friends elsewhere, and have never had any trouble before.

Well. No more.

I had a go at making small talk with various people, but quickly became a bit hoarse. We couldn't find anybody there at all from Faye's generation. Neighbour (who lives on the other side of a field from us, and who has children the same gender, and almost the same age) had, yet again, invited all the local teenagers around for a sleepover at her house, except for my precious, sweet, gentle, in-offensive, warm and friendly daughter.

Should we just give up and go home?

"If you snooze, you lose," remarked Faye, as she headed off on a circuit of the carpark in a valiant last attempt to track down just somebody that she knew of her own age. No one.

She's only 13. She was tired and in pain. She looked like Elephant Woman beneath the scarf. I couldn't believe how determined and brave she was. I smiled. What a proud Mum.

But we're not going back to that party again next year. Because we are going to have moved to Haldon Brake, finally to live in a thriving community of friendly, open, like-minded people who are genuinely pleased to see us.

God I just so can't wait to move. Nowhere can be as bad as this. Sell, Wydemeet! Sell!

DaDaDaDaDa
03/08/2015

"You're always saying that," comments Will, as for the nth time I try to reassure him that I'm highly busy and efficient - that the hours and hours I spend tapping away on the computer instead of entertaining him during his all too short holidays isn't just flirting online with potential computer dates.

Truly though, each day does seem to be dadadadadadada, from preparing B&B breakfasts, to collapsing in front of the telly with a plate of microwaved leftovers at 9pm.

This week's B&Bers have been the most wonderful family. They used to stay a couple of times a year at Wydemeet with their friends who owned the house before it became an Adventure Centre.

That would have been thirty years ago! Wydemeet was a comfortable, much loved and very happy family home back then, they told me.

I was surprised by this, because when Ex and I moved in, back in 1995, the house was practically derelict! I was scared to go upstairs because I thought the floor might cave in! There were bunk-beds for 36 stuck in every conceivable nook and cranny. Wind whistled through the windows, walls and floors. The kitchen was dark brown and covered in grease, with a hole in the wall where presumably the defunct Rayburn's chimney once went. The water supply required regular priming outside, with the use of a hand pump and three pieces of string holding up various bits and pieces in the holding tank - normally in Gale Force 10 and lashing rain. The house hadn't been over-wintered in for two years. It felt to me as though it had been gradually falling to pieces, the electrics and plumbing remaining untouched, since it was built during the first World War. But now it would appear that actually, it only took a couple of years for the house to simply fall to bits. Scary how quickly decay can set in.

Cooked breakfast for four at once may not sound too challenging, but it still makes me feel as though I've run a marathon. Well perhaps 100 metres. And 'refreshing' two bedrooms is not exactly hard - it's just that at my great age I feel quite tired once all that is done, and the day has hardly started.

And of course I spend a great deal of time chatting to my guests.
I love the idea of getting paid to chat to nice people.

The upside of the rationalisation of my recent marketing efforts (I'm now relying solely on TripAdvisor for publicity, having sacked all the horrible greedy agents), has been that without exception, all guests who booked direct through my website entirely 'get' the concept of Wydemeet B&B, and are a genuine pleasure to have around the house.

The downside is that I am empty for the whole of August. August?!
EMPTY!!!!

And Wydemeet has now slithered right down to Number 11 on
TripAdvisor, despite reviews that would make you weep with touchedness.

I have spent a long time working out whether there is something wrong
with my booking form or email communications resulting in this total
dearth of bookings during peak season on Dartmoor, but no. It is as clear
as crystal, not mud. Nobody has booked to stay at the fantastic
Wydemeet for the whole of, no - not January - August!!!

I have altered my website and booking conditions to say how much we
love all sweet little children and gorgeous small dogs, and then finally,
most reluctantly, I've allowed TripAdvisor to take bookings direct, for a
12% commission.

All is so uncertain with the house on the market that I have taken my eye
off the ball, and this is the result. Eeek!

Dartmoor vs The New Forest
03/08/2015

This renting out my entire house for a massive sum for a week lark is
getting easier. Sashka does everything these days. She likes me out of her
hair so that she can concentrate properly. This means that I can go away
on holiday for even longer, while she gets the house ready before our
guests arrive.

It's important to me to feel that I am enjoying myself during the times that
my home is being lived in by somebody else.

I'm back home again now from my latest little trip, this time to The New
Forest, and I loved it so much that I'm wondering whether we made a
mistake in choosing to live on Dartmoor.

The New Forest is a bit like Dartmoor having been stamped on by some giant. Rather as the Evoque is a bit like a stamped on Range Rover.

The New Forest boasts the best riding I've ever done in my life - you can gallop without stopping for miles, and not get lost, you don't drown in bogs, or even have to go the same way twice; and there's nobody else anywhere around. And I appreciate the well managed, straight paths which actually lead to places; the signage; and the 1000s of healthy, pretty wild ponies which, unlike the Dartmoor ones, don't attack you, the stallions being properly graded and kept off the moor for most of the year.

Except for. The donkeys.

I set out alone on a long expedition riding my horse, Mad Vegas, to a pub called "The Fighting Cockerels". Vegas trod on Twiglet the dog, but otherwise didn't seem to be too crazy that day. As we approached our destination, though, I realised that this must be one of the busiest days of the year in the Forest. People and traffic everywhere, the pub located on a main road.

Vegas and I bounced towards it, aiming for something to tie her up to. Nothing. While some guard dogs growled at us, and all the tourists stared. Twiglet out of control in the middle of the road. And suddenly, completely out of nowhere, a honking, braying donkey charged up right behind us. Vegas bolted. The donkey galloped after, screaming. Twiglet leaped about in the middle of the traffic. Vegas and I went flying down the road, the donkey galloping after. I turned in the saddle to see the donkey mounting another one, still braying its stupid head off, while the onlookers gasped. Twiglet appeared still to be 3D as opposed to squashed flat in the middle of the highway.

God, I really needed a drink now! But the group of donkeys had gravitated towards what I could see was the horse tying-up place. Nightmare city.

Time to give up and head for home.

£775,000
14/08/2015

They've put in an offer of £775,000 for Wydemeet.

Only £775,000 for my beautiful home? What an insult!

But of course it isn't - it's just a toe in the water.

After a bit of bartering, the final offer from my lovely little B&B family is £800,000, as one might have predicted. That's a whopping £50,000 below the asking price!

I don't feel elated at all, and rather fearfully email the lady who sells me sausages, asking for her off-the-record advice about whether I should accept this (her other job is estate agent).

I tell her that the Daily Mail says we're in a sellers' market, that I have heard that the property market will wake up in September, and, most importantly, Wydemeet is due to be featured on Channel Four's reality TV programme, Four In A Bed!

"Good buyers are few and far between," she says. "Accept their offer, but tell them that you will put your house back on the market in September if you haven't exchanged by then."

So that's what I've done. Ooh er missus.

Taking a Horse to Water
14/08/2015

A couple of tears slide down my face, as I hide in the horses' barn.

I have to face it. My rural dream for my children hasn't worked.

They never take the dog for a walk. As a family we've only ever been on two - what I would term 'proper expeditions'. They never go out of the garden gate of their own volition. They have never made camps in the rough field between Wydemeet and the river. They don't fish. They don't go for bicycle rides. They don't make dams in the river. They don't explore. They don't know the names of any of the tors or birds or flowers or grasses or trees.

They would rather live in Surbiton next to a bus-stop and a railway station, with teenage friends, cinemas and cafes down the road, than here in the middle of remotest Dartmoor.

Sending them 100 miles away to boarding school doesn't help with local friends either. Why do we do it? I still can't answer that exactly.

Faye is a bit of a Devon Girl because of the horses. She knows more 13 year old girls on the moor than anyone else, with her heritage of local village school, local prep school and the pony club, which draws in girls from every conceivable background and from every corner of East Dartmoor. She likes riding to places across the moor too. So all has not been lost there, and her new school isn't all that far away, so she will always have lots of friends round about.

But when I sell the house there is no going back. Neither child will ever know every inch of their heritage, as I did when I was a child.

Does it matter? If your children are balanced, kind and confident - perhaps that's enough?

One In A Million!
14/08/2015

"I've done this psycho-thing and I've come out at one in five thousand for original lateral thought," comments Ex this morning, over his boiled egg and soldiers.

"Only one in five thousand?!" I splutter. "You're one in a million! Any of those identikit blue chip companies would benefit from having you on their board, bringing with you a spot of fresh thinking and individuality."

It's nice to be able to rave about the children's father in front of them. We are in a place now where it is a genuine pleasure having him to stay, and even better if his new girlfriend and her daughters can come along too.

Courage is like a muscle - it improves with use
14/08/2015

"See that girl over there? Would you believe that she used to be a nervous rider too?" instructor Jenny encouraged a terrified twelve year old on her naughty little bay pony.

Meanwhile, across the field, Mad Vegas of the Rolling Eye was jumping up and down making sure that everyone was admiring her, while Faye sat firmly astride, laughing her head off.

It's been a long old haul and lots of tears to get this far.

"Don't take any notice of her crying - that's what she does," I've said to many a music teacher and riding instructor along the way.

And here we are now. A happy, confident, able rider, musician and performer.

"Character forming - that's what it is," I inform Will, when he queries why anyone on earth would ever want to get involved with horses.

Early Onset Dementia
19/08/2015

Is it?

Or is it just too much for one middle-aged brain to take on board?

I'm sitting here at my Mum's house in Dorset, bashing away on this utterly fantastic new laptop I've just bought, which has completely changed my entire attitude to the world.

It's called an Acer Chromebook and I bought it in a 30 minute slot I had yesterday at 'Curry's PC World' in the arse-end of Exeter. But now I've bought this laptop I am happy, in a situation that I might otherwise be a bit miserable in.

My Mum (85) is upstairs with a cracked vertebrae and a very upset tum resulting from her meds. She will now only eat rice, and drink Lucozade Sport (orange). I gave her long grain with soy sauce for main course, and short grain with bananas for pudding.

Meanwhile, from this satellite headquarters, I'm dealing with collecting my children from Ex's house, cancelling most of the social life I'd planned for this week, and in the meantime September's B&B bookings appear to be going ballistic for some reason.

I've just come off the phone to The Telegraph, who, on September 12th, are to publish a feature on Wydemeet B&B in their property section.

We're also going to be on telly. And hopefully my first book, "Dare B&B", will be published shortly after!

Followed, with a bit of luck, by the sale of Wydemeet!

I also have a change of health club imminent - to the Exeter Golf and Country Club where people actually speak to each other. I might even meet a man in a zig-zag jumper!

And then finally yesterday, in the middle of Curry's PC World, whilst testing out laptops, I was called by Knight Frank. The conversation resulted in a compromise regarding my taking Wydemeet off the market whilst my B&B buyers, my rock star and I all work towards a mutual fast completion.

We have agreed that Knight Frank will take the contact details of anyone interested in buying Wydemeet, but won't conduct any viewings until the Telegraph article gets published, by which time my buyers should have sorted themselves out.

By then, they should be so close to exchange that only a Russian oligarch appearing at my front door with a suitcase of £900,000 in notes, would be able to deflect things.

So I've just changed the front page of my B&B website to say:

"Quick! This is probably your last chance to experience maybe the most remote, comfortable, and romantic luxury B&B in all Dartmoor!

We have just two rooms available, and we are taking bookings only until end-September, as Wydemeet is now under offer.

Come Spring 2016, however, we hope to offer you something even more special! Your own totally private cabin, sheltered in two acres of secret woodland glade, everything done new to the highest possible spec, a herd of wild deer peeping through your door, views stretching 30 miles across the Exe Valley. Total privacy, little swimming pool, hot tub, sun deck, incredible walking, cycling and riding in the Haldon Forest, fantastic nearby eating and drinking, and Twiglet, Faye and Me, wanting to be taken for walk, and preparing your scrumptious breakfast respectively, as ever!

All just a convenient 20 minute bus-ride direct to the end of the drive from Exeter St Davids railway station!

I'll probably charge £150 B&B for two, for a minimum of two nights.

You'll need to move fast, though, as we can only accommodate one couple at a time (we're only doing this at all because we enjoy having you to stay so much!) and I think demand is likely to go through the roof, because:

Our participation in Channel 4's 'Four In A Bed' B&B reality competition is to be broadcast sometime this September. And it's seriously funny! (if you can be 'seriously' funny). Also shocking. And moving, too.

Wydemeet B&B is to be featured in The Daily Telegraph on September 12th.

And my first book, 'Dare B&B', is, at last, nearly ready for publication!

So please supply your contact details if you'd like to reserve a stay in my Secret Retreat, or buy a book, and I'll be in touch in due course.

Alternatively make your reservation online now, to be sure to enjoy Wydemeet just one more time!"

Hmmmm. We'll see. Not your average home page for a B&B, but hey! Life's an experiment!

I've already received a booking for two days' time, so perhaps my new approach is working?!

And in the meantime, how many things have I forgotten?

To hang up Mum's washing.

To water the beans.

To take the black sack to the end of the lane.

To book the taxi driver for the eye appointment.

To get some cash out for Mum to pay the cleaner.

To take some more bog roll upstairs.

And that is only the things I can remember that I have forgotten.

Two nights ago my sister and I stood in the grounds of her new palace, watching the sun setting across the valley over neighbouring Highclere/Downton Abbey, and agreed that we were both rather proud to be turning into our mother.

Today, provided she steers clear of the nightmare painkilling drugs, it would appear that my Mum is rather more on the ball than I am!

In Pain
20/08/2015

These days I appear to be constantly suffering from something.

I had been about to announce that for once I felt fine. And then my golfers' elbow came back.

But I have found a cure. It's really rather simple. Now that I prop up my new laptop against the breadboard, the pain has gone away again.

8.15am
26/08/2015

"How are you, Mum?" It's Will on the phone.

"I don't really know yet, I haven't woken up properly," I yawn.

"Would you like to hear my GSCE results?" he casually continues.

Yikes! God I'm such a hopeless mother! It's Thursday! Results day! Tell me! Tell me!

He's done great. The relief is overwhelming.

"You're not to go around telling everyone," he warns me sternly.

"OK - only Granny," I reluctantly acquiesce.

Granny, so small, so ill, so vulnerable, lying in her bed, offers herself up for a hug, grins broadly and nearly falls onto the floor with excitement at the news.

And then, silence. I'm not allowed to find out how his results compare with everybody else's.

So now I am in limbo. Desperate to know what my friends' children have achieved, in this, the first, national, objective, overview of academic ability. But that's forbidden.

There's More
26/08/2015

That car ahead of you, indicating left but going straight on, will be a Peugeot, according to Clarkson.

I have found myself reading another of his books. Everything he's written has the same cover and the same name - "Oh God I Can't Stand Any More" or something, so I was disappointed that when I got this particular one home, it turned out to be all about cars.

So now I know quite a lot about the various makes and models that were launched between 2011 and 2013, especially supercars (I really hadn't appreciated that most of them cost nearly £1/4 million) and I've found the book actually quite gripping. Although I'm not sure about the Peugeots. I've been cut in front of twice this week by something called a Suzuki Swift.

It's such a treat to have a book you look forward to reading, and at the moment, I've got two!

The other one's called "Wife in the North". This has made me terribly excited, and put me in a sunny mood.
It was recommended to me by my latest lovely B&B couple, who said it was written by a woman, in blog form, similar to mine.

So I immediately looked it up on Amazon. It turns out that it was published by Penguin in 2008, and it was read out on Book of the Week on Radio 4! So I devoured the sample pages that you're allowed to see online, to discover that it was all about this woman who had moved to Northumberland because her husband wanted her to, and how much she hated it, moaning on and on.

Anyhow - that's why I'm so excited at the moment. If they haven't become bored with this genre in the ensuing years, there might be a place in

Penguin's library for my little tome! Because Michael Joseph, which owns Penguin, was the company responsible for publishing Ex's best seller back in 2005, and the editors there, who I have met, said they were highly interested in taking a look at anything I might produce! So hah! I must hurry! Sort out my scribblings and see what they think!

Red Rose and Fried Egg
04/09/2015

Now I know all about self publishing.

It's so easy it's frightening!

I have discovered Chrome Documents on my fantastic new Chromebook, and moved the text of my book onto it/them. This means that I can easily amend the copy anytime, from anywhere. And then if I turn it into 'Word', I can move it direct to Amazon's kindle! So I've done that, and I think it looks really good!

So now I need a 'Kindle Cover'. There are several libraries of pics you can download, some for free, to make up the template of the cover, and also some specialist designers who could do it all for you, who advertise themselves on the web.

I had initially asked Will whether he might draw a cover for me, including cartoons of me stamping on a mole, him slouching off looking grunge, Faye smiling and waving a broom; Sashka waving a mop, Twiglet leaping around carrying a 'B&B Vacancies' sign in his mouth, and the two horses looking on, bemused,

But we decided it was all a bit difficult.

So later that night, at around 1am, when I'm still obsessively progressing the whole thing, I stumble across a picture of a single red rose above a fried egg in the shape of a heart. Hah!

'Dare B&B' is ready to go live!

Daily Telegraph Pic
04/09/2015

I wash my hair for the first time in a week.

I have tried to sack myself from my health club in order to join the new one, but I'm not sure whether the contract allows this, and daren't visit either one until I have found out, in case I end up having to pay for both at once. Hence I have finally succumbed to bathing at home, and have just got the hairdryer out as Twiglet goes ballistic, because a car is pulling up outside.

I wander down in my 'Four In A Bed' uniform: black cowl neck jumper, black M&S Per Una Trousers, and black high heeled suede boots. It is unbelievable how much thinner I look in this outfit than in anything else.

"Could you possibly not wear black?" asks the photographer, very politely.

"If we were the Daily Mail I would have to ask you to wear a floral dress, but in the Telegraph's case, just anything but black," he begs.

"Oh alright - what about grey?" I reply. That seems to be OK so I put on my grey sloppy top which keeps falling off my shoulders and revealing a black bra strap. I hope that's not too sexy for the Telegraph, and doesn't make me look like a slapper.

I have a coffee to calm my nerves, while Faye, in little floral skirt, catches Vegas for the Big Shoot. The instructions are that the picture should also include Twiglet. Justin, the photographer, is braced to work with both animals and children. We could be here all day!
Anyhow, Mad Vegas is behaving remarkably well, as Faye hops onto her, no hat, no tack, and I lead her by a rope attached to a head collar.

We keep having to wait for the sun to go in, to get a good pic without too many contrasting shadows. So backwards and forwards we walk, about ten times in all, up and down the drive, with Twiglet in front of us and Wydemeet behind.

"Nice! This could be a full page picture if we're lucky," comments Justin.

Yikes!!! I'd thought it was going to be a little thing similar to The Times using Wydemeet as 'Property of the Week'.

I've already spent 45 minutes boring the property correspondent of The Telegraph stupid about my B&B. I'd better get my act together and ask her to include a sentence promoting the imminent publication of my book too! This could Go Large!

Disaster!
04/09/2015

Rockstar's taken his house off the market.

The job he had anticipated in Florida has been put on hold for a year, and so he wants to stay in the home that he has created for himself. This whole property buying business seems to be a bit more like online dating than I had thought.

So I've searched my soul and decided that £800,000 is not enough to make me want to leave Wydemeet and camp somewhere else for who knows how long until something I love as much as Haldon Brake comes onto the market. I've just told the nice little family who want to buy Wydemeet as much. They have been extraordinarily fatalistic about it, but haven't offered me any more money. I'm not convinced that Wydemeet really is their dream home - possibly more of an investment, if that is possible in central Dartmoor.

Call me over-emotional, but I would prefer to sell Wydemeet to someone who arrives literally jumping up and down with unsuppressed excitement when they see it. They'll probably look a bit eccentric and be slightly off the wall. No one like that has come to see it yet. Most viewers have looked rather smart, and not very outdoorsy. Nobody has leaped out of a beaten up old 4x4 with a "I'm Perfect for Wydemeet!" vibe coming off them - but I suppose you can never tell for sure.

And the next few weeks could change all that.

You know PR companies organise promotions with names such as 'Bramley Apple Week' or 'Breast Cancer Month', with all their efforts focussed into a short space of time to maximise the impact of their efforts?

Well this September is going to be 'Mary Hadow Awareness Month'. Quite inadvertently as it happens.

I am very curious indeed as to how things are going to stand at the end of it.

But for the time being we are back to the drawing board. Wydemeet is on the market again, and I must return to the hunt for a new home in the desirable 'Dunchideock Triangle'.

Exploiting Contacts
05/09/2015

Heart in mouth I email the Chief Executive of arguably the biggest publishing house in the country, if not the world.

"Back in the hazy mists of time when we were both young(er), you may remember a handsome, charming polar explorer popping in and out of your offices. Sometimes he was accompanied by his wife. Me.

On one of those visits, his editor introduced us all, and when I said I was working on a book, you kindly suggested that I should send it to you.

Well, more than a decade later, here it is - interrupting your summer break... blah blah blah"

And she's replied, saying of course she'll take a look at it! Wow! Wow! Wow!

But time is of the essence. I'm not sure what she can do really, except advise me that it's garbage and to forget all about it. Because my plan is to launch 'Dare B&B' via Kindle, the very minute that the final 'Four In A Bed' denouement fifth episode has been broadcast.

The magic of the thing. It's so amazing that today you can get a book printed for free, in five minutes, rather than the five months plus of yore that it used to take. There must be some major disadvantages to all this. I wonder what they are going to be?

Not content with that, I have also emailed a top national newspaper columnist who is a novelist as well, who I met once at Dartington Ways with Words. I've asked her to endorse my book with the words 'utterly hilarious' or something along those lines. I wonder whether she will even ever get to see my email?

Anyhow - they can only say 'non', and then I will have another idea.

Mafia
09/09/2015

Both my nephew and niece (different families) have elected to hold extended family lunches as their 21st birthday celebrations of choice.

How special is that? What a credit to the family as a whole, their parents, their sisters and their cousins whom they reckon up by dozens. And their aunts! As well as brothers, uncles, godparents, and most of all those grandparents who have all instilled such strong family values in them.

And I am touched/chuffed to bits because both children wanted to sit next to me for the pudding course. That is because I am a larf.
I gave my niece £21 towards a pair of shoes off a special site I've found on the internet which makes them in huge sizes which fit us both. And for my nephew I bought a little practice golf green which fits round the loo, to practise on while he's sitting on the throne.

Meanwhile the tragedy is that Granny the Matriarch, who is so responsible for all of this stability and solidarity, is still confined to barracks with her cracked vertebrae.

We are all a little tearful as we raise our glasses to absent friends, wondering what the future holds.

Granny has been incredibly grateful to the three of us, her children, who have taken it in turns to stay with her. "What goes around comes around Granny" I tell her.

Oh dear. If that's true, then my old age is not looking hopeful!

Room Freshener
09/09/2015

I looked at two houses for sale in my special triangle this week.

One is an architecturally designed garden shed cum portakabin in its own delightful valley with lots of room for the horses, but it smells of vegetarian cooking and people's used bedrooms.

And the fake Aga is greasy. If it had a more fastidious owner, it could arouse the same sort of reaction in me as Haldon Brake did, but I cannot see past the immediateness of the people living in it to imagine that.

The second one is a proper house, a bit like Wydemeet in that it is basically cubic, with one of the corners pointing south. But they've designed it all wrong by putting the staircase on the southwest side, meaning that nearly all the main rooms have to go at the back of the house, with no views nor light.

This one has belonged to the same family for sixty years, and has two acres of glorious gardens complete with huge immaculate lawn in a sort of amphitheatre shape, two ornamental ponds, a fountain, a river, and secret pathways zig-zagging through woodland. I feel really bad that should I become the proud new owner, I shall erect an electric fence along the entire length of the lawn and stick my horses in the whole lot. I know from experience that I don't walk around pretty garden paths. I am much more excited by fields.

But on my visit, what appealed to me most about this house was that it was immaculate. Unstained white carpet throughout, despite the owner having two toddlers and two puppies. How on earth does she do it? And she had left lots of lights on and squirted room spray everywhere so that everything felt loved and fresh, and as though she really wanted to sell it. I could tell that she must have spent a long time getting everything ready for my visit, just as I do for my potential purchasers, so that she'd made me feel special, and want it.

So I've spoken to her estate agent and explained that I need a significant differential between what I sell mine for, and what I buy a new one for, including allowing practically £50,000 just to cover the cost of the sale, moving, stamp-duty, bits and bobs of repair-work/alterations etc. And that should she take a look at my website, she can work out for herself how much more she thinks Wydemeet might be worth than her less nice house.

I advised her estate agent that I will be in a much better position to know how things stand by the end of Mary Hadow Awareness Month - what with the piece in the Telegraph, the launch of the book, and the telly thing, and hopefully his client in turn, may know what she is willing to accept by then.

Crazy September
13/09/2015

Mary Hadow Awareness Month has begun.

With beating heart I flicked through Saturday's Telegraph in the garage yesterday. I wasn't going to buy it if I wasn't in it. I couldn't find the Property Section and the whole thing weighed a ton and bits advertising chair lifts and comfortable shoes were beginning to slip out of it onto my car's floor. So finally, somewhat flustered, I coughed up the requisite £2 and retreated back to the car to search through the paper which must have used up an entire forest in its production, for the Piece on Me.

And blow me down - there it was! A postage stamp picture on the front of the Property Section, and a double page spread inside! As promised, they used a huge picture of Wydemeet, Faye, Vegas, Twiglet and me, and two more little pictures, one of our Visitors Book, and one of our White Company toiletries.

It is a long article, and fair. Its only problems are that my hair looks a bit stupid and my grey falling-off top is really very falling-offy - but it does make it impossible to tell how fat I am underneath it. The other thing is that in the copy, the writer uses my mouldy lemon curd story. Perhaps I shouldn't have mentioned that to her. Hopefully it won't matter too much. And in any case, my guests were lucky to be offered home made lemon curd in the first place.

So. Guess how many enquiries about buying the house, and booking in for some B&B nights, I've received in the last 24hrs as a result of this article?

NONE!

PR is Dead
17/09/2015

I've still not received a smidgeon of interest resulting from my full colour double page spread in last Saturday's Telegraph. PR is dead. But there is now a rather smart For Sale sign erected outside my front gate. That will bring in the punters! Not. The only people ever to pass my house are Neighbour, a handful of walkers, and sheep.

Hugh Laurie
21/09/2015

This morning my alarm clock roused me out of a dream in which Hugh Laurie had invited me to dinner, and I was so excited by this that I completely forgot that it was the first evening's showing of 'Four In A Bed'.

In my dream, it wasn't until twenty minutes after the programme began that I suddenly remembered it was on, and rushed upstairs to catch the last few minutes, surrounded by all Mr Laurie's B&B guests.

Blimey - I must be anxious! Or going potty.

This week is becoming surreal.

In the lead-up to broadcast-day, I have been living what feels like three days within each one.

In just the last week my B&B has turned over nearly £1200, which, if you extrapolate that out, is the equivalent of earning over £50,000pa.

During that time I've watched Faye getting thrashed in the U14Bs' hockey in East Dorset; lunched with Ex and Will and his friends who are beginning to get taller than him; ridden with Faye in a hunter trial; driven to both children's schools several times (100/200 mile round trip); prepared the house for two viewings; chatted and chatted and chatted to B&B guests because they are so especially nice and interesting, etc etc.

I wonder whether I am tired because

a) I do too much
b) I am old - 56 tomorrow
c) I drink too much Cava

I think it might be all three.

My new builder, Peter, has just told me that I have a special 'aura' about me. He always says nice things to me. He came on Friday because the rain is pouring through the new roof into the smart cloakroom. My Jaeger pink jacket is now discoloured and covered in mildew. The dry cleaner lady made me put it in the litter bin just by the bus-stop outside her launderette in Chudleigh Ouch!

Meanwhile repairing the roof is likely to cost £several thousand. Peter tells me that the insurance will probably pay and has taken some pictures of the damage.

It's A Non
21/09/2015

Boo hoo. The publisher has turned down my book. No reason given. I suppose they just think it's rubbish. I think it was nice of them to check it out in the first place actually - I think I was quite lucky that they did. They suggest I take it to an agent if I'm not going the vanity publishing route.

Well I am going the vanity publishing route.

What I think would be completely brilliant is if I could get enough of my email contacts from the last decade to order a copy, and take it straight into the Best Sellers list.

I've had another look at it and decided the first entry is boring, even though I have spent several days perfecting it. So I've deleted it. If I keep on doing that, there will be no book left!

I have sent the draft to an extremely nice lawyer friend from many years back, who specialises in slander and libel (I always forget which is which), and he has extraordinarily kindly agreed to look through it, to see how much trouble I am likely to get myself into with it, and the gorgeous, lovely, utterly wonderful man has said that legally it should be OK! If people are recognisable even if you use false names, and take you to task for defamatory comments that aren't justified, then you could be in trouble. But if She tried any of that nonsense I could easily line up about 100 witnesses who would all say that She got off lightly. In fact, by the endless use of capital S, and capital H for 'Her' - She has actually become deified!

I have also now completed all the online forms for making it go public on Kindle (they are remarkably straightforward - they take about five minutes), so we are all systems go!

5.30pm Friday September 25th my first book should be in the Public Domain! Just as the closing music for the final episode of Four In A Bed fades away.

Oooh!
28/09/2015

Amazon Bestsellers Rank: #19,178 Paid in Kindle Store
#20 in Kindle Store > Books > Humour > Parenting & Families
#96 in Books > Humour > Love, Sex & Marriage
#257 in Kindle Store > Books > Nonfiction > Self-Help & Counselling > Self-Help

I'm so excited watching my book whistling up the charts, that I have to share these figures with you. Fancy reaching the Number Nineteen Thousand One Hundred and Seventy-Eighth slot?!

Rant
28/09/2015

Yesterday morning I lay in bed, sweating. With anger and frustration. Clare Balding was chatting to an Indian guru bloke on her Radio 2 Show, Sunday Best.

Clare once visited us to go Rambling on Radio 4 with Ex. Although I think she actually preferred me.

She thought it was really funny when I said that his rugby-flattened cauliflower ears meant anything I said passed him completely by. And she was very nice about her strange tasting tea - we found out after she'd left that Will, aged 9, had added salt to the sugar bowl.

My sister has suggested that for future television appearances, I ask her how to talk posh without sounding silly.

I've also met, very briefly, the guru bloke she was interviewing, although he wouldn't remember.

Anyhow, I apologise now if I've got any of my facts wrong, or completely missed his point; but I'm quite clear about my sentiments.

Here was this chap on a sleepy Sunday morning, exhorting us all to spend more time communing with nature, while he deplored the 9-5 job.

Well that's OK if you live in a mud hut somewhere warm. Or you're a monk with no dependents, partners, or fun mates - whose monastic accommodation and living expenses are funded by some goodly wealthy soul who's derived a fat income in the commercial world (or you're a wealthy monk because you sell tanker-loads of mead laced with caffeine to Glaswegian alcoholics).

And this sort of thing always sounds good, if you're an idealistic idiot who doesn't bother to think it through properly. Because actually, it's not.

Not in the temperate Western World anyway, and I'm fed up with narrow-minded judgmental liberal socialists who sneer at others for doing a proper day's work, and then scrounge off their partners, friends, or the state.

Personally speaking, I think it would be highly romantic to live with someone who had a 9-5 job. To kiss him goodbye. And later, hello again; and then be able to discuss your mutual day together in the wonderful security of knowing his salary will arrive in his bank account at the end of the month. Something that I've never known, and yearn for.

In my opinion, the only way you can spend loads of time 'communing with nature' responsibly, if you have a partner and children, is if you're lucky enough to enjoy inherited wealth, or have won the lottery, or have retired.

Otherwise who is going to pay your rent, fuel bill, your council tax, your dentist bills, for your children to have a car like all their friends do, for your own transport, for emergency operations when you or your children fall ill, for your glasses, for tennis racquets or musical instruments for your children to learn new skills on, your meals if your friends invite you to eat out, a computer, for your holidays if your friends want you to come on one with them, your watch, for your nursing home, and how are you ever going to entertain or look after your friends in return? On and on and on the endless list of every day expenses in a Western World goes.

The 9-5 job means that you have only the very early mornings, your strict one hour lunch break, your evenings and weekends free for your hobbies, shopping, coffee breaks, household and social admin, housework, electrician's appointments and deliveries, socialising, exercising, dentist and doctors' appointments, being kind to other people, and, if there's any time left, in an ideal world, finally you can spend a couple of minutes communing with nature.

Naked?!
28/09/2015

"That all sounds fine. Did you come across us through the telly?" I queried this morning, of a Scottish bloke who called about staying at Wydemeet.

"No - have you been on telly?" he said.

I suggested that he watch 'Four In A Bed' on catch-up, and that if he liked the look of us, that he books direct, online - that it's a minimum of two nights for two people, and I explained to him that he could find our website by googling 'Luxury Dartmoor B&B'.

"Oh - just before you go. My partner and I are naturists," he said. "Is that OK with you?"

"Well, errrrrrrrrrr, no ...... not around the house at any rate, even if it's illegal to stipulate that," I said, a bit flustered. "There are children here. Is this a piss-take?"

He earnestly assured me that it was not.

"Well you could go without any clothes on in the river, I suppose," I went on. "Although, at this time of year, I think you might be better off in a wetsuit."

What a Flop!
01/10/2015

So, September is over and it's time to take stock after all that.

The Results.

B&B Website hits: 3,500

Supportive Emails of Encouragement From Four In A Bed Viewers: about 12

New Suitors: 1

Hate Mail: 0

Kindle Book Sales: 16

B&B Bookings: 0

House Sales Enquiries: 0

Further Media Enquiries: 0

Job Offers: 0

What a flop!!

Hmmm. Looks like we're back to the drawing board. I'm going to have to have a new idea. Roll on the printed physical manifestation of my book and we'll see what I can do with that. I have worked out how to produce a paper copy. It's very straightforward through Amazon's 'CreateSpace' arm, and doesn't cost anything to do; and the proof is winging its way over to me from the States right now! It only cost £3 to print! Can't wait to see it!

I am disappointed I have only sold 16 Kindle copies so far - that's a grand total of about £30 profit as a result of all my hard work! And looking at some of the other similar books on offer - there's one called "A Year in the Life of a Playground Mother" ranking Number 11 in the Kindle Store - well I know that I'm a bit of a crap writer, but hers is so bad I couldn't make it past the second boring page! Huh!

Once I've succeeded in making the paperback version of my book look halfway decent, I shall finally use my database of over 2,000 contacts, and anyone else I can think of such as the Old Etonian Association, as well as journalists and the media book clubs, and ugh! even the social meedja, in a last-ditch attempt to get everyone to buy a couple of copies of it for Christmas presents! Oh - and they could think about buying my house too, while they're at it.

I might have to sell Wydemeet for less than I thought after all.

What Really Matters
01/10/2015

It's all about the children. While the whole of September was all about Me, Me, Me; my Revered Son and Beloved Daughter were performing out of their skins!

Will played 'Punga' - a highly technical and massively exciting house music sax solo which I've heard blaring through the changing rooms of 'Next' - to his entire school, and he was so 'in the zone' that when he was kneeling on the stage, his head almost crashed on the floor! Parents were not welcome but he allowed his Dad in, provided he hid at the back, and I gather was very polite and courteous to him despite the embarrassment of his being there at all.

I have looked up every connotation of "Cool dude playing a sax solo" on YouTube, and all I can find are "Epic Sax Man" - a plonker playing a few notes on stage in a Eurovision Song Contest entry; and "Sexy Sax Man" - someone who only ever plays a few lines of 'Careless Whisper', and is buzzed off "America's Got Talent". There is most definitely a space out there in the musical world for Will (in my opinion) if he cares to follow it up.

While Will was playing his heart out on stage in East Dorset, Faye was busy proving them all wrong about both her and Vegas' ability as a partnership, by completing a Clear Round in a hunter trial, Mad Vegas of the Rolling Eye leaping over jumps that I wouldn't attempt in a million years.

It is such a delight when your children become better at things than you are.

Having spent a large fortune on our children's education, it felt a bit nuts not to cough up an extra £90 for the re-marking of three of Will's GCSE's, so we did, and guess what? An extra A* came out of the bag!

And finally, given the option of an appointment with the Flat Feet Man, or playing in the school First XV rugby match, Will has opted for the latter! So I am going in great excitement to watch him play Centre this afternoon!

Let's just hope we don't end the day in Yeovil's A&E.

A Weighty Tome
07/10/2015

Thump!

It landed on the kitchen table, looking like a proper book.

The proof had arrived, all the way from America.
"Blimey - I hadn't realised I'd written that much!" I thought. "No wonder my friends are a bit loathe to wade all the way through it online."

The book must comprise 350 pages of solid, uninterrupted typing, in quite a small font, without much space around the edge of the page. Seriously daunting to even start reading that lot! On and on and on and on it goes, all about me. How incredibly self-indulgent!

If you dip into it though, it's quite jolly, catchy and addictive. It's a loo book. Hardly high literature. I can't see how it could work on Kindle really. In fact, I've never come across anything quite like it.

So now I've got to tweak it a bit, to make it more readable. The 'Mary Hadow' on the front cover needs to come down a bit. The blurb on the back needs tidying up. And the inside needs separating into different sections. With pages numbered, titles of each entry at the top of each page as in Jeremy Clarkson's book; and attractive little squiggles inserted here and there, as there are in the book I am currently reading, which is called "Getting Rid of Matthew".

The trouble is, I don't know how to do any of this, and I've got to find an inexpensive and quick way, that works well with supplying books as and when required by Amazon. I've also got to proof-read the entire thing yet again, because where I crossed out all mentions of the word 'kind', when I decided to stop calling my neighbours 'Kind Neighbour' - it's caused a lot of trouble in the rest of the copy. As a result there are now missed out words, or simply 'ly' or 'ness' left, where it once read 'kind', 'kindly' or 'kindness'.

Crumbling B&B
11/10/2015

My home is almost uninhabitable. Lucky I still haven't got any guests.

Peter, my lovely buddhist builder, kindly stuck together the cracks in the roof tiles, and sent me a quote for proper repair. £8000! Gasp! It is the new part of the roof that's gone - it was only built seven years ago! The tiles are plastic and screwed together in a special way apparently. They are particularly expensive tiles, for unusually shallow roofs, and aren't made anymore. We have told the insurance company that we think they were cracked by some detritus falling off the higher roof above, which is 100 years old and fine.

The nice man from the insurance company has said the house and contents are under-insured at £650,000 for buildings, and £50,000 for contents. I told him that I could replace all the contents from eBay for less than £50,000, but that's not the point apparently. So they will cover £5000 of the repair costs. Well that's £5000 more than I was expecting, and I'm very pleased!

While I continue to pray for no more rain, so that the roof can be mended, I can't cook because I've got no hot water, as the AGA's gone funny . The kitchen is full of fumes which are wafting up through the whole house. Gary, my plumber friend, says it's a leaking flue, and hasn't come, nor returned a phone call, for ten days now. I'm amazed my carbon monoxide alarm hasn't melted!

Nor can I wash, because our water has gone yellow, with silt in it. So I can't fill up the jacuzzi or have a bath, and I'm drinking Tesco's Aqua Pura from bottles.

And finally, there doesn't seem to be a single plumber within a 50 mile radius who has any clue about water neutralisers. The chap who fitted mine has suffered from a series of mental breakdowns ever since, and never returns a phone call. Gary is flummoxed and says it will cost £400 to import a replacement cartridge from the States.

And then I got through to Miles - a chap who lives in Widecombe who represents England in the World Lightweight Tug O War Championships. He says all you have to do is pour 'media' into the top of the blue cannister, which will cost £50 all in; and that the yellow water and silt are caused by the current 'media' needing replacing. He will pop round to do it when he has a moment. Well I wish he'd hurry up.

Faye's school is 53 miles away, which is a long journey for a coffee morning; and her weekly riding lessons are 63 miles away. It takes me eight hours, from 12.45pm to 8.45pm, to bring in the horses, get them to beyond Tiverton for an hour's tuition, and back home again. Every Tuesday.

"Dear Mummy

Thank you for everything that you do for me. I love you very much. You are the best Mummy.

Love from Faye" she texted me the other day.

"I do it all for ME! Hadn't you noticed?! PS I love you more," I texted her straight back, and wiped a tear from my cheek.

"Your brake pads should be fine, we only changed them recently," said Super Sexy Dick, opening up The Golden Monster's bonnet. "Oh, you've done 16,000 miles since we last had a look," he looked up in surprise.

"So now you know why I can never get the thing to you, I'm always in it," I replied.

I just can't wait to sell this place. It's completely stupid living here, and now there's a new pile of council gravel piled up outside the gate, and I see that Neighbour has also started taking delivery of big tree trunks again, even though there is still a sea of old ones reaching to the sky all higgledy piggledy on the right hand side as you go out of our garden and onto the moor.

My nice estate agent has left his company, and his replacement hasn't yet called me in nearly six weeks, nor has he arranged any further viewings.

Maybe I'm stuck here forever.

Ex To The Rescue!
19/10/2015

I'm going to Spain.

Only for four days, but it feels as though I'm to be away for a year!

The Aga still doesn't work. There's no heat in it, and the kitchen stinks of oil.

None of the telly's work, nor does any catch-up via Sky Plus; nor does the internet through either a laptop, nor the PC, nor the new Chrome notebook thing. All this despite four lengthy expensive visits from my IT man.

The media in the water neutraliser has finally been changed, but it's still running a light, silty yellow, like wee wee after you've had a lot to drink.

The new roof has started leaking again, despite its £5000 repair.

Sashka is away this week.

I've got guests coming at the weekend and I won't be here.

Ex to the rescue!

I leave him three pages of 'crises' notes and instructions on what to give them for breakfast. Faye will 'refresh' their rooms and the paying guests will house-sit and look after Twiglet, left alone, to their own devices, on Sunday night.It's taken me all week to get this far. I think I might be going bald.

Goodbye Cruel World
19/10/2015

They call it a mobile phone upgrade but they're lying. It's a downgrade. They've delivered me this huge brick of plastic, bigger and slower than its hideous predecessor, and once I work out how to use one or two of its functions I discover that it only accepts a gigabyte of memory or something, before you have to start paying a daily fiver for more. So I can't look anything up on it. I hate it with such violent passion that I don't bother to recharge it.

The result is that here I am, wandering around the vast waiting area of Bristol airport, wondering how I am going to find my best mate Judith for a little drinky before we board our plane for Spain, and jet away from the horror that is all things Wydemeet.

NICKERSOFF!!!!!!!!!!!!!!!!!!!!!!!!!!!!!!!

I stop and rotate slowly. The sound could be coming from in front of me, behind me, above or below me.

And suddenly, from behind a large glass of what is probably Chilean Sauvignon blanc and a square dish of roasted almonds, erupts the chic, slender frame of my great friend, resplendent in canary yellow mini-coat, spray on black leggings and boots; a vast pair of (genuine) Prada sunnies perched on her head. Bloody Hell she looks good! No wonder I don't have a queue of men after me if she doesn't.

I stand in my black, feeling like an elephant, grinning at her stupidly. I am so very pleased to see her again.

The book, the book
19/10/2015

One of the most exciting things that has ever happened to me in my whole life took place last week.

Here is the sentence that changed my whole attitude:

"I spent three hours yesterday reading random excerpts from your book. I hadn't intended to spend so long but I did find it difficult to put down. Had I started from the beginning I'd probably not have gone to bed!"

Written by a bloke called Dave who lives in a small village outside Exeter, who doesn't know me from a hole in the ground, whose profession is preparing books for print, to whom I'd sent a proof of my book, to check out whether I should be printing it direct, or continue with CreateSpace.

So this came from a bloke who sees a lot of books ....

Well!!!!!!!

He is hardly my target market of chick-lit-loving recently dumped girlie-wirlies is he?

So if he liked it - probably loads and loads and loads of people might! I really had never quite dared to believe such a thing. I was so excited I went all jittery. Comparing potential publishing costs, though, I worked out that the Amazon route looked a lot cheaper. So I was straight back to the drawing board of how to produce a professional finished printed edition myself, via CreateSpace.

I've discovered how to get the copy into their 6" x 9" template, and have put together loads of introductory pages like they have in normal books. Faye and I didn't get up until 6.45pm last Sunday, when I had to take her back to school, and I spent the whole time checking the thing again for typo's, and finished the entire book before bedtime! Couldn't put it down actually, but I thought that might just be me being interested in me.

Arriving in Spain my closest, oldest, most loving and caring mates - all Exeter University Alumni from 35 years ago - are quizzing me about my progress. I am shy about producing the three proof copies that I have squeezed into the 55 x 40 x 20cm overnight case permitted by Ryanair. On the second day, however I quietly dish them out, and by the third, nobody appears for breakfast. They are all riveted by my book! This is just too, too good to be true! They all rave about it! Wow!

I've got to change some names, take out the last entry, and the last line of the description on the back cover, and make the front cover funny, and off we go!

Well I've managed to close my mind off to the horrors back home, and now I daren't think of what I should do next as an author either, or I will become so excited that there will be no chance at all of a much-needed recuperative sleep!

Sense and Sensibility
19/10/2015

A dark red, cloth-bound copy of Sense and Sensibility lies on the Spanish kitchen breakfast table, really rather miles away from the Cotswolds, or wherever Jane Austen originally wrote it.

On the first page inside, in royal blue fountain pen ink, is written: Nicholson 1930. My maiden name.

So it would seem that at some stage I lent or gave this book to our hostess, Lindsey.

And in return, she says she would like me to take home the huge, flat, weird-looking stainless steel implement that proved so useful in removing some poached eggs from a pan-full of simmering water this morning.

I wonder what the bloke looking through the x-ray camera in customs will make of it?

How Many Shades?
21/10/2015

"Was it ten? Fifteen? Twenty-five?" I ask my son.

I genuinely can't remember how many shades of grey there were.

He is now really worried about me. There could be no clearer proof that I truly am suffering from early onset dementia.

A Flexible Business
21/10/2015

Booking.com, the world's foremost agency for hotels, guesthouses and B&Bs, with a daily turnover of millions, can't spell accommodation. They've got it wrong three times - twice in their standard contract, and once in their accompanying email.

I have commented before how satisfactory it is that you can turn the B&B business up and down, like the flow of water out of a tap.

Well, over the past year I think I have turned mine rather too far down. So now I am back on with Booking.com - the necessary evil - the experts without whom I find I cannot function properly however hard I try.

I must say that they have become considerably more efficient over the past few months that I've been away, and appear to have blossomed into a courteous, intelligent and professional company, even if they can't spell the most important word in their vocabulary.

I said as much to the nice young man who spoke English properly (rather than the usual Dutch of yore), who proved so helpful to me. But I couldn't help adding that his company might learn how to spell, and had he ever stopped to think how much his bosses must be raking in on a nightly basis, at a conservative guess of five rooms, occupied at £100 each, in half a million properties, worldwide. The total sum still goes right off my calculator!

Well the other thing about running your own B&B business is that you can treat every visitor completely individually according to whatever suits them and you best.

My first set of returns had the house completely to themselves for the entire weekend.

I left breakfast ingredients out each morning for the second returns we've just had, but they had the house to themselves for a night, and had to cook for themselves.

And now I've got a lady coming from Germany.

Could she book five nights, just for her, she queried.

"I don't normally cater for singles, but what the heck," I replied, and gave her a quote for about 2/3rds of the normal charge.

"Ah - that's very thoughtful, but with the Forest Inn down the road closed, I think you might be too far to travel out each evening for dinner," she came back to me.

Kerching! Or not! I am panicking to myself. This will be deathly quiet midweek November we're talking about, and no agents' fees involved.

"Ah - it'll only be the two of us in the whole house," I tell her. "Why don't you use the kitchen? I tend to eat late in front of the telly, so I'm sure we won't get in each other's way."

So that's what's happening. Company for both us, pleasant and convenient for her, cash for me! And she's chosen the more expensive Hexworthy Room, too! Hurray!

And now the latest thing is that we've got our first ever THIRD TIMERS wanting to come to stay!!! They've just got married, and want to come back yet again! What an honour! I love them both! Since they were last here, he's learned to ride, so their plan is to book a couple of hirelings and we shall all go hunting together! Now there's something to look forward to! Hope I've sorted out all Wydemeet's wretched glitches by then!

Faye's Parties
31/10/2015

"One of my friends got kissed by two people, and the other three were kissed by one each, but nobody knew anybody's name," Faye informs me. The party season has begun!

At this particular jamboree, which is held every year in London for posh young teens, at over £50 a ticket, no alcohol available, I gather the idea is to swap saliva with as many people as possible in the couple of hours allowed. The system is that one boy stands in front of a girl, and if she is sufficiently pretty, waves to his friend who is waiting behind her, who, at the thumbs up, then swoops round to the front, gives her a tongue sandwich, and moves on to the next one.

I know of a boy who managed to swap spit like this with 17 girls in one evening!

It's the sort of reason why I was keen for Faye to go to a school on the west side of the M5, with hopefully less of the London influence of schools nearer to the capital. Unlike her brother at his trendy school in East Dorset, she wasn't invited to this particular party, and hardly knows anybody who was. Hurrah! My little plan has worked!

Last week, during Big School half-term, we finally had a little party for the leavers of her first school, inviting the other eleven children from her year-group, who left with her, to come to Wydemeet and catch up on everybody's news. Two boys and five girls stayed the night, all wrapped up in sleeping bags, onesies, pillows, duvets and cushions in Will's cosy Bothy, complete with its semi-naked posters of Cheryl Whatevershecallsherselfthesedays, lava lamps and flashing fairy lights.

I took a picture of them all in the morning because they all looked so sweet together.

There's a 'marine drive' around a peninsula outside Torquay that, in twenty years of living here, I was totally unaware of until yesterday. On one side it drops down a cliff into the sea. And on the other are some Very Posh Houses Indeed, where Faye's last night's new school's Hallowe'en party was being held. The whole effect reminds me very much of the French Riviera, and today the late October sun was blazing hot, the bright blue sky reflected in the gently swelling sea. Quite a contrast with the chilly grey fog that I had left behind, 45 minutes earlier, on high Dartmoor.

We were warmly greeted by the party-girl's glamorous parents and their friends, all of whom appeared to be two decades younger than me. Faye was immediately whisked away to join the singing along to a massive sub-woofer echoing all around the bay. And then. Gasp! Seven young men walked through the kitchen. And they're only Year 9! Whoa! This was a bit different to Wydemeet's innocent little prep school leavers' party! No wonder party-girl's Dad was planning to sleep on the stair-landing between the boys' and the girls' 'dorms'.

"Is that beer?" I whispered to one of the Mums.

"No, it's Seven-Up," she breathed back.

This morning, last, as ever, to collect my beloved daughter, I discovered that, having gone to bed at 3am after two scary films, the 'boys dorm' had all risen at 7am, and without anybody asking them to, had cleared up the whole party!

I am really having trouble getting my head around this young generation.

Doom
31/10/2015

"The gate's broken!

There are two wild ponies on the lawn
I have tried sweeping up the leaves but it doesn't make any difference!

Sorry to be the harbinger of doom," says the hand-written note that Sashka has left out for me on the kitchen table.

Well this is on top of a leaking roof, a leaking Aga, leaking front door which is already beginning to smell of mildew, leaves in the leaking hot tub because the lid's blown off again, faulty wifi, and a still-problematic Sky Box.

I have just got back from Torquay. It took me nearly 1 1/2hrs to get there, including finding it; 1 1/2 hrs to get home late last night, following fellow-Mum Gillian who's sat-nav appeared to have gone bonkers; 1 1/2 hrs to plough through Newton Abbot which was at a standstill this morning; and 1 1/4hrs to drive back over the Berry Pomeroy speed bumps route, arriving home to find all of this.

I am really fed up with living in the back of beyond.

I'm going to research the rental market.

Book Cover
04/11/2015

I'm going bananas trying to work out how to make my book look more professional. And wondering how to communicate on the cover straightaway that it's supposed to be funny. I have decided that the picture of a rose and a fried egg makes it look like something that might appeal to the recently bereaved.

The cover templates provided by Amazon's CreateSpace are terribly limited, and I've experimented with every single one of them using my copy and pics, and none is ideal. Interestingly, there aren't any that imply a sense of humour, using jolly fonts. Most convey a sense of mystery, which isn't quite me really. It would seem that hardly anybody writes funny books.

On Google there is only one other company that promises easy cover templates for idiots that can be used direct in Amazon's CreateSpace publishing. Their choice is not that great either, but I am so desperate I coughed up 45 dollars for one. It says that you can create a new cover in under an hour. I've now spent several days trying to work out how to use the thing. I've had to download a free photoshop-type programme called 'Grim' or something, to make it work, but I'm still getting nowhere and in despair forwarded the download to my IT man, who has come up with something even worse than my original.

I have also asked him to insert page numbers and page titles into my 'interior' - the insides of the book. What he has sent back has turned it into a total dogs dinner.

Every time I have a spare moment I am trying to come up with something funny to replace the words, "Broke, bewildered and alone?" My Exeter friends suggested "Broke, bewildered, and bonkers," but I'm not keen.

Last night, discussing all of this over delicious sea bream, with my friend Malcolm and his lovely girlfriend, Malcolm came up with the idea of a fag-end stubbed out in a fried egg yolk. I airily and probably rather rudely dismissed this at the time, but now quite like the concept and am wondering whether I can work out the graphics myself on my new Grim programme.

If I download Windows 10 I might be able to manage page numbers as well!

And finally, after days and days of hard concentration and lots of sleepless nights of rubbish potential slogans going round and round in my head, I have come up with the perfect subtitle which says it all:

"A Very Funny Book."

So now hopefully I can get the thing finished, and out just in time to catch the Christmas market.

Eight Hours - Worth It
04/11/2015

Since September I must have done at least six eight-hour days, getting Mad Vegas to Faye's riding lesson.

Am I completely potty?

Well, as a result, I have now finally worked out how to stop the crazy mare from kicking my trailer to bits.

I had tried giving her nicer stuff to eat, changing the side she travels on, removing the partition, moving the hay nets so she could see out of the little window in the front. Nothing's worked, I have to take her friend Panda everywhere with her so she's not frightened, and so she will get into the trailer in the first place. Both horses regularly arrive at their final destination sweating and with cuts on their legs, me an exhausted nervous wreck.

But now, bingo! It's sorted!

I simply needed to tie them up tighter. So they can't bite each other.

The results have been so miraculous that yesterday I managed to load the mad mare on her own by myself, with builder Peter looking on and brandishing a long whip like a circus master. In she went and there she stood - a 2 1/2 hour journey each way - still as a statue. Me arriving at the lesson, and then home again, cheerful and refreshed.

And over the weeks, Vegas and Faye have been on 'a journey' together, both of them gradually gaining confidence, each in the other, both jumping far higher, brighter things than they ever thought they could.

Faye has now been promoted up two rides in the pony club, and such is the bug that she has caught, she insisted on riding all the way home from her 'C test', which she passed; and from her pony club rally - all alone nearly twelve miles across central Dartmoor!

"Your father gets his vicarious pleasure through your rugby," I said to Will over his half-term last week. "I get mine from Faye's riding."

"What does 'vicarious' mean?" he said.

Dollop
05/11/2015

Faye's Pony Club riding teacher called her 'a dollop' during her lesson last week.
That's what I like to hear! And so does she!

For most people, I think, but perhaps especially for Faye, the teacher is so key to whether she learns anything and progresses.

Faye responds well to affectionate jovial bullying, empathy, an obvious personal commitment to her, and a firm hand. I wonder where she gets that from. Or, alternatively, to very beautiful, gentle, ethereal feminine teachers. No idea where she gets that.

So Joy - shouting and laughing at and with her at the top of her voice, "I can't do it" not being an option, had her jumping the biggest things she's ever done, remembering what she had been taught afterwards, and so inspired that, yet again, she wanted to ride twelve miles home, after a 1 1/2hr lesson.

Faye's musical progress, on the other hand, has ground to a complete halt.

"Play me all the things that you've learned at your new school over the past seven weeks," I ordered her during half-term, settling myself down for 30 minutes of pleasure. Nothing. Not one single thing. She hasn't learned anything at all. After all that! And what's going to happen now, with her scholarship and all, if she isn't contributing anything musically back to the school?

This has to be sorted out. She clearly hasn't bonded with one of her teachers, and has just played or sung through some jolly stuff with the other, no clear, bossy directions for practice, nor apprehension of the consequences if she doesn't do any. And no fun, nor feelings of achievement derived from learning something new and well that she likes either. In fact she started to cry and finally admitted that she was hating it.

Oh dear! This calls for a special meeting in Tiverton - perhaps a little drinkie with my online friend Little John on one side or the other, to cheer things up.

Meanwhile I have joined the school choir, so I will be singing with Faye every Monday until the school carol service in Exeter Cathedral at the end of term. That will be another couple of hundred visits to the garage for more petrol then.

My Dad, sitting on his cloud in Heaven, will be smiling from ear to ear, to see his heathen middle daughter setting foot inside a church of her own volition!

Half Price
05/11/2015

Tell me something's half price and I'll buy it - doesn't really matter what it is.

This week I've bought myself the most extraordinary load of stuff.

On my way to Spain, customs wouldn't let me take through my very expensive pot of 'Label M' hair conditioning mask - the only one I've found that works on my hair - and made me throw it away. Agonising! Anyway, I ordered two more pots through eBay and they arrived alongside some very upmarket-looking vouchers with silver numbers on, saying '£50 off!'

The dark blue one offered me 50% off a box of three meals for two. The meals offered were things like curried chicken, parsnip risotto, 'bangin sausages in ciabatta rolls' etc; each portion size normally costing £5.38, but half price for your first box.

The catch is, you have to assemble all the ingredients and make up these meals yourself.

Anyway - the box duly arrives and I say! What a triumph of presentation over substance! Every single ingredient - right down to a teaspoon of paprika, is individually wrapped, there are three little ice-packs included, and pages and pages of mouthwatering literature. There are about six teeny pouches of spices, two individual cloves of garlic, four tiny pots of things like balsamic vinegar, a parsnip, two sachets of rice, and most extraordinary of all - one chicken breast and four sausages. This package would normally retail at nearly £40!!

In astonishment, I worked out how much the parsnip risotto would have cost if I'd bought all the ingredients from Tesco, and it came to £11.08 for enough for six.

So I emailed them and said so, adding that I couldn't think what Dragons Den was playing at, supporting this extraordinary business, and that if it succeeded I'd eat my hat.

Then I set to, making up their chicken curry, using all the tiddly widdly bits and pieces, and the beautifully presented step by step recipe card, and I must say that it was very quick and easy, with everything being to hand and measured out for you; and the end result was substantial and delicious. As it should be, with half a pot of double cream in it, at 1000 calories a serving!

But if you're going to eat like this - 'Cook' is your puppy, in my opinion.

Deep frozen, ready-made - cheaper, quicker, more convenient, easy to store, even more reliable, and no washing up!

Anyhow, so not content with that, my larder is now also bulging with £50 off a £92 crate of wine from Laithwaites. The Mum of their owner, Tony Laithwaite, was my teacher at Eton Porney School (yes that is its real name), the local primary school I attended back in the sixties. She had pink hair and always wore a mixture of pink and beige or grey clothes, and smelled strongly of perfume.

Lastly, I have also found myself with £50 worth of coffee pouches from some company called Little Cup Large Cup or something. This one's a particularly mad purchase because nobody uses the many Nespresso machines I bought off eBay by mistake, thank God. They are a fiddle and leave a horrid mess on my mahogany surfaces.

Renting Out Wydemeet
04/11/2015

I have bitten the bullet.

I have emailed the people who put in the original offer on Wydemeet, suggesting that they might like to rent it - either to test it out, or to live in while they continue their search for that perfect home in the West Country.

Well blow me down with a feather.

They had been wondering about just the same thing! And then, even better, they asked whether they might rent Wydemeet over Christmas Week! The only week that I do actually want to let it. And just that very morning I had been considering whether to re-sign up to Owners Direct, with their £300-odd down-payment required, or just to continue with TripAdvisor's Holiday Lettings which demands such a horrendously high commission from their customers, that so far it has put off three potential enquirers.

Well now all is arranged to everybody's immense satisfaction. My nice little family of potential purchasers get to test out Wydemeet for Christmas, at a substantially reduced rental rate as there are no agency fees required. Meanwhile, in effect I get to have some friends paying for the privilege of house-sitting for me while I'm away celebrating Christmas at my sister's mansion. They've even offered to decorate the tree!

Which means I now have a very serious deadline. I've got to make sure everything is working properly by December 23rd, all smells of mildew annihilated!

Property Merry-Go-Round
08/11/2015

Helen is spiritual. So I think she will buy my Mum's house.

Helen knows all about the tiny hamlet my mum lives in, because her daughter works for the racehorse trainer there. And she loves it.

What were the chances that Mum's house - a perfect project for Helen - is just about to come onto the market, right when she's looking for something, and is at a complete crossroads as to where to go?

"It's meant to be," says Helen.

Helen has been forced into selling her beloved five-bedroom home just outside Widecombe for the same reasons as I have. She has just accepted an offer for it from her next door neighbours.

The odd thing is that, of all the houses on sale within a 15 mile radius of the local prep school, the little family who are trying out Wydemeet this Christmas have been torn between buying Helen's house and mine, all this time!

Change Required
08/11/2015

Will's best friend and room-mate has broken his neck.

That is what people think, anyway.

It happened yesterday afternoon, in front of all of us, when they were both playing rugby.

Finally somebody noticed that Jim was lying on his back, prone in the mud, and the game was stopped. A neck brace came out of somewhere, and after about ten minutes a black car appeared and a sort of camp bed was produced. Then someone thought of putting a coat over him. I saw him wiggling his feet, which was something.

No ambulance appeared for another twenty minutes or so. Now we are all wondering how bad things are.

Play resumed and the opposing side scored and converted another try, I haven't seen Will's side win a rugby match for three years now.
I asked him why he doesn't wear a skull cap. He said they are uncomfortable, hot and sweaty. Nobody appears to know why they aren't compulsory in schoolboy rugby - after all, riding hats, skiing helmets and even those ridiculous cycling helmets are de rigeur these days. Ex says it's because the stick-in-the-muds that run schoolboy rugby think that what was good enough for them is good enough for ours. But they didn't weigh 16 stone aged 17, they didn't deliberately 'bulk up', body-building daily in the gym, eating special diets comprising steak, steak, more steak and protein drinks, like so many A'level schoolboy rugby players do now.

These days schoolboy rugby players are huge, massive chaps - two of them on our side have full beards!

Will, once known as 'Tank', who hasn't grown since he was thirteen and who now has the frame more of a soccer player than a rugby player, isn't keen on walking funny with bulbous thigh muscles, nor having the neck of a tree trunk, nor weird swingy arms like a baboon, having bulked up to some massive, unnatural frame and no doubt popped a steroid or two.

Nor is he keen on suffering permanent injury, or even dying, for the sake of a sport. It is extraordinary how enough of them do actually make it through to representing their country.

You see the mothers lined up along the touchline at the beginning of each game, understandably white with fear on behalf of their cherished boys.

I don't suppose the currently empty bed in Will's room will contribute much to his enthusiasm for the sport.

Bang
10/11/2015

The Golden Monster's exploded.

I was driving along the A38 in the dark and the rain last night, having not been able to sing a note in the choir practice (I mouthed along, but the other singers were totally out of my league), and an exclamation mark, a picture of a battery, and 'check trans' started flashing in red from the dashboard at me.

Atypically quick-thinking, I came off the dual carriageway early, and set off home cross country driving as quickly as I could, before all the car's lights went out. First the radio went funny, then the dash said ABS in orange, then it told me that my seatbelt was undone when it wasn't, the windscreen wipers slowed almost to a halt, and I started praying to God, just in case He exists, to get me home in one piece across the desolate, dark, barren moor.

Well, out of the several billion people asking God for special favours at any one time, He heard me, just as I was wondering whether the power assisted brakes would give out as I careered down the last hill towards the still-broken Wydemeet gate. I had arrived, and to celebrate, every light on my dash started flashing its head off. I tried reversing so that the car would be well placed to be towed away in the morning, and the engine died.

Time to test out Green Flag, which I have recently signed up to because it's half the cost of its more famous sister rescue services. They got here in an hour and yes - it was the alternator. Which was only replaced less than a year ago. So now the Golden Monster is back at Super Sexy Dick's garage, and I am stranded.

Which means ... yes! I have a clear window to get my book completed and onto Amazon!! I am SO excited! This could be the beginning of the Third Chapter of My Life.

Vulgar
10/11/2015

I saw through the window that the postman was bearing with him a small package, and I leaped down the stairs to grab it off him.
It was the second proof of my book, hot off the press from the States, sent express delivery for a very large sum of money (about £10).

I have designed a new cover for it in shocking pink. The picture is, as suggested by Malcolm, an egg with a Consulate Menthol butt-end covered in pink lipstick, stuck in the middle of the yolk, and there are even a few droplets of ash on the white!

It is truly vulgar.

I was desperate to know whether my design had worked, or whether it would be back to the drawing board again.

I tore open the cardboard and Sashka and I gazed at the contents.

Well you can't miss it. Then Sashka burst out laughing. Which is exactly the reaction I wanted.

So we're all systems go! I've made a couple of tweaks to the 'interior' and the cover, and now the final thing has been submitted for review. Oh how

I wish they'd hurry up at Amazon and tell me it's good to go. I simply can't wait to put it up on their site!

In the meantime, I've drafted the email promoting it, to go to all the email addresses stored on my computer. It goes like this:

To: Mary of the Moor

From: Mary Hadow

Subject: New Book

Ta dah!

It's done!

I've just written a book!

And it's really funny! (I hope)

You can buy it now, by pressing here:

Tell you what - perhaps you might actually buy a couple, for your friends and family for Christmas, and we'll see if between us we can get it into Amazon's Best Sellers list as an experiment.

I've sent this email to everyone I've been in contact with over the past decade (that's around 2,000 'contacts') including people I've sued, people I don't like, and people who think I'm an idiot, so it's a bit of a punt - but very exciting all the same.

I would be incredibly grateful if you could bear to 'share' news of my book with your Friends on Facebook, I'll have a bit of a go at sprinkling my old PR fairydust on it, and hey presto! We have the next 50 Shades!

Or not. Channel 4's "Four In a Bed" resulted in a resounding silence after 2 1/2hrs of international broadcasting time, as did September's DPS in the property section of the Daily Telegraph. There are never any guarantees.

So while I'm bothering you, just to let you know that I run a very well reviewed B&B, if you'd like to come to stay (unless you are a predatory single male); or perhaps you might like to buy Wydemeet, which is now very sadly up for sale after twenty years of living here, for reasons too numerous to mention.

So I hope you don't mind my bothering you with all of this - I have held back for three years until now, and don't plan to be sending such a Round Robin again. But if you'd rather never hear from me, please email me back saying so.

Either way, I wish you a very Happy Christmas (especially if you buy the book), and Prosperous New Year.

Start All Over Again?
11/11/2015

I've just discovered that I'm going to make minus 6p on every copy of my new book that I sell.

Why didn't I read the 'do you understand this bit' small print on Amazon's CreateSpace website?

The company tells me that it's going to charge 40% for something they call a 'sales channel'; a 70p 'fixed charge' on every book sold; and, worst of all, 1p per page for printing the thing, on top of all that! In my reckoning, this comes to £7.56 for every book sold! AAGGGHHH! After everything I've done - I really can't make a loss on this whole enterprise can I?

So here I am, back emailing the wonderful 'Knows-All-About-The-Whole-Thing' Dave, detailing the above, pleading that I've made the most terrible mistake after all his kindness, and how long and how much would it cost for him to do the whole thing properly with a professionally produced dust cover, and printing done by the small company just outside Exeter?

Dave emails me back within two hours, detailing his costs and timings. A minimum of 19 days. And, even if I had 500 copies printed, printing costs alone would still be £3.50 per book, plus Amazon's 40% commission for retailing it.

Oh no. Back to where we started! This Vanity Publishing game is very expensive!

"Charge more," is Dave's advice.

So, my book will be up on sale on Amazon over the next 3 - 5 days, at a whopping £9.99. That's ten pounds for a book where the front cover photo is only 40kb and fuzzy, the cover itself picks up marks before you can say Jack Robinson, the inside paper, on which there are no page numbers, is so thin you can see through it, and the copy is printed in a stupid yankee font.

I hope somebody still buys it!

Stranded
11/11/2015

£365 for a new alternator.

I email my lovely accountant, Michael, who checks my paperwork, and confirms that it was only January when the last one was done.

Sigh. More agro to get my money back or whatever.

But in the meantime the Golden Monster is still residing at Dick's, my truck's home from home, and I remain stranded at Wydemeet, wondering what to do with myself as Hexworthy's customary horizontal rain swirls around the house outside, and in under the ill-fitting, new, £3000, bespoke front door.

So far I have missed a riding lesson, a lunch with 'The Jilted Wives Club', and a hockey match. If it goes on like this, I shall also miss going to visit Mum tomorrow.

Better take my mind off things with Sir Alan and his extraordinarily thick Apprentices.

Google Gives the Heave-Ho
13/11/2015

"We're going to turn you off if you do that," says a stern message from Google, wiping everything else off my computer's screen.
They didn't like me trying to send out 2000 messages at once, mostly to defunct email addresses, and announced 'non'.

So now, like stone-age man, I'm having to trawl through all my contacts, ticking one at a time, adding new ones as I go. There's a vast amount of missing names off the list - all my B&Bers for a start. I don't know how to get them back. What a waste.

And so in an enormously heavy-handed way, I am sending out my message to one letter of the alphabet at a time. So far I've covered the As, Bs and Cs. About 400 in all, of which 300 emails have been returned as 'undeliverable'.

I've been sent three sweet replies, one from my brother-in-law's sister, one from the ex of one my friends, and one from the primary school teacher of both my children from five years ago. This is getting very close to home. I am playing with fire. Something is going to go horribly wrong any minute. I can feel it in my bones. Somebody is going to be highly offended - I don't know how or why, but they are. Not one of this lot is going to like the pink vulgar cover either.

CreateSpace has got back to me almost by return when I asked them to change the sub-heading from "Broke, bewildered and alone" to "A Very Funny Book"; and for them to remove a stray typo. Thank goodness for that!

So far my sales figures are impressive too! Not.

As of 11.15am, Friday, November 13th, 2015, I have sold one book.

Cunning Plan
16/11/2015

I'm going spinning.

My Exeter health club holds 23 'group cycling' classes a week. That's cycling, while stationary, to music, I think.

My assumption is that these classes will be full of hunky men.

So my plan is to go and spy on a few, to find out what you're supposed to wear, check that there are some fat old women like me around, and to gauge which class has got the most attractive men in it.

Unfortunately none of the classes coincides with my swim today, prior to Choir rehearsal, but Friday looks promising.

Hi-Tech Jacuzzi
17/11/2015

I tried to snuggle down deep into the hot bubbles and relax, but it was difficult.

To one side of me were three Dads examining one of those rubber wrist-straps that tell you how many steps you do a day. One of them, talking very fast at the top of his voice so I couldn't help but hear, apparently does 20,000 daily steps, runs a bike shop, and takes part in triathlons.

On my other side, a bit too close for comfort but the tub was very full of people, was a young man who first, carefully removed his signet rings, and then proceeded to use his mobile phone, regularly dipping it into the steaming chloriney bubbly water to clear its cloudy face, and then tapping in more messages. I quite wanted to ask him where you find such a water-proof, chemical-proof, heat-proof piece of equipment, but, surrounded by all this testosterone, I was too shy.

I checked out the 'group cyclists' spinning away, on my way out of the health club, and on to choir practice. The room was full, and all the participants were standing up on their bikes' pedals! That wasn't part of the plan at all! Why bother having a saddle if that's what you're going to do? Even the fat people were cycling away like maniacs on what looked to me like a steep uphill incline. I don't cycle uphill. That's what horses are for. God I would die doing this! Perhaps a daytime session might be a bit less demanding/embarrassing. I'll check in on one of those next and hope it's full of women knitting and chatting.

Cyclops
15/11/2015

Play had stopped as yet another boy lay in the mud, injured, surrounded by the rugby coaches.

I scurried past, bent double against the hurricane, my new £18 eBay Burberry leopard-spot umbrella already wrecked by the gale, looking for Ex and Faye somewhere along the touchline, as they crouched together behind another equally useless brolly, supporting Our Boy doing his best for his school's First XV.

It was only when I finally found them that we all realised the injured player still lying there was our Will! We ran over, slipping and sliding in the mud - I was wearing some rather smart leather boots more suitable for carpets, and couldn't run anyway, because I hadn't been to the loo recently enough.

We saw Will in the distance get up and jog off to the paramedics' cosy little hut about a mile away, so we all hurried after him, to find him prone on a stretcher, requiring three stitches just above his right eye, where a metal stud had caught him and made a gash about 2mm deep.

There was jolly talk about how Ex used to practise sewing up a gashed banana in case of similar incidents prior to his solo trips to the North Pole. I felt a bit faint and queasy, and was no help to anyone, hearing my big macho boy sucking air between clenched teeth as the local anaesthetic went in.

Thirty minutes later we were all sitting around sipping cappuccinos in the school's Costa franchise.

"Rugby's not worth losing your looks for," Will observed.

"Rugby's not worth losing your eye for," I replied, finishing off a chocolate cookie.

Next term Will has opted to play squash instead.

A Most Remarkable Letter
15/11/2015

I've got to 'C' in sending out my letters alerting all contacts to my new book.

'C' for Customer Services.

And yesterday I received the following from Tesco:

"Dear Mary

Thanks for getting in touch with us,

Congratulations and many thanks for letting us know about your book. I bet your absolutely thrilled Mary I know I would be.

Many thanks too about letting us know about the bed and breakfast and sorry that it is now up for sale. Fingers crossed the book sale makes you lots of money.

Good luck with them both and if there is anything I can ever do for you, let me know.

Have a great weekend

Kind regards,

Susan Jones
Tesco Customer Service"

So, assuming this was some kind of sarky wind-up, I emailed her back saying:

"Thanks Susan - what a remarkable email! I'll write about it in my next book!"

But it wasn't a wind-up. Susan replied straight back, again applauding me for managing to write a book, and promising to buy a copy. So that will bring my number of sales up to eleven. Meanwhile, I've kept my promise.

Trapped in an Apron
18/11/2015

The worst thing about being on your own all the time is having to make endless decisions for yourself - what feels like every hour, every day. It's exhausting!

I have never felt frightened. Bringing the horses in from their field, in a pitch black gale, living in the middle of the moor behind an electric gate, the wind whistling around your ears and the rain pouring down, is much less scary than living in Fulham next to a council estate with strange people going backwards and forwards just outside your window, separated from you only by a pane of glass.

I have never felt threatened - the media assure me that nearly all murders and rapes are carried out by people who know each other. And I am too far away for any of my friends or family to bother to make it over here to rape or murder me, I reassure myself.

And anyway, I may be able to succeed in talking them out of it, should they, or indeed should any thieves appear.

No, my main fear has been the great big spiders that love running across the carpets of this house so much. But now we've got Twiglet-The-Spider-

Eater - so that's dealt with.

I am far too busy ever to feel bored or lonely.

But I have just come across another, much more serious, problem. The bow on the back of my apron has turned itself into a tight knot, and I can't untie it. So this hour's decision is whether to go to bed with my pinny on, or cut the tie. Or ask neighbour to come and undo me. I think I've decided on the middle option.

Hush, not a word...
18/11/2015

They just played this on Radio 2 - a sad haunting song by some yodelling cowboy called John Rowles. He's had a million views on YouTube, so he must be a bit famous, but I'd never heard of him before:

"Hush, not a word to Mary
She means the world to me
Don't wanna lose her

Oh, hush, not a word to Mary
Don't let her know
I stayed here with you

Mary's gone visiting
All the folks at home
Kind of you to ask me around
Knowing I'm alone

A cigarette, a glass of wine
A little harmless fun
A cosy chat about this and that
Never could hurt anyone

Oh, hush, not a word to Mary
She may not understand
And she may worry

Oh, hush, not a word to Mary
Don't want her crying
Over nothing at all

Mary does everything
Keeping me in mind
Loving me so faithfully
That constantly I find
I think of her and long for her
When she's not around
I love her so, I'm sure you know
I never could let her down

So, hush, not a word to Mary
Don't wanna break her heart
All over nothing

Oh, hush, not a word to Mary
Show me the door
It's time I went home"

Six years on now, and the hurt still hasn't gone away.

I think it's time I went to watch Lord Sugar and his idiotic sycophants to cheer myself up.

An Essay on Hunting
19/11/2015

What I like about hunting is riding along quite fast on my beloved horse through the most glorious countryside, chatting to my mates.

I like this new(ish) trail hunting lark because it means that you're more likely to follow a sensible route across safe ground and over some proper, well-made jumps.

Foxes, on the other hand, tend to run round in circles and then go down a hole, while you have to stand about catching norovirus from sharing other people's hip-flasks of whisky mixed with sloe gin, and the huntsman gathers all the hounds back together again.

I would hate to see a fox killed, but I believe them when they say that fox-hunting was a form of natural selection because they only caught the manky old ill ones, and it was a quick clean kill, unlike some bullets.

But this is an area where I can't manage to get too impassioned.

I don't like hunting enough to cough up £65+ a day, spending up to six hours, twice a week, riding around looking fat in about ten layers of clothing, still freezing wet in a horizontal gale, hail or blizzard.

And it's difficult for me to completely enter into the spirit of the thing, because when I hear the unbeatable sound of the hounds crying out as they find the trail, and the horn telling everybody that we're off for a really good gallop, I think, 'Oh no - that's the end of my jolly conversation with her, and the start of that risky business of charging down an uneven hill at full tilt, being a woman in late middle age who gave birth for the first time aged 39 to a baby with a huge head who weighed 10lb 5 oz. Why oh why couldn't they have given me a cesarean??'

What is truly astonishing about hunting is the colossal time, effort, money and discomfort that goes into it. You've got to buy the weird kit, which is simply what people wore 100 years ago and hasn't been changed much since, pay the subs (literally £1000s a year for the smart hunts), the transport, the horse, its gear, its food, shoes, vets bills ... There are enormous amounts of heavy lifting involved when you're looking after horses, and unbelievable quantities of mud and poo that have to be disposed of somehow. The hay and straw get everywhere, and if you do it all yourself, you permanently smell.

You can't really do hunting in a half-hearted way because if your horse isn't kept fit, warm and mollycoddled, it can't keep up and will explode or go lame or catch a cold before you can say Jack Robinson.

So you have to cut all its hair off til it's basically naked, let it in and out of fields and stables according to the time of day and the weather, keep changing what it's wearing according to the temperature, bandage up its legs, and keep it ridiculously clean even though it lives outside in the rain and mud half the time.

This all requires several hours' a day input, so either it takes up half your week, or half your savings if you pay somebody else to do it.

I quite fancy the idea of being a young, fit fox living in Gloucestershire in the olden days, with one of the poshest hunts comprising several hundred squillionaires, chasing after me, when it was allowed. One of them would be Her - I hear She's joined one of the smartest hunts there is - good hunting ground for another peer I would imagine, but She's not a terribly good rider so instead of habitually falling off, she now goes around and through the gates, my moles tell me. Pathetic.

Anyway, were I this young fox, I would be dead chuffed to know that these people, collectively worth billions, had put all this massive, inconvenient, hard work and expensive effort into chasing after little old me. I am a complete sucker for being centre of attention. I would run in a few circles around the roads, and then go down a hole and laugh at them. And then I would go and eat their chickens that night as a punishment for putting me through it.

When I got old and ill I think I would prefer to sit in front of a farmer's gun and be shot, at point blank range.

Most hunts are awash with such vast quantities of testosterone and pheromones that you can almost smell it, and you'll often get couples who won't speak to each other - one at the front and one at the back of the field, after some shagfest disaster. This all used to provide great fodder for Nigel Dempster's column.

The number of riders in any hunt varies from 100s in the smart ones, to sometimes one, two or none at all in the smaller outfits.

Last year I found myself spending the whole day with only one other rider - a chap I had heard had attacked his partner with an axe.

"Is it true you attacked your partner with an axe?" I asked innocently.

"Well she'd locked the door, so what else was I supposed to do?" he replied.

What I really, really, really love about hunting, though, is how happy it makes my beloved horse. The minute she gets wind of where she's going she starts trembling with excitement, and when we get there, she almost dances with joy. As I down as much free port and as many sausage rolls as quickly as I can, before we all canter off.

Marriage Foundation
23/11/2015

Marriage Foundation is a charity whose mission is to be 'a national champion for marriage'. I think it is something that everyone should have heard of, but they haven't.

It was established about five years ago by the country's two leading family law barristers - Sir Paul Coleridge, and Baroness Shackleton (Fiona) who has represented almost every famous divorced person you have ever heard of.

Apparently during their thirty years' practice in family law (each of them presumably making a fortune out of their chosen careers along the way), they became increasingly concerned by how easily and casually so many couples appear to make the decision to get divorced, and the terrible fall-out that it has on the children involved.

According to research conducted last month by Marriage Foundation, 60% of couples separating were getting along fine only the year prior to making their decision, and 54% subsequently regretted it.

I have been skirting around getting involved with Marriage Foundation since it was first established. I even wrote a letter to Sir Paul offering my services, but never sent it.

I actually met 'Baroness Butler-Sloss of Marsh Green', who is one of the patrons, at a drinks party, just after Faye and I had been checking out a potential pony to loan nearby. She appeared to be rather more interested in the pony than the marriage thing, but never mind. I have had a brainwave.

I am thinking of sending my book to her with a letter suggesting that Marriage Foundation might use me, as a published author, to be a spokesman talking about the perils of divorce, and suggesting people read my book to find out what the fall-out can be.

I might be much more light-hearted, OK idiotic then, than some of the lawyers and intellectual erudite people that currently comprise the Foundation's board. And equally off-putting, middle-class and posh for the general public to want to take any notice of. As well as a ticking time-bomb for saying the wrong thing. But I might make good telly. The Four In A Bed thing has given me a bit confidence actually.

I have just checked with Sashka whether I sound mad. She said it was a 'Maryism' but it did sound a go-er, rather than being a completely bonkers surreal idea.

It would be really scary. But if I could just avert one family from unnecessary divorce I would die happy in the knowledge that I had done a small worthwhile thing for mankind.

So I am going to send Ms Butler-Sloss that letter. And then, if she wants to follow it up, I am going to have to have a serious chat with Ex about what I can and can't say publicly about our experiences.

Poor Creatives
23/11/2015

If I succeed in selling 1000 copies of my book (dream on) I will make £1500, while Amazon takes a stonking £8500 from this unknown failure-author; whose book ranks 25,000th at most in their Best Sellers list.

So the mind boggles at how much Amazon is raking in altogether from exploiting us anonymous Vanity Publishers. The company lists several million books! Respect!

It's the same for journalists, musicians, actors, people on telly, artists, sculptors. Nearly all the wedge goes to the manufacturers and sales effort, rather than to the creatives - the people who provide whatever it is that the public are paying to see, read or hear.

Fair enough, I say. Loads of people want to write, paint, make music etc. Fun, lots of them doing it, mostly at relatively little risk or up-front cost. Whereas the business entrepreneurs stake their livelihoods on investing in structures through which the finished product might be displayed, whether it's a printing press, theatre, television channel, art gallery or whatever, that might easily go bust. Meanwhile effective salespeople are a rare, charming breed unafraid of the word 'non'. If you want to make money, be one of them, I say.

So I am particularly excited by my son Will's announcement that he wants to go into Band Management as a career. He has already started researching for universities that run a course called 'Music Business', and is keen to start managing a promising band in his school for practice. Hurray! He will make loads of dosh and be able to fund my nursing home in due course. How lovely to have something to plan for, and to look forward to, three years ahead.

So far, our research has led us to 120 such courses, mostly run by bodies with names that sound suspiciously like the real thing, but aren't, eg Southampton Solent University, University of Brighton, which I suspect aren't Southampton or Sussex Uni's at all. I had to explain to him the difference between proper universities and poly's - call me old fashioned. I think it would be nice for him to go somewhere where he'll be surrounded by other people who have also had millions and trillions invested into ensuring they get good A'level grades, whereas a 3 B's requirement is typical of most of the courses on offer. Keele and Falmouth look promising. More research required. We've got over 3 years to sort this out so it's hardly urgent,

An Essay on Divorce
26/11/2015

This is me practising what I'm going to say when/if I get an interview with Marriage Foundation.
Five divorces happened all at once in my son Will's year at prep school. Of these I would say that one was inevitable and unavoidable. Of the other four, I think, although they may argue, that out of the eighteen people involved including parents and children, six years later only two are significantly happier now than they would have been had everyone stayed put.

One poor little eight year old girl found herself having to suddenly share her parents every alternate weekend, at each of their homes, with one of two new 'nearly sisters' from her class at school. Of these, one has indeed turned out to be a 'nearly sister', the other hasn't.

Leaving aside intimacy issues and emotional turmoil, to follow is a personal list of the practical consequences of separation as experienced by me. So don't expect it to be in the least bit comprehensive, nor applicable to all. It's just my perspective:

CONS

You feel as though you're being severely punished. Almost every waking moment of your life is affected by the separation in some way or another - for doing what wrong? All these years later, you're still not quite sure what you've done to deserve all this.

Christmas

Christmas will never be quite the same ever again for anybody in the family. Arguments as to who goes where. Every second year you find yourself home alone, tucking into a poussin in front of The Sound Of Music. If you're lucky, at tea-time you receive a series of phone calls from jolly friends and families with lots of loud happiness going on in the background. Otherwise they have kindly invited you to join in on their Christmas, where you feel like some rejected, failure, lonely old maiden aunt. With no Christmas stocking.

Poverty

You couldn't afford two houses, two cars, two sets of fuel bills, two holidays, two sets of children's clothes, two sets of Christmas and birthday presents, massive transport costs etc before, let alone after you've paid all the lawyers' fees - how can you now?

So you have to sell the family home that you've known and loved all these years, leave the local community with whom you've been building up relationships for a decade or more, uproot the family to somewhere else smaller and nastier, and start all over again.

You have to start working in order to cover the bills, so have less time to concentrate on the children, meanwhile you morph into a stressy person.

Suddenly the idea of funding yourself all alone in your old age becomes very frightening.

Social Ostracism

Life becomes an endless series of lone decision-making and responsibility. See 'Trapped in an Apron'.

Your children are too old now for the village toddler group, where lifelong relationships are formed, so becoming an integral part of the new community has become much more difficult. You are a divorcee. "It takes two." There must be something wrong with you, living all alone like that. They say the stigma of divorce has gone, but I don't agree.

You're not seen as a 'threat', it's more that you no longer fit into the social of norm of being a traditional proper family, so you don't get asked to things so much anymore. The Dads like to have other Dads they've known for years around for Sunday lunch, or dinner, or days out. New partners don't quite cut it. Your erstwhile friends simply forget you exist. Your new social life works better with other people in a situation similar to yours.

The above impacts on your children, eg in school/clubs where Dads and Mums take it in turns to bring the children, bond with each other, and start getting together socially, with their children, outside whatever the key activity is. You can't get properly involved because of time/baby-sitting issues. Your children miss half the fixtures because they're at Dad's.

"Blame Mummy, it's not you," I explain to Faye when she's crying because she hasn't been invited to the Hallowe'en party, the birthday party, the camping weekend or the sleepover. "It's not because they don't think you're nice, it's because I haven't bonded properly with their parents, so you weren't on their radar."

As a single Mum you have to go to everything on own, or stay at home watching Casualty. You have to walk in to parties on your own with your head held high, stand on the touchline on your own cheering them on in your silly, high, girlie voice, go to the healthclub on your own, on holiday on your own, cinemas, theatre, beaches, soft play areas, adventure parks and zoos and other similar 'treats'. And you'll probably give up going to the pub altogether.

You are stuck at home every night. Night after night after night after night, for years on end, unless you get a babysitter, but you can't afford one anymore.

Alternatively, when your ex has the children and you are free as a bird and ready to play 24/7, everybody else is busy doing family things.

There is no one to share the driving - to and from school, long distance to see relatives, get to airports etc; and never anybody to drive you home from any parties you might be invited to, so you can never enjoy a drink.

You find yourself changing light-bulbs and fuses, doing the gutters, the drains and the mowing, painting, putting up shelves, topping up the oil in your car and changing its wheel after a puncture.

Inviting people round to your house is difficult, because the Dads don't want to come, and the invitations, shopping, cooking, laying the table, entertaining and clearing up afterwards all on your own fill you with dread. You struggle to afford it anyway. So you no longer entertain. And other people don't entertain you in return.

You don't have any time or money left for a hobby anymore. Known these days, I believe, as 'me time'.

Relationships with the Children

Your time spent with the children is halved. If they are at boarding school this leaves you with literally just a few weeks of them being at home over a whole year. Even worse if they start wanting to stay with friends or BF/GF, where proper family life is more fun, more relaxed and more full of jolly people.

You spend most of your day arranging their travel and pick-up dates and times with your ex.

Input into homework, music practice, discipline etc is all down to you. You are Mrs Bad Guy. There is no one to share the nagging.

This all takes place after you've done a day's work, collected them from school, done their shopping and washing, at the same time as you're trying to cook your and their supper (you eat fish fingers with them these days) and clear it up, read them a story and finally get them into bed.

You turn into an alcoholic.

Effects on the Children

They spend most of their lives packing, unpacking, travelling and losing things.

They never know where they are going to be for Christmas

PROS

The children get very good at packing and using trains.
They mature and become self-reliant quickly.

They become worldly-wise and perceptive.

The loo seat is only left up if you left it up.

Nobody squashes the toothpaste tube, leaves rings around the bath, hair in the basin, or muddy footprints up the stairs.

If the kettle boils dry on the Aga, or the door of the deep freeze is left open, it's your fault. In fact anything which goes wrong is your fault so there is nobody there to make you cross.

You can paint your bedroom pink and it always smells nice.

You can read your romantic novel with the light on, well into the early hours, without being disturbed.

You can fantasize about the ultimate perfect non-existent mate who may one day share your new world.

You only lose things if it was you who mislaid them in the first place.

You can eat the same weird stuff every single day and never wash up.

You can listen to Radio 2 all around the house, and watch reality TV and Rom Coms whenever you like.

You are entirely free to do whatever you like, and go wherever you like, whenever you like. (Although you don't have the time or the money, and you can't leave the children)

How long you spend on the phone is entirely your business. In fact how much you spend on anything is completely up to you. You can go and buy a horse or a car without asking anybody's permission. Oh - except you can't afford either.

Nobody criticises you, puts you or your ideas down, or spoils the mood if you're feeling happy.

You can be OCD about what goes where in the fridge and cupboards - or the opposite if you prefer.
You know exactly how much money there is, or isn't, in the bank - because it was you who did or didn't spend it.

Hmmmm. Perhaps this singledom thing isn't too bad after all!

Or actually, looking at these lists again, do the Pros seem a bit trivial compared with the Cons?

Lady C
28/11/2015

"You're like Lady C, you just don't say it to their faces," observes my loving supportive daughter, Faye.

Extraordinary how the telly viewing public loves a posho with character. Perhaps there's hope for me yet. All on her own, Lady C must be bringing in £millions in both advertising revenue and viewership to ITV, in her role as controversial aristo on "I'm a Celebrity". And I couldn't help agreeing with what she said to that ex-pop-star bloke. Trouble is, I suspect he knows that she's right and it's just what he's afraid of acknowledging as the truth. "Boring oik" she called him, amongst a lot of other things. Nevertheless, I suppose that is a bit rude.

Meanwhile my vote is for Louise. It's amazing how few people who can really sing are also easy on the eye. But hey ho, I suppose that big black bloke who sings 'Crazy' managed OK somehow, and he's hardly a stunner.

And lastly, I've done something mischievous. I've donated a signed first edition of my book for auction at tonight's hunt pledges evening. That could cause a stir. Half the people there are mentioned in it! Richard's idea, backed up by Sashka. Naughty pair! Perhaps no one will buy it and I can have it back and make a fiver on it myself. Meanwhile lovely Flora at Prince Hall Hotel up the road has offered to sell signed copies for me without even taking a commission!

Another Murder in Hexworthy?
28/11/2015

"MARY!!!" belts out Sashka.

"Get in your car NOW! I've heard unearthly screaming coming out of Paula's house!"

I am still in bed as usual, wearing my shiny nylon baby-blue faux-silk pyjamas bought for Four In A Bed. I throw on an anorak and some wellies, getting mud on my PJs, and hurl the finally mended Golden Monster through the still-broken gate, and up the hill to the lone grey cottage which for the last twenty years has been as silent as a grave.

A bloke beat his wife to death twenty years ago in the house opposite Paula's. I am worried that it might have happened again.

The screaming must have been pretty loud for Sashka to have heard it across their garden, through the gale, and through her riding hat.

Sashka rushes up their garden and into their house, while I thoughtfully turn the truck round, Chris Evans bantering (if that's a verb) away with David Walliams on Radio 2.

Within less than five minutes Sashka returns.

"It was BT," she explains, breathlessly.

"Paula was completely hysterical, crying and berating and beside herself. The phone's been off for a week now. I told her I'd seen OpenReach down the road this morning, mending a telegraph pole."

"She needs a complimentary copy of my book," I replied. "It might cheer her up to read all about my problems with BT last year. Actually cancel that. I don't do complimentary copies."

Holy Cow!
02/12/2015

The government is spending out even more on TB compensation than it did on Foot & Mouth.

In 2011, DEFRA anticipated paying over a £1 billion of taxpayers money to farmers, in compensation for their cattle slaughtered because they'd contracted TB, over the ensuing ten years. (I think I've got my facts right, but I'd consumed quite a lot of merlot when this conversation was taking place last night).

Each infected slaughtered cow, the boffins straight out of university with their first class honours degrees at DEFRA have decided, is worth £1500.

So that's handy for people like Neighbour, as his healthy little belted galloways will typically fetch less than £1000 each, dead or alive. He might as well deliberately infect them with TB and make a profit on their useless carcasses!

Or I might get some and do just that! What a great new business idea!

Meanwhile my mate's Devon Red's are worth over £3000 each. That's more than a decentish horse! And although both his herds of cattle, and his sheep, have been isolated for twenty years, there is TB on his farm. Yet the pop stars still want to save what Neighbour refers to as 'the black and white fox'.

What's worse - losing a few badgers? Or tens of thousands of cattle?

Seven Reviews!
02/12/2015

My newly published book seems to be getting almost more reviews than sales! Now there are seven listed on Amazon!
Extraordinarily enough, of those seven, five of them are by men! Not my target audience at all! And not all the reviews have been contributed by my friends either - in fact I have only ever met three of the reviewers!

I am touched to the core by how enthusiastic about the book everybody seems to be - and the sentiments expressed appear to be genuine and heartfelt, each review largely reflecting the last. Perhaps my first book will become a best seller somehow after all!

At the moment I have sold a combined total (paperbacks and kindle) of 79 - about half of each. Which has achieved a stratospheric £156.30 in royalties - that will be enough to cover the cost of new tyre for the Golden Monster then.

My favourite review is the first one, put up by my great mate Richard:

5 out of 5 stars: *Buy it.*
Almost certainly the best book ever written on this or any other subject.

(I don't believe Richard has actually read the thing)

My second favourite review is a mystery one:

Hilarious and moving
By Mme La Bonne on 26 Nov. 2015
This book is a diary written by Mary who is focused on coping with changes after divorce. She describes trying to find a man to love while juggling the finances, sorting out her messy lair and taking care of the children. I thought it was hilarious and deeply moving. It made me laugh out loud and also pop out a few tears. It reminded me of a combination of the classic

Withnail And I [1986] [DVD] and the wonderful The Rosie Project: Don Tillman 1. It was definitely a page turner and I really enjoyed it.

I was so excited by this anonymous review that my heart started beating thumpity thump, while my brain said, "What if! What if!"

So then, being totally ignorant generally, and particularly hopeless at quiz nights, I looked up WIthnail And I; and The Rose Project: Don Tillman 1" on Amazon.

Well.

Withnail and I is a cult film from the late '80s described thus:

London, 1969 - two 'resting' (unemployed and unemployable) actors, Withnail and Marwood, fed up with damp, cold, piles of washing-up, mad drug dealers and psychotic Irishmen, decide to leave their squalid Camden flat for an idyllic holiday in the countryside, courtesy of Withnail's uncle Monty's country cottage. But when they get there, it rains non-stop, there's no food, and their basic survival skills turn out to be somewhat limited. Matters are not helped by the arrival of Uncle Monty, who shows an uncomfortably keen interest in Marwood...

Why have I come across like them? Help!

It gets worse.

"The voice is first person from Don's crippling matter-of-fact Aspergers point of view," goes the first review of 'The Rose Project: Don Tillman 1.'

Which is clearly doing really well because it's currently at 596 on Amazon's Best Sellers list.

So, as narrator in my book, I come across as Aspergers do I? Oh dear! No wonder there are no men beating a path through the mud to my door!

Ready Brek
06/12/2015

The neck of my fibula measures -1.7.

Oh no! What a shock!

I'd waltzed into Torbay hospital - well that's not quite true. I'd driven round and round and round and round Torbay hospital looking for a parking space; and then set off on an unsponsored marathon walk to find the department for rheumatics. And then had this dexa-scan thing - a routine scan for middle-aged women with osteoporosis in the family. "I take after my father's side of the family," I announced cheerfully.

Oops.

Well according to the results I'm in the 'osteopenia' bit of the graph. So that means no more fags or cava, and Ready Brek with sardines for breakfast every morning. I'm also going to be prescribed some monthly pill, and vitamin D. More walking (I hate walking - that's what horses are for), while this is one area where swimming's not particularly helpful. I need 'bumpy' exercise, apparently. And a lot more holidays in the sun.

The irony is that thirty years ago, when I was doing PR for Lyons Tetley, I was tasked with preparing a reserve statement in case of a possible calcium overdose as a result of consuming too much Ready Brek. One assumes that chalk must be cheaper than oats. Anyway, my research revealed that it is almost impossible to OD on calcium, and one child's serving of Ready Brek supplies half their daily calcium requirements, and over a quarter of the Vitamin D they need. So - I guess it's lucky I like Ready Brek!

But nothing, not even the threat of my backbone dissolving into powder, will get me anywhere near a sardine.

Rutter vs Shakin
06/12/2015

Yesterday was each child's School Christmas concert.

I was 40 minutes late for my final choir practice, having tried four different routes into Exeter - all gridlocked by Christmas shoppers.

But the service itself was spectacular, with a massed choir of 120, ranked on scaffolding in the middle of Exeter cathedral, a 22 year old ex-Kings College Cambridge organ scholar belting the carols out through the cathedral's massive organ pipes. "Big enough to hide in," commented one young chorister. The school service was a ticketed sell-out - I would imagine there were 2000 people in the congregation.

We sang Rutter and Britten and a modern particularly ding-dongy version of Ding Dong Merrily, and we all had to wear black, with the school choir wearing black or white surplices over their blazers and ties.

A quick cup of lapsang and half a clotted cream scone each later, it's on for my sister and me to the next concert at Will's very different kind of school.

Will is to play a 'cheeky solo', in a 'dirty' or 'growling' style of play on his tenor sax, during Shakin Stevens' "Merry Christmas Everyone". The children have to wear black, whether it's strapless tops, Doc Martens, bow ties or no ties.

"Really excellent, really tight," comments my sister.

"Round pegs in round holes," I think to myself proudly. "The right school for the right child."

!
06/12/2015

Today is the last rugby match of the season for Will. Against his neighbouring school. Will and the rest of the 1st XV rugby squad are 'pumped'. So are the Mums and Dads. Will's school has had to invest in railings to prevent the parents from the opposing schools fighting each other.

I set off to this important match, down the bumpy lane from Granny's house, Twiglet running along by the side of the car as usual - the only exercise he's going to get during these two days of keen parenting.

At the end of the lane I stop, let him in, get back into the Golden Monster, and it's showing a red exclamation mark on the dashboard again. I put on and release the handbrake but no - the horrid little sign stubbornly remains.

"Ah - I know!" I remember, as I head on to the rugby game. And as I drive, slightly nervously, but reassuring myself this must be a simple case of worn brake pads from towing around too many horses up and down too many hills, it strikes me."Brake fluid!" I turn into the nearest garage in Sturminster Newton.

"Have you got any brake fluid for a diesel truck?" I enquire.

Two blokes come out with me, and we pour some in. "Not to the top because there needs to be some air in there," I say knowledgeably. I turn on the ignition and bingo! The exclamation mark has gone! The brake fluid only costs £3.99. "I would have given you £50 for that!" I exclaim to the garage owner.

Anyhow, so disaster averted, I reach the rugby game before it starts in the normal hurricane. Will is subbing today - good - perhaps he won't have to play at all, won't get over-exhausted, and won't contract ME after all.

Well - this is the first exciting match I've witnessed in three years, with injured music scholar, Andrew, playing Jerusalem on his trumpet from the touchline, while another boy bangs a plastic bin, the rest of the school chanting and singing "In Dublin's fair city" for some reason. I think some of them might have been to the pub for lunch.

But best of all - there's a fight! All the supporters rush over to watch, and to egg them on as suddenly, in the middle of the match, each entire team lays into the other.

The whole game is most intense, with lots of running, a couple of tries, and ending in a draw, everybody's honour satisfied. There's a bald section of mud afterwards where the fight took place, and Ex takes it upon himself to find a black bag and to collect up empty beer cans. I like that about him. He does things that the usual crowd behaviour people overlook.

At the celebratory team tea afterwards, the school athletics lady stands on a table to make a speech and congratulate everybody. I can't hear what she's saying, but all those assembled - about 150 people, school children and parents combined - suddenly turn to me, and start laughing and clapping.

It turns out that far from giving a congratulatory speech, the lady was asking who the Golden Monster belongs to, because it's blocking in the other school's coach.

Viewings
06/12/2015

I'm cleaning my teeth when the estate agent bangs on Mum's front door. He's come 30 minutes early to have a look around her house before the first viewer of the day arrives.

After they've finished looking over the place, I have a little chat with the potential purchaser. I like her. She lives in East Sheen, is divorced, and is wearing a well cut Barbour quilted jacket.

"Well to be honest, if it were mine, I might just get rid of the entire new half," she says. "It feels like being at boarding school with all those rooms leading off the passage like that, and those awful windows."

Well that's one take on it I suppose.

What's amazing though, is that Mum has had seven viewings of her £475,000 four bedroom house in the middle of nowhere in West Dorset in a week, whereas in a whole year I've only had seven viewings of my beautiful Dartmoor home altogether!

School Newsletters
06/12/2015

The trouble is that they're always so predictably full of good news.

If only they reported that the School Fete resulted in food poisoning, 43% pupils fell asleep during Henry V on the school trip to Stratford, and the real reason why we said such a sudden goodbye to Charlene Smythe was ... they might be more readable.

Worst Christmas Party
06/12/2015

I'm doing quite well for Christmas parties this year.

I was two hours late for the first one, last Tuesday, having scampered home after Faye's riding lesson and turned straight round again to retrace my journey for my local friends' annual get-together at Riverford's Organic Kitchen. (I must sell this house, it's so far from everything, daily mantra). When I finally got there, I headed straight for where all the husbands were sitting, and was last to leave, feeling warm and loved. And there are still three drinks parties to come! Hurray!

Last night, on the way back from Will's rugby match, having collected Faye from her school en route, was the option of dropping by on my health club's Christmas party. Would we? Wouldn't we? Hell - we're us! We can't resist a party! So no bath nor shower, no washed hair nor party frocks, in we went, £15 each, for a good boogie and possibly to make some new friends.

Well I got recognised! A friendly lady called Ann approached me, asking if I was from 'Four In A Bed'! And it turned out that she was single, and had come to the party with two other single girlfriends. So that made five of us, and I don't suppose we were the only single ladies there. Meanwhile all the men were at a much better party across the road at Exeter Chiefs.

Not Much Of A Year
09/12/2015

This time last year I was so excited about what the future held.

"In twelve months' time I'll have a whole new life. I'll be living in a new house, and embarking on a new relationship - the beginning of Chapter Three!" I thought.

Well I'm feeling sad today, because looking back over the last year, I don't feel I've got very far at all. No house sale. No boyfriend.

I'm glad that the book's out, but I'm only selling one a day, after all my efforts. About 85 so far, instead of the 1,000 that I'd optimistically envisaged.

In fact I feel I've made so much effort over everything and it's got me nowhere really. I'm not sure what more I can do. Just keep going and hope things work out next year instead.

And remind myself that actually, thinking about it, in the general scheme of things, I am rather a lucky bunny.

B&B Stress
09/12/2015

Much as I love running the B&B, I can't tell you what a relief it is when something goes wrong, and there are no guests here.

At the moment the house reeks of oil.

Last year I sacked my oil deliverers in a rage, because first they didn't top up my oil tanks despite supplying what they called a 'top up' service, so I ran out. And then they filled both tanks instead of one, as is the arrangement, resulting in a bill of £1000, just when I was going through a poor patch.

Well on Sunday both Aga and boiler went out as there was no oil getting to them. Despite there being a full tank of oil - but without its tap turned on. So I was without heat or cooker - thank God it was so mild. And then I had to urgently get otherwise-engaged-Gary-the-plumber over to bleed the system yet again, and turn the tap on, at vast inconvenience to him, and expense to me.

The result is that we're warm again, but the entire place stinks of oil and mildew, as Storm Desmond continues to rush in under the front door.

It's livable with, but if there were guests here, I would definitely be bald by now!

Black
15/12/2015

I have just taken delivery of the most expensive jar of cranberry sauce known to man. It cost £6.75 and was hand delivered on its own, by Tesco. Just like the bunch of bananas I ordered last year.

This time the cranberry sauce jar came on its own because my broadband ran out last night, so I was unable to complete my order.

No broadband out here is like having no arms, legs, or head.

After five hours of nothing, at 10.30pm I put on my wellies and went out into the rain and dark in my white dressing gown and nightie, with a torch and my rather nice replacement new mobile phone, pushed open the still-broken heavy mildewed gate, squelched through the mud, and started screaming my head off at God - or whoever - into nothingness. And cursing my broadband provider, and Faye for streaming too many films, and anybody else I could think of, as no blobs signifying a mobile signal appeared, and the torchlight faltered.

I am so utterly, completely, totally, fanatically fed up with nothing ever working here, and every single thing I try to do proving to be such an uphill struggle and just so, so difficult. To be honest, I nearly cried, which I normally only ever do when I'm on the telly. I am so desperate to move.

As I reached the top of the six acre field, finally up came the blobs, just as the torchlight went out, and I sent my rather important text.

I swore at sweet Herbie the pony, who'd suddenly emerged like a silent white ghost through the darkness for a nuzzle; and went back to bed for a restless, sleepless night, furious at everyone and everything.

This morning I went out in my nightclothes and wellies again to check the internet connection one more time, to discover that somebody who shall remain nameless had turned a minute little switch off, on one of the little black boxes that connects it to the house, rendering it useless.

Europasat and Faye - sorry.

Third Most Expensive Thing on eBay
15/12/2016

I've taken Wydemeet off the market. It will come across better on RIghtMove in the Spring if it looks as though it's only just gone on sale for the first time then.

Over the past year its most likely buyers were generated by me anyway, rather than the estate agent.

So I've popped it back on eBay where it is currently the third most expensive thing on sale, just in case there might be another jolly little billionaire out there. eBay only charges £35 a month to advertise property.

Well guess what. My little eBay ad has generated '5 people watching'.

And then a 'Best Offer' came in - of £50,000. Eeek! How do I stop this going through? I am facing total and utter ruin for being so sloppy and not ticking the box preventing Best Offers! Do I have to ask a friend to put in another Best Offer of £800,000? If we do that, will I have to pay Stamp Duty when I pay them back? What to do?

Finally I track down the 'Help' people at eBay. They call back and gently explain the Best Offers only last 48hrs and you can 'decline' them. Pheweee! So I messaged back my optimistic potential purchaser with "Nice try, mate. Better luck next time. Respect."

And then the next thing that's happening is a chap called Alan has booked to view the place just after New Year. How exciting is that?!

Laters Baby
09/12/2015

At 13, is Faye old enough to watch 50 Shades of Grey?

Mary Whitehouse-esque, I decided that the only way to find out was to watch it myself.

A treat I'd been looking forward to for months, as I loved the book trilogy, but am the only person that I've ever met who admits to doing so, and I couldn't find any mates prepared to come with me to see the film at the cinema.

So some time ago I bought the DVD off Amazon.

Will (then 16) first viewed 50 Shades prior to its release, on some pirated download on his laptop. He said it was so rubbish that he dropped my new DVD in a flower pot, where Faye wouldn't find it.

Well last week I retrieved the DVD and ...

What a disappointment!

The story-line (what story-line) keeps close to the narrative of the book

(I'm currently reading the fourth one, 'Grey', which is how I know) but in my eyes is devoid of chemistry, romance, intensity.. and then the whole thing suddenly ends while the story is still in the middle, which I'd forgotten would happen. When Christian moves the end of his hacking crop over Ana it looks ridiculous more than anything. You would be laughing if you hadn't fallen asleep.

I think the problem is in the casting. The stars are both too short and too young. No way would that muscular little boy be running a global empire. The only person who could possibly find him 'hot' is someone the same age as Faye!

The DVD is now back in the flower pot - the best place for it.

Marriage Foundation
18/12/2015

A couple of weeks ago I sent a copy of my book, a DVD of 'Four In A Bed', my 'Essay on Divorce', and a covering letter saying I'm a bit like Lady C, to Sir Paul Coleridge, Founder and Chairman of Marriage Foundation, retired judge, and family barrister of the highest standing of 30 years, to a Box Number taken from the Foundation's website. The whole package took me a day to put together, including working out how to up- and download again the 'Four In A Bed' DVD, and it cost a fortune to post because my book is so thick and heavy.

And then I sat and waited. And heard nothing. Perhaps I should have sent it recorded delivery. Perhaps that Box Number was out of date. Perhaps the whole Foundation has folded. Perhaps I didn't put enough postage on. Perhaps they just think I'm some weirdo and threw away my precious package.

So after some more sitting and some more waiting and daily rifling through all the Christmas card post looking for a proper, serious letter from them, I finally bit the bullet and wrote direct to Sir Paul's email address given on the website, attaching links to everything I had initially gone to such trouble to package up.

Well.

Blow me down.

Within a couple of hours I received a reply direct from the great man himself, saying he'd like to meet me and put me forward for a BBC 1 Discussion Programme in early January! Eeeek!!!

Gone With the Wind
19/12/2015

"You can start on '50 Shades' when you've read 'Gone With the Wind' from cover to cover, and learned what proper romance is all about," I said to Faye.

I read 'Gone With The Wind' when I was about Faye's age, when there was no telly to distract me at my horrible boarding school, only to find out that the last page, page 999 or something, was missing. So I never got as far as 'Tomorrow Is Another Day' after all that.

Faye has now ordered the great tome off Amazon (£7.49; No 6,441 in the Bestsellers List), and, while waiting for it to arrive, has started to re-write it for the modern young teenager, using Amazon's 'Look Inside' feature for reference. She has been typing away now, copying her Mum, sitting up in bed, still in her nightie, tap, tap, tapping on her AppleMac, every day til teatime.

This is how Faye's version goes:

Gone With The Wind

(Modern Day)

Belle O'Hara a fit young lady with a hypnotizing smile that she used to capture men with, like the Tarleton boys, as well as her mesmerising face that was absolutely perfect on all areas including shamrock green eyes with dark lashes that were long and curled with brows that were perfect with a high arch, with no work done, this all matched her black hair which made her green eyes stand out. Her complexion of olive skin, highly maintained by a hot Miami private beach house and low SPF sun cream. Everyone who saw her was jealous of her perfect hourglass, curvaceous body.

The Tameton boys, Stuart and Brent were sunbathing in out on the patio of Tara house, above dad's private beach, on a bright sunny day in august 2015, for many this was a great sight. Belle strutted down the porch stairs in her new tightly fitting black cocktail dress, black flats with matching earrings and a necklace, all from Gucci where her dad bought them. The dress really brought out her award winning 17-inch waist that everyone admired (as it was the smallest in three counties), and showed off her boobs that were big for a sixteen year old. Her bold choice of a twisted bun showed that she wasn't afraid to be her self, even though she carefully sat down trying not to draw lots of attention to her self you could see the eagerness to explore in her eyes also with a wilful and defying look. She had the manners of a proper lady but the heart of a lion. She was the type to look but not to encourage as she learnt how to entice from her mother, if she wanted a man she would get the pick of her choice taken or not taken.

On either side of her the boys were sunbathing happily squinting through their Ray Bans as they talked and laughed together. Their long legs thick from muscle. The boys were nineteen and six ft two and hunky, ripped bodies with sunburnt faces with a messy heep of dark auburn hair, their eyes gleaming with tears of laughter, their shorts the same billabong design.

The sunlight beamed down on the beach reflecting off the white sand with a blue backdrop. The boys jet skies were tied to the pontoon. Even though these teenagers were raised in the sweet life they wouldn't rely on people doing everything for them. They would often help as much as they could....... etc etc

This could run and run! I've suggested to Faye that she publishes on Amazon Kindle!

Falling Down
24/12/2015

"There's water coming into the sunroom!" called out Faye.

I don't know how long we've been having this horizontal rain, but it feels as though there's never been anything else. Global warming gone ballistic.

The house has given up and is now leaking like a sieve. And reeking of mildew the minute you come through the back door. I'm not going to bother mending the 'ram' on the gate as that will cost £700. With the little family who is/was interested in buying Wydemeet arriving on Wednesday to spend Christmas week here at vast expense, things are not looking promising.

Last week we successfully negotiated the sleepover of six 17 year-old friends of Will's, with only one of them being sick, and, after using the hot tub, they were good about putting the barricade back in front of the door to keep the rain from coming in under it; but something appears to have gone wrong. The carpet is soaking again.

On closer inspection, we now discover that the rain is actually making its way through the double glazing panes of the £3000 door - actually it's gushing through. Peter builder is away on some building project in Hungary.

I have already hinted to our delightful rental family that all might not be quite as I would like on their arrival.

While I sit here tapping away on my Chromebook in my Mum's cosy kitchen 100 miles away from the disaster zone that is my home, it's Sashka, with flu, on the phone.

"Peter's Away. The carpet in the hall is soaking. The whole house smells. So I've nailed up a tarpaulin across the front door. Have a very happy Christmas!" She's laughing. Is it hysteria?

Arguing About Divorce
24/12/2015

I think my Mum's quite proud about my Marriage Foundation project.

So now I want to argue about it with everyone, to get me into practice, should I really find myself appearing on TV talking about divorce.

I will need to learn the stats: 60% of couples separating were fine the previous year, and 54% regret their decision, wasn't it? This kind of thing is difficult when you suffer from early onset dementia.

A friend has expressed concern that I should not get stuck in a rut and define myself forever as the 'sad divorcee', so perhaps a year or two of it would be enough.

I took a breath and called Ex to update him, and to ask him whether he would like to appear with me. "It would be good for your profile," I said, not believing for a minute that he would jump at the opportunity. Which he didn't, obviously. But he did reiterate how important it is that I don't bring the children into public discussions.

So is it contradictory that, as a divorced woman, I am proposing to represent the Marriage Foundation whose aim is to champion long-lasting stable relationships within marriage? I've just checked the precise wording on their website and they've changed it. I shall never be able to keep up at this rate! And all this without bringing my own family's experience into the equation?

My intention is to publicly draw attention to the realities of post-divorce life as listed in my Essay on Divorce. But will I be able to commit everything I've written to memory? I can't go live on tv carrying notes!

Over the past couple of weeks the main fallouts of my divorce are turning out to be:

1) Faye is backwards and forwards between Mum and Dad to such an

extent that she will only be able to ride once - no pony club, no hunting, no learning to look after her horse herself, always tired, no continuity, no enthusiasm to do anything except collapse in front of Disney Channel

2) Will will only be home for four days of the entire holiday period

3) I have already done the 60 mile round trip to Exeter Railway Station seven times in ten days

4) We have no home to live in over Christmas because we have to rent our house out to make ends meet

5) I will struggle to afford to re-roof the still leaking sun(rain)room

6) While my home is rented out, I am doing a 166 mile round trip from Mums to a drinks party near Wydemeet, because a lot of my mates from all around Devon, who I haven't seen for ages, will be gathered together there

7) I am missing a second party with my closest South Devon friends (important to attend, in order to remind them of my existence) because all this driving is becoming bonkers!

A Better Christmas
28/12/2015

The mad maiden aunt (ie me) had a better Christmas at my hospitable sister's mansion, this year than last.

Braced for nights spent alone on the sofa, and bumping into devoted husbands in the kitchen at 9am making cups of tea while their loving wives waited for them in bed, this year I found myself with my own room, and I didn't come across a single early morning husband!

Feeling much loved and indulged, I even found myself with a very personal Christmas stocking containing CowPat body cream, L'Occitaine bath gel, and best of all, The Ladybird Book of Mindfulness. If you aren't already aware, Amazon's Top Twenty is comprised almost entirely of colouring-in and Ladybird books. No wonder my own tome hasn't made it as Best Seller yet. It is clearly far too grown up for today's average adult reader. I will have to add some colouring-in sections and some old pics from the sixties original Ladybird books that Granny still has stored in her attic.

I would imagine that most of the copies of Ladybird's mindfulness book are at this moment being used to light fires with, in Totnes. Some of the observations in there might actually incite murder as opposed to contemplation. I was particularly pleased to see a picture in it of two cereal boxes turned into masks of old men's faces, the beards, moustaches and hair all made from cotton wool - efforts that my sister and I attempted to recreate in 1965 using the Ladybird Book of Things To Make. In 2015 the picture was used to illustrate tips on re-focussing your energy.

The trouble is, I don't seem to have any. I have been shut out of my home while it's being rented out to our nice little family, away from all the leaks, my dying computers and lame horses, and haven't done anything but eat, drink and sit down, for exactly a week. The result is that I am completely exhausted. The less I do, the less I want to do. No wonder really fat people just get fatter and fatter and fatter. By the end, it must be as much as they can manage to raise a doughnut to their mouth.

The one thing that might get me out of bed tomorrow is the need to take Twiglet to the vet. He has torn about two square inches of skin off the inside of his leg, so that you can see right through to the muscle - like when you're pulling apart a chicken leg. My children keep taking pictures of it which make me feel sick. There has been no blood, and Twiglet is quite cheerful, so I am loathe to spend £100 on a vet on a Sunday or Bank Holiday Monday, but now the children are close to tears, because they think he is going to die.
So tomorrow.

The Vet.

Probably followed by a visit to the bank manager.

Wet
01/01/2016

As I reached for the bog-roll, the wooden loo seat stuck to my damp bum, and then clattered to the floor beneath the basin, its hinges sheared. Just another casualty of falling down Wydemeet.

I'd raced into the lavatory after half a day's hunting in 'Storm Frank' - I can never really manage past 1pm after a good tipple at the meet, or several goes at reformed-alcoholic Richard's hipflask, which I assume he carries around with him for old times' sake and to make people like me happy, or happier than ever.

Today BBC Weather had forecast heavy rain and wind speeds of 45 mph across the highest, bleakest part of the moor where we were scheduled to be riding. But because it's New Year's Day, and because daughter Faye has only been able to get on a horse once throughout the holidays, and because if an adult accompanies a child to the hunt meet it's only £15 cap money, we were going to go despite Hell and High Water.

The big question in such circumstances is what to wear.

I have done a great deal of research into how to look like a hunting person but stay dry-ish and warm-ish out all day in these conditions, and the unanimous answer is something called a 'Ri-Dry' - a waterproof jacket that comes in hunting colours (red or black for men; black or blue for ladies) and is designed to go over a hunt coat, They're £150 a pop, but I have persuaded my Mum to cover two-thirds of the cost as my Christmas present. The trouble is, I haven't bought it yet. So for the first time ever this morning, I waved goodbye to dignity and hauled on a pair of those hideous waterproof trousers. I had also bought three different types of waterproof gloves varying in price from £10 to £30 a pair, off eBay.

Well. Guess what? The gear worked and I stayed quite dry and warm in the worst weather that God could think of! Long enough to make it until loo-time, anyway.

But despite all of that, most of my headspace this morning was taken up with what happened last night.

Just as Faye and I were setting off for our New Year's Eve roast grouse at Richard's cottage, I received an email from the family who stayed in Wydemeet over Christmas.
I've spent the whole of the Christmas period anxious, forlorn, and mortified about the state that this nice family was going to find the house in.

And now they'd sent me this email. And in it, they'd made me another offer (they did include in their message that they are known by some to be a bit crazy).

But so, having lived in dilapidated Wydemeet in these conditions for a week, they are now offering me £100,000 even less than last time! And part of the deal is that I am to move out by mid-February, taking all curtains and carpets with me, and leaving outbuildings absolutely clear.

My regard for my ex-friend the rockstar, who messed up all of our original, perfectly satisfactory arrangements by pulling out of his house-sale, has plummeted lower than ever.

And now the thing is, I am so very desperate to move that I am tempted just to take the money and run.

Thoroughly Modern Mary
02/01/2016

Anything rather than get up...

I'm tap tap tapping away on my laptop in bed, even though it's lunchtime, and my excuse today is that I am beginning the Herculean task of drumming up sales for my book. So far I have been selling roughly a copy a day, resulting in my positioning on the Amazon Best Sellers list hovering between 41,000th and 131,274th. Agh! I had anticipated ten times that!

Meanwhile the reviews are completely fantastic! Ten now! Lots from people I haven't met, and mostly from men - totally outside my target audience of sad and lonely single Mums. Nearly all the readers say the same sort of thing: they can't put it down, it's funny, gutsy, affecting, why isn't there a film of it etc, etc. I am totally and utterly chuffed to bits with how nice and enthusiastic everybody has been about it, and as a result am finally persuaded to have faith in my product. So this gives me courage to get out there and flog the thing to the world, his wife, cousins, uncles, aunts and everybody else.

Most importantly, I want to send copies of it direct to all the specialist publishers of chick lit, and even to Penguin again, but to do that I'd have to get out of bed in order to pack up all the books, which isn't really my bag at this moment on a Saturday.

So I've been doing research on the internet instead, and am now on my third cup of coffee.

I've been reading about some very famous biker-bloke called Guy Martin who uses a lot of the same expressions as mine, such as 'shit', 'can't be bothered', 'don't know what's coming next' etc. His book, 'When You Dead You Dead' is at Number 211 in Amazon's Best Sellers list, not far behind all the colouring-in ones. So I might be OK if I can only get mine out into the public domain somehow. Guy Martin presents on telly apparently, and was nominated for a BAFTA, so it's no wonder he's got 612 reviews on Amazon, compared with my 10.

I've also checked out the author of the 'Mum In A Playground' books, to discover an online group called 'Goodreads'. She's received 682 Amazon reviews. I am intrigued as to how she got started and plan to send whoever 'Goodreads' is a copy too.

But I've had an idea of my own. With beating heart, I've looked up comments about my telly appearance on Four In A Bed's Fan Club group. I seem to have got away with it with them, quite lightly for a posh person, so I've just 'posted' a message telling all the members to buy my book.

Energised and encouraged, I then joined MumsNet - for which my username appears to be LadyMuck2 - and told its members to buy the book. Then I got completely carried away and 'shared' that message with Facebook, Twitter, and Google+1.

Blimey I am getting modern! What if it all backfires? The thing is, all this social media stuff is so alien to me and feels just so far away that I don't think I'll mind all that much what happens. Famous last self-deceptive words. Eeeek!!!

Properly Scared
03/01/2016

I struggled to open the car door against the horizontal rain and 30mph wind, and yelled 'Faye' hopelessly into the darkness, waving the weak flickering torchlight around feebly,

I mean really. What on earth was the point? She could be absolutely anywhere.

My old next door neighbour of the first twenty years of my life, Sue, had made a special visit from Kent to see me, but on her arrival I'd leaped into her bright red Shogun and ordered her to turn it around and help me search for my daughter out on her own, dressed only in running gear, who was wandering around somewhere on the moor, in the middle of the continuing Storm Frank.

As we progressed up towards Combestone Tor, following the route that Faye and I would normally take on our horses, a terrifying vision of my beautiful girl getting washed off the stepping stones and away down the Dart in full spate suddenly flashed before me. We were going to have to call out Devon's Search and Rescue Helicopter sharpish.
Sue and I turned for home.

Meanwhile Ex was back at Wydemeet, manning the landline.

Ring! Ring! Finally, finally a call from Faye, explaining that she had been sheltering in a barn, where she had been found by some neighbours popping out for a fag. Well. Blimey. Phew.

This had all erupted because I had shouted at her. We never argue, so she was terrified. Just as Panda and Twiglet are if I ever raise my voice, as all any of them ever want to do is to please.

She wanted to get away as far as possible from me. "I saw the hatred in your eyes," she said.

"You are just so lazy!" I had screamed at her, and subsequently googled "Do all teenage girls do nothing?"

Netmums rushed to my rescue, confirming that their daughters were all rude, did nothing, and grunted. Not like my lovely Faye at all! She is a total delight! Simply needs telling what to do all the time when there's no routine, thanks to being all over England throughout the holiday. I find it hard enough to make myself do anything, let alone energise a second party, and I was fed up with it.

None of this was a problem for me at her age, when Sue and I lived next to each other. I drafted up daily timetables of so many things to do to fill the days that my mother would only take me to a fraction of them. Our gang of girls would cycle, draw, pretend to be horses, act, sing, play the piano, violin, listen to records, play ping-pong, swim, play tennis, squash, read; and had any of us been lucky enough to own a pony we would have spent all day every day involved with that.

My parents must have been so grateful to Sue for inspiring my sister and me to be constantly occupied, just sad that she made us wriggle and giggle and snort with laughter throughout any church services she attended with us, and that she put us off the vicar whom we all referred to as 'Jonnybum', and in the end, contributed to our equivocal attitude toward God Himself.

Faye's problem, I have now realised, is that she doesn't have a Sue living next door to her to share things with. Deeply frustrating – because of

Neighbour's daughter, who isn't much older, being just 100 yards up the road, but refusing to be friendly! What were the chances of finding that, here in the middle of nowhere?! But sadly, it is not to be, and none of the activities I've listed has much appeal if you are a 13yr old girl on your own.

So. What to do? I must move!

Results of Social Media Sales Campaign
04/01/2016

Sales of the paperback version of my book, during the first three days of January 2016: 0

Sales of the kindle edition of my book via my social media campaign, on the day of January 2nd: 5

Comments on MumsNet saying: "Are you the agony aunt from The Spectator? If so you are really funny": 1

Almost worth it then.

Death, Divorce and e-Cigs
08/01/2016

You've guessed it - I'm stressed out.

So much so in fact, that I'm researching an e-Cig thing that I confiscated off Will after he had used my eBay details to buy it for a friend. Faye expertly charged this pen-like thing up for me and filled it with some yellow liquid from a little bottle that came with it, and handed it over. I tentatively put the black plastic end to my lips and breathed in.

AGGHH!!!! I jumped backwards, knocking over a chair. "It's disgusting!" I shrieked at her. "Why would anybody ever want to deliberately breathe in apple-flavoured steam?"

Since then, the weird-looking piece of apparatus has wandered around between kitchen, office, and that place on the stairs, wondering where it lives, if anywhere.

Back from boarding school, young Will spotted it, lying around in its nomadic homelessness. He explained that it is indeed currently supplying just apple flavoured steam, and that it can be used for tricks. He showed me how you have to press down the blue button so that it makes a gurgly noise, close your throat, and blow lots of vapour around, in and out through your mouth and nose. I was slightly alarmed at how expert at this he seems to be.

Ten minutes later he reappeared with some similar-looking implement, although this one looked a lot more worn. Instead of jolly yellow liquid in the middle, this one was filled with brown stuff. I pressed the button and breathed in. "Ach, ach," I coughed, like a first time smoker.

So this one is clearly the business. Red Bull flavoured nicotine. Yum! Much more like it.

So now, if I ever feel the urge, which is not often, I can pop down and take two breaths out of Will's gadget, and pretend to myself that I've had a fag. The difference is, the e-version is almost free, you can use it inside instead of outside in the hail, you don't reek like a bonfire afterwards, and you don't get osteoporosis or cancer or any of all those other things as a punishment for using it. The downside is that it makes you look like a complete moron.

The reason why I am stressed out is because everything appears to be moving rather fast. After a roller coaster that you wouldn't believe.

I told my nice family that it was a 'non' to their paltry offer.

Then a friend of a friend came out of the woodwork, desperate to buy Wydemeet even though she hadn't even seen it. She's a publishing agent (negotiated Ex's book rights, small world), which could come in handy if I play my cards right. She booked herself in for the weekend.

I reported all this to my nice family who upped their offer by small increments during the course of that day, until we reached an agreement at 5.30 in the morning, and, rather embarrassed, I had to email my publishing agent back to cancel her visit.

So now I needed to find somewhere to live - ready to move into by Valentine's Day, the day my family has to complete on Wydemeet.

Full of hope and optimism, I immediately made paltry offers on the two houses I like. No dice. I upped my offers to the maximum I could afford. No response.

A very long stay at Mum's house, all my belongings in storage, loomed.

Then the estate agent for one of the houses finally came back and told me that my offer was so pathetic that I couldn't even have a second viewing.

And then finally rockstar came back and said overnight he would consider the revised offer I had made on Haldon Brake. And now he's just said yes!!!

So here we are today. Me £100,000 the poorer than I would have been, had our original arrangement gone through.

Planning to move into my romantic woodland Scandinavian love-nest, perched on the side of the hill with views right across the whole of the Exe Valley - just in time for Valentine's Day!

And no one to share it with.

2 KEEP THE DAY JOB?

Hilarious - moi?
08/01/2016

An ex-copper has just called me.

He tracked me down using his professional detective skills, our first communication having taken place over Encounters some time ago, it turns out.

He is utterly courteous, modest and charming.

"I'm not 5'4", I don't have a beard and I don't wear silly shoes," he says.

"But your name's Keith," I reply.

He asks me extremely politely whether I would do him the honour of joining him for a cup of tea in Ashburton one day soon.

"I'd rather get pissed in a pub," I respond.

Keith explains that the reason he has gone to such trouble to find me is because he finds my book so funny.

Well that's absolutely great - I am so grateful and flattered, that he has spurred me on to write four new blog entries, instead of getting on with opening the post.

But why is it that the main market for my bright pink book about girlie stuff appears to comprise middle-aged men?

I am going to put a picture of a car, or a rugby ball on the front of the next one, and give it a blue cover. Perhaps then it might appeal to sad, lonely, single women, like it's supposed to.

Private Blog
08/01/2016

I attempted to set up a private blog, which turns out to be the least private thing in the world!

I blame my piano bloke.

For some reason, if anyone googles my married name, up comes a blog I wrote about him, dating back nearly a year.

Almost everyone I speak to these days appears to be quietly reading my blog, without making any comments on it. I am being stalked!

Even the lovely little family buying Wydemeet is following my hallowed prose.

Well. I would hardly say that what I've written constitutes the average sales pitch for selling a house.

I go back through what I've said.

Words such as 'dilapidated' and 'falling down' leap up before my eyes.

And this is on top of their horrendous Christmas experience of the house.

So actually, things should all be plain sailing and a delight for them from here. Nothing could get much worse really. No surprises and no disappointments. Management of expectations - my favourite phrase. How extraordinary. March on!

He Hates It!
09/01/2016

"You're moving, Dad's moving, and Granny's moving," Will observes sadly.

I am hoping that the children have had their home in Wydemeet long enough for their general stability not to be affected too badly by the general migration of all around them. But I understand that it must be upsetting for them, everything happening at once.

Will and I are on the way home from the railway station, after his final visit to his Dad's lovely flat in London. Ex is due to move out of that, and in with his new girlfriend at the end of the month.

"Judging by the particulars, I much prefer that other house you were looking at," he continues.

My body freezes. I am suddenly cold all over. What's left of my hair is standing on end, and there's a wooshing noise rushing around my head. After all that. I can't bear it.

Dusk is falling.

"OK, we'll go and look again at all the properties for sale in the area before we drive home, if you like," I say cheerfully. Will proves keen and off we wind through the increasingly familiar lanes of the Dunchideock triangle, wrapped between the A30, the A38 and Haldon Forest, just south west of Exeter.

As far as I can work out from 'mouseprice', not one single four bedroomed detached house has sold here over the whole of 2015. I think the fact that most of the properties available are hideous gentrified cardboard characterless farm labourers' bungalows built cheaply in the '50s might be the reason why.

We drive past a house which I think has been on the market for a couple of years, that we've seen a few times before, and then find ourselves on the lane leading to the 'Second Choice' that I have been forbidden to view by the estate agent, because my offer for it is so pathetic.

"Shall we knock on the door?" I ask WIll.

"OK, if you like," he replies, so we undo the elastic thing holding closed the metal gate, crunch up the drive, and bang on the door of the lean-to conservatory at the front of the house. Dogs bark. A curtain twitches. Will looks around at the amphitheatre of garden and mutters, "It's not quite what I'd imagined".

After a long wait a young woman holding a pretty little toddler arrives at the door. I apologise profusely for our scary and probably illegal intrusion at putting-to-bed time, and cheerfully lie in a jolly way that of course everything we do is for our children, and if my children want me to buy her house, well, I come from a rich family so I am sure that it can be arranged.

Phew. We've achieved it. Will has seen it. At least from the outside. I would never have dared to have done that on my own.

Will has gone a little quiet in the car. "It's not nearly as nice as Wydemeet," he ventures.

We drive past seven more properties available in the area in my price range, even motoring up the drive in the dark to a couple of them.

Two are for sale through 'Purple Bricks' - that online do-it-yourself estate agent. One of these has 59 pictures on its website, all taken in the rain, still managing to miss out shots of the two things I wanted to see: the stable and the workshop. This one wouldn't let me view it, when I told them it was overpriced by £200,000.

"God no, drive on," orders Wilf as we slow down in front of it.
He is becoming ever more quiet. Perhaps he is car-sick. Or is having a sugar low since he had no lunch on the train.

The next day we're with an old boyfriend of mine who is in the music business and who lives up the road, discussing a possible career in Band Management for Will. I think it might be a good idea to pop in to Haldon Brake on the way home, just to remind ourselves of its appeal.

Will appears a lot more enthusiastic now, and is clearly intrigued and impressed by Rockstar's coolness. The final seal of approval comes when Rockstar suggests putting a door between Will's potential new bedroom and the shower, turning it into an en suite.

Thank goodness for that! What a relief! I think we might be alright after all.

Last Night Together
09/01/2016

Will, Faye and I have just spent probably our final evening ever, all together, here at Wydemeet. Both children have lived here since they were born. Bitter-sweet. Exciting, but melancholy. We tried to swap stories about our times here over all these years, as we shared out a rather excellent Tesco Peking duck, but couldn't really think of any.

Mostly it was a series of jolly, extended family Christmas's.

A double chocolate cheesecake later, and Will and I have now agreed where all the curtains will go in the new house.

And on Wednesday I have my meeting with Marriage Foundation. Eeeek!

And on Valentine's day, before the children come home for half-term, I complete.

This simply does not feel real.

GOOD!
14/01/2016

They want me.

I'm going to be on telly on the Victoria Derbyshire Show on BBC 2, one morning in February, with Sir Paul Coleridge, founder of Marriage Foundation (it looks like that at the moment, anyway.)

Doing just what I wanted, which is to stand up and say:

"Think very carefully before deciding to divorce. You will be poorer, your children will cry, and Christmas will never be the same again.

"Look at your Christmas card list. Is there anyone on there whose happy lives you envy? Yet they've stayed together appear to be reasonably content with the arrangement. The grass isn't greener post-divorce, just different. Do not have unrealistically high expectations of life in general and marriage in particular," or something along those lines.

Sir Paul had a lot of interesting things to say, all backed up with properly researched statistics, as he briefed me, over a flat white, in a large, warm cafe on the Aldwych. His key point is that 'poorer people' are tending to have children without even considering a long term relationship with the father, married or unmarried. These are the people we need to reach most of all, he says, but how?

It's all too easy to preach to the converted, and Marriage Foundation (not the Marriage Foundation, because the word 'the' is becoming a bit old-fashioned, apparently, and we want to concentrate on word-play re 'Foundation' - eg marriage should be the foundation of our lives) comprises mostly posh, ageing, out-of-date, and out-of-touch types like Sir Paul and little old me. A fat lot of good getting loads of column inches in The Times is going to prove in reaching the 'poorer people'! And I do wonder how many of them tune into a news discussion programme on BBC 2 of a morning...

Still - we're making progress. The powers that be at the BBC view Marriage Foundation as a pretty reactionary group. The Beeb, would, said Sir Paul, much prefer to focus on discriminated against social minorities, rather than smug, solvent, hard-working, middle class, normal people.

The way to reach our young underprivileged audience, we agreed, is via the social media, whatever that is/are. Paul tells me of the banks of under 18s he has seen working at computers, Tweeting and Instagramming and Snapchatting or whatever, in an attempt to get their employer's message to go viral. Even Paul's 30 year-old children are out of touch with this world.

Oh dear, what a challenge - but then Sir Paul and his ilk wouldn't be needed if it weren't.

"Which is worse, bereavement or divorce?" I query, as I've got a blind date with a Mr I-only-like-women-sized-twenty widower tomorrow.

"Divorce is worse by miiiiiiiiiiiiiles!!!!" exclaims Sir Paul. "Organising the funeral and everything before and after the death of your spouse would be absolutely horrendous, of course," he continues, "but death is completely out of anybody's control. In divorce, not only do you experience loss, but somebody has made a decision, and the resulting guilt and/or feelings of rejection go on more or less forever."

There is a core of people who devote their entire working lives to Marriage Foundation, who are paid, hence its need for funding. But I didn't want a paid position. I would hate to have that sort of responsibility for the Foundation and its supporters.

Sir Paul and I shake hands. I am so very chuffed that he has taken time out to see me, and paid for my avocado sandwich.

Radon
21/01/2016

"The information that you have provided shows that Radon is an issue in the area There is the likelihood that even a retention of £5000 will not be sufficient to eradicate the radon problem It is now imperative that you speak to the HPA asap as well a specialist in radon. You are right you may not be able to sell the property or you may have to reduce the price substantially in respect of a sale. Also a lender may refuse to lend against

the property.

You now may have to consider not to proceed with the purchase of the property. I await hearing from you"

That's what I woke up to yesterday. An email from my buyers' idiotic, narrow-minded, urbanite, poxy, thick, Reading-based solicitor. Telling them not to buy my house because there's radon gas in the area.

Of course there is! My house is made of granite!!! And guess what? There is still a property market on the moor! And we are not all dead! (even if we are all a bit potty and likely to die of cancer in the end). AGGGHHH!

So vast swathes of my day and emotional energy were wasted in an attempt to calm my buyers' understandable hysteria. Whoever heard of a solicitor telling their clients not to buy the house of their dreams for such a stupid reason?

"Our radon measurement is quite low, as the house is currently so drafty," I reassured them. "If you make everything airtight, then you might need to invest in a sump pump which goes under the floor, and costs about £1000.

"Radon in the water supply has been considered so low-risk they haven't even bothered measuring for it until this year," I continued.

The previous day my buyers had attempted to get me to reduce my price by £10,000 after their survey revealed not very much bad at all.

"It's £750,000 and no less whatever comes up," I have had to repeat firmly about three times so far. Why won't they believe me?

Meanwhile a lovely girl, Cathy, visited yesterday, telling me that she can deal with every aspect of the moving issue with a couple of vans and a Luton. Well that might take her some time.

But she's going to coordinate rubbish collection, with packaging and removals, with taking stuff to auction, and taking Ex's stuff for storage in

Salisbury.

"So all I have to do is sit on a stool for five days, and point?" I said.

"That's right," she confirmed. "And you might need several bottles of wine."

Ten Million More Reasons Not To Get Divorced
24/01/2016

"When all of this is over, I think you will come out of it worst, then the children, and I will be fine - it's just that I didn't choose it and don't want it," I informed Ex, as our marriage finally unravelled.

But six years later, actually I think I am the worst off, however bright a picture I have tried to paint.

Last night I pre-warned Ex of what I was planning to say on telly for Marriage Foundation - "Whatever else happens, you will be poorer, your children will cry, and Christmas will never be the same again," blah blah blah.

"I don't see the children crying," he replied, as they merrily tucked into a delicious spag bol, prepared by Will, who is practising cooking on us, in preparation for becoming a chalet boy in his gap-year.

"Well they would have been much happier if it had never happened ..." I started, but six warning eyes swivelled in my direction, so I returned to twiddling spaghetti around my fork.

I have to admit that the children have (so far) dealt with it all a lot better than I had anticipated.

Meanwhile Ex and I might both now be broke, but he appears to be very happy with his lovely girlfriend of a year now.

Anyway.

My book was meant to be an inspiration for people recently out of a relationship, who are/were feeling wobbly and broke. Its purpose was to demonstrate that life post-breakup can be fun; sorting yourself out financially can prove most rewarding in every sense; and then finally it was meant to end up with me meeting a new bloke and living happily ever after. I had planned to complete the book on a most jolly note of wedding bells.

What a shame that real life hasn't quite turned out that way.

There are five destinations for all the possessions this broken family has accumulated over two decades.

The rubbish dump (or landfill as I think they refer to it these days); the auction house; removals of Ex's furniture to a barn belonging to his girlfriend's parents somewhere near Shaftesbury; removals to my new house; and removals of ordinary furniture which I will no longer have room for to lovely house-clearance Cathy's headquarters, from where she will sell it.

We have just said goodbye to the auction man who kindly came out on a Sunday afternoon to look at all Ex's stuff.

"There's no market at all for big furniture anymore," he said cheerfully.

The beautiful inlaid painted mahogany Georgian card table is now only worth a few hundred quid, thanks to a crack in the veneer due to central heating, he told us, not the £3,000 we thought it would fetch. Bang goes Ex's share of the school fees.

The most valuable item of all appears to be a tortoiseshell cigar box.

It is really horrible going through these much loved belongings, knowing that we have to say 'goodbye' to over half of them. And all because Ex decided that he would rather live with Her, or possibly anywhere, in preference to staying with me and the children. Today marks the final end to what we had worked so hard to build into a calm, ordered, stable family home.

I still don't even know for sure where or when I am going! All I do know is that if exchange doesn't take place this Friday because of the radon issue or something equally banal, we will be all ready for when I do finally move - whether that turns out to be in the next few months, or the next few years.

So guess what. No surprises. I have succumbed to that weirdest of gadgets. I am inhaling the odd puff of strawberry-flavoured yellow liquid nicotine, steaming out of the end of a silver and black pen-like thing. I hope I don't get caught looking this ridiculous!

Death, Divorce and Moving House
27/01/2016

They say that death, divorce and moving house are the three most stressful events of life.

Well as of February 19th I will have a five-bedroomed-house-worth of furniture, two children, a dog and two horses, oh and me, with nowhere to go. Rockstar now refuses to exchange on Haldon Brake until he has found himself a new home. Well that's not going to be sorted in just three weeks is it?

So I've submitted another derisory offer for the other house that I like. And have found a third one that might be OK which I will go to look at today.

Meanwhile it has finally dawned on me that, while the children, Twiglet and I are lucky enough to be able to decamp any old time to Mum's, I really do have to find somewhere for the horses to go. So last night, in the gathering gloom, I went and banged on the doors of a couple of liveries within sight of both of my preferred potential new homes.

The cost is eye-watering. At least £200pw, probably more. Agghh!

And then one of the livery owners, who happens also to be a local parish councillor, informed me that Haldon Brake was originally built as a holiday house, with a maximum residency of ten months a year, and lots of 'bits added' since. Even though it was owned by a judge who lived there. Hmmm.

But hey, guess what. The stress of all this is nothing - just nothing - compared with that of getting divorced.

I toss and turn a bit at night, wondering where we are all going to end up eventually.

But I do not sit for hour after hour dissecting the past fifteen years, wondering how and why it all went wrong; agonising how damaged the children are going to be; mourning the loss of our relatively normal, happy family; quaking under the stigma and shame of being a divorcee; forcing myself not to shout and scream at Ex while divvying up what's left of our combined possessions/wealth; terrified of the impending penury, loneliness and general insecurity of an empty future.

Hector
30/01/2016

Houses bought and sold: 0. E-cigs re-charged: 1. Proper fags (bummed off Sashka) 3

Wednesday 9.30am: email pings in to say exchange is delayed by a month

Wednesday 10.30pm: email says exchange due this Friday after all
Wednesday 11.00pm: eureka moment. Just realised that since August, the differential between Haldon Brake and the bigger house a mile down the hill, which faces south and has a garage perfect for horses, has shrunk from £150,000 to £50,000.

Sleepless night envisioning where light fittings and curtains will go if I buy the bigger house

Thursday 10.30am: email says exchange is delayed by a month

Thursday 11am: viewing arranged, with both children in attendance, on their Open Weekends home, of the bigger house, for 3pm Saturday

Saturday (today): Meet representative from Estate Agent in grotty conservatory of bigger house. Shock horror! She isn't lovely posh granny Liz who showed me round before. It's 'Horrid Hilda'! The person I hate most in the whole world second only to Her! Who, for legal reasons, I cannot elaborate upon further. Suffice to say, when I mentioned her name ten years ago at a drinks party 150 miles away in Cornwall someone yelled, "Two faced, duplicitous bitch!!!" which I found most reassuring.

I stamp on my shock having only just recognised her, and am entirely civil. I hope she is wetting herself at the thought of what I might say or do to her, after the way she treated me a decade ago.

Shock horror number 2. The house does not have central heating! What??!! It's 2016!!!

Builder Perfect Peter is going to love this! He has a thing about a special kind of electrically powered oil-filled radiator. So that's alright.

Super-Steph horsewoman has joined us and is jumping up and down with excitement about what a fantastic stable the triple garage is going to make.

Meanwhile Will has spotted the perfect potential teenage den in an old shed.

Faye thinks the house is 'cold and grungy' and prefers the wow factor of Haldon Brake. But I reassure her that we will clean the thin metal-framed windows and that I will only live somewhere warm.

Will plus girlfriend have just provided the most beautifully prepared rather late dinner of toad-in-the-hole and potato-dauphinoise and frozen peas (despite a fridge-full of emergency-pre-ordered fresh veg from Tesco's). I think he is going to crack being a chalet-boy, if that's what he really wants to do during his gap year.

Another mega-jumping competition for Faye on her horse in the gale, bloody miles away, at dawn tomorrow. She will be jumping 3' on Perfect Panda. Measure your dining room table. It is bigger than that, and just as wide. Gulp.

Time for bed. This evening, new, sensible house sorted, surrounded by enthusiastic warm young things, I'm just a Happy Old Hector.

Met Office Weather Warning
06/02/2016

Higher ground in southern parts of Devon and Somerset are likely to see the highest totals of rain, in excess of 80 mm possible over parts of Dartmoor. In addition, southerly gales or severe gales are expected with gusts of 65 mph over higher ground

What's going on?

It feels as though we've been having weather like this every day since the end of October! Is it me? Is it just Dartmoor? Or everywhere? Is it global warming? Is it always going to be like this? If it's as freaky as it's beginning to feel, why does the front page of the Daily Mail shout, "Vindicated Surgeon!" instead of "Why bother to go outside ever again?" or "Has your house started leaking?!"

They must be just about running out of names for all these storms. Yesterday's one was called 'Henry', I think. I don't know why they always seem to be boys.

Back in November I was saying "this weather's weird, it can't go on for much longer", but as far as I can tell, it's never really stopped since, and there's water running down inside our sunroom again, despite Builder Peter's best, very recent efforts.

If things don't change next winter, or the one after that, what's the point of living in the UK? I might have to re-think my house purchase plans yet again! A Radio 2 'shout out' has just said it's lovely in the Dominican Republic.

I blame myself actually. I shouldn't have kept on using that hair spray aerosol.

It's All Over
08/02/2016

They've pulled out.

After a year in which they've changed their minds three times, they've just sent me an email to say they're not buying it. Five days before the delayed exchange date.

I am livid, raging, impotent.
"...alternatively you could ask Builder Peter to provide you with a costed plan of works within your budget, so you would know exactly where you are..." I emailed them back nicely, with gritted teeth.

Pathetic.

They've always had the wrong mindset. I was never confident about this sale. I mean freaking about radon, if you're going to live on Dartmoor? Planning to fence a seven acre field to keep in your stupid dogs? Anti-hunt - around here?? They read my blog. Didn't they believe all the things I said on there, ages ago?

Sigh.

So now I am going to sort out the roof and the door and the windows, replace the oil tank, tart up the drive and barn, and put the house back on the market at a sensible price.

Meanwhile Marriage Foundation has just been on telly, without needing me, but I missed it because there was a power cut caused by Storm Imogen (oh it's a girl this time) with her 80mph winds.

My agent-friend has said 'non' to my book.

There appears to be no market for my latest business idea, which is writing online profiles for inarticulate people who want to do online dating.

Nor for my book.

And I've got no B&Bs or house rentals booked because I haven't been able to market either properly because of the bloody non-sale.

I'm having my first argument with Ex - about whether Faye should have to travel up to London to see him, when she's so tired. She didn't ask him to move 150 miles away, and she wants to stay at Wydemeet with her cousins who are coming for their 'Last Non-Hurrah-Goodbye-to-Wydemeet' .

The roof is leaking again, the front door has blown open behind its polythene, the lid of the jacuzzi has flown off, and the trampoline has broken its moorings and flown into the cows' field next door where it's lying upside down, having left behind a few of its legs.

And finally, my favourite online date, Charioteer, has gone cold, as has another great hope who I met over Christmas and who lives in West Sussex.

Neither of them can cope with the idea of committing to somebody who is so far away, "We'd have to go from 0-60 spending days together at each end," observes Mr Sussex, and he's quite right. I understand. Somehow I just have to move.

They Said To Give You A Massive Big One, Mary
09/02/2016

"Excuuuuuuse me?"

Ten 50-something Thunderbirds (my group of girlfriends from the South Hams) look up, astonished to hear these words from the young and nervous wine waiter.

The poor chap, hardly out of his teens, is scarlet, realizing what he's just said, and so am I, but luckily it is too dark in the pub for it to show.

In some confusion, I accept the 250ml glass of Chilean Sauvignon, and apologise for embarrassing us both by being a bit over the top, having laughed so loudly at his courtesy, in a public place.

Spring Clean
20/02/2016

Everywhere I look, everything I think about, is affected by my failure to sell this house.

Sitting here in bed, tap tap tapping away, I look at my dressing table, which actually belongs to Ex, and is due to go into storage, and listen to my rattling windows, which will now have to be repaired before they fall into the garden, and my heart sinks as I confirm with myself that the curtains, window seats and carpets are all in need of an overdue, urgent, deep clean.

So my next project, starting from the broken electric gate, and slowly walking up the garden taking in a need for raking, removal of molehills, broken flower pots, broken trampoline, broken front door, broken roof tiles, knackered barn etc must all be taken in hand.

I've received an email from an ex-prep-school Mum telling me that she's keen to buy Wydemeet, so she's coming to visit next weekend. If that goes through you can call me Donald Duck.

Unmumsy Mum
20/02/2016

Steve Wright said he'd been talking to the 'Unmumsy Mum', Sarah Turner, on his show last Thursday.

I've just looked up her book.

She's No 8 on Amazon's Bestsellers list and she lives in Exeter. I checked out what she'd written on their 'Look Inside' facility, and, like "Adventures of a Playground Mother", call me up my own arse, but I don't think it's that good.

Also, I am fairly boiling because the agent I wrote to told me that mine is a difficult genre for mainline publishers.

Eh? "The Unmumsy Mum" and my effort are exactly the same 'genre' - non-fiction/humour/sex, love & relationships, derived from blogs written by two mothers living thirty miles apart in Devon!

And another thing. Both Sophie Kinsella and Sarah Turner happen to be published by Bantam Books.

So guess who I'm about to email now?

Blocked Again
20/02/2016

"So you ARE promoting your book!!!!!! Sorry don't suffer fools or players. Goodbye", and with that, my latest online date, Thebodyguard2, blocks me, so I can't email him again.

Well good riddance.

I have been conducting further experiments into making a sales pitch for my book online, with no success whatsoever. I've talked about it on my dating site 'profile', and I have been giving out details of how to buy it in my messages.

Until finally the Big Brothers who run the site, and read all of their clients' private messages, threatened to de-list me because I was contravening their terms & conditions by attempting to use the service for commercial purposes.

Nosy buggers. Imagine being paid to read "I like your profile", "I like walking my dog", "I have all the normal interests", "I think I'd like to shag you" and all the other standard messages that potential online dates exchange between each other, two million times a day. I think they should be grateful for my divergence from the norm, making life more interesting for everybody.

So far not one of my multiple sales campaigns is working. Not the house, not the B&B, not the house rental, not the online dating, not the book, and not the profile-writing.

I've spent a long time developing 200+ keywords for my AdWords listing for www.profile-writer.com. And then even longer working out how to use Google Analytics to discover how many people have visited my new website for it. Answer: 2.

So I've had another brainwave and amalgamated pushing the book and the profile-writing service together on one website: survivingsolo.co.uk. Number of visits so far: 12.

I spent all last Sunday emailing features editors with my first press release for eight years: "How (not) To Be Single", linking my new website with the release last Thursday of a recently released film called "How To Be Single" starring the bland Dakota Johnson from 50 Shades. Yet I haven't even received a single acknowledgement back from any of them. Perhaps my sales pitch wasn't up to my standards of yore. The film, certainly, doesn't appear to be up to much, according to the Daily Mail, which awarded it just two blobs yesterday.

But I have sold one paperback and one kindle copy of my book this week, so perhaps I haven't got things completely wrong.

Certainly my most specific target audience: divorced Mums running B&Bs on their own (of whom there are two, Lucille and Serena reader-buyers so far), have proved most enthusiastic supporters!

I will find a way forwards through what at the moment feels like a morass of sludge, somehow. I always have before. It's just that the years are beginning to tick on by!

Five Bottles of Wine
20/02/2016

I'm onto my fifth bottle of 'good' wine.

This one's called 'Jactone Ranch Viognier Reserve California 2007'.

It's absolutely disgusting.

Just like the last four.

What can I cook that's going to use up this much wine?

I'm thinking that if I'm going to move house I need to deplete my plonk cellar a bit.

So I've started on all the nicer ones that I've been storing for when some Esteemed Guest arrives.

The thing is, that Esteemed Guest always brings something better, so in the corner all these bottles have remained - getting old.

And now they're past it.

Rewrite It!
24/02/2016

I went to a Guardian Members' Club dinner last night - a vegetarian affair, at Totnes' Riverford Organic Kitchen, of course. It wasn't very well attended.

Those female guests who did turn up were thin and had short, straight, white hair; while one of the men had a bushy grey beard, and the other, an earring. You could tell that it wasn't a Daily Mail gathering.

"You'll need to cut your book down by 30-40% and re-write it seven or eight times," Malcolm's girlfriend, whom I love and respect and who knows about these things, informed me. "No author can edit her own work. One spelling or grammatical mistake, and it's straight into the publisher's bin."

Before I left, I sought out the organiser of the dinner and said, "The trouble is, your Club members are already regulars at Riverford, so it isn't a particularly interesting venue to tempt them to. You'd have done much better if you'd arranged a Guardian Soulmates singles evening."

And with that, I climbed into the Gold Monstrosity, feeling thoughtful and rather deflated.

Decisions Decisions
25/02/2016

I've said it before. The worst thing about being on your own is that you have to make all your decisions on your own. Every second, minute, hour, day, week, month and year.

Today I've got lots to make.

Do I go to Mum's early, because my oil's run out again, so I've got no central heating and it's less than 5 degrees outside.

Do I pay the £11,347 deposit to get the windows, roof, door, barn, yard, and house interior building works on the go?

Do I agree to meet my latest online date, who calls himself YAH?

Do I book flights and accommodation for a week's economy skiing in Andorra in the Easter holidays?

Do I re-write my book eight times?

Answers: no, yes, yes, yes, no.

According to Google Analytics, 117 people so far have clicked onto my new website. Not one of them has bought anything. So my brilliant brainwave is to reduce the price of the book. Perhaps someone might be tempted, now it's only 99p on Kindle, and £7.50 in paperback. Who cares that this means my royalties are 4p for every copy sold? I just need to get it out there.

I can drive For Miles and Miles and Miles and Miles and Miles and Miles and Miles and miles....
02/03/2016

Netball for Faye at Will's school on Saturday.
Dressage competition, then school run Sunday.
Granny solicitors meeting Monday.
Horse riding lesson trip to Faye's school Tuesday.
Spring concert at Faye's school Today.
Parents Disco at Faye's school Friday.
Cross Country Running Day at Faye's school on Saturday.
Will's jazz concert in London Sunday.

That's nearly 1,500 miles in nine days.

If there's a murder reported in Reading it'll be those people who didn't buy my house who are dead.

Meanwhile I shall be residing in the Spanish Riviera with all the other wanted crims, with no sense of guilt, topping up my Vitamin D supplies in the vain hope that I will be able to avoid osteoporosis in later years.

No Sales
02/03/2016

Everything is still at a complete standstill, no sales of absolutely anything whatsoever. Time for a new approach.

I know. I will bombard the publishing world with copies of my book.

I've now spent the most enormous amount of time researching who the specialist agents are for my 'genre', which I believe might be called 'humorous memoir', and the people who publish my kind of stuff.

Recently I have been buying lots of this type of book, and instead of reading them, I just turn straight to the acknowledgements, for inside info on the authors' editors.

I have decided to ignore the professionals' advice of re-writing the thing a million times, and instead to rely on a really fresh, unusual and targeted covering letter sent direct to each thoroughly researched agent.

I've done two so far, one to the agent responsible for "Wife in the North", and the other whose agency was behind the success of "The Unmumsy Mum".

And when they both say 'non' I shall approach Penguin's Transworld, based at Random House in Ealing, which seems to be the publisher of every other book I've ever bought.

Girlie Wirlies and Ladz
10/03/2016

I don't think my children, nor their cousins, nor my best friends' children, are normal.

None of them are giggly girly-wirlies, nor ladz.

I don't know whether this is a Good or a Bad Thing.

"Celebrate that Faye is not Best Friend material!" cried a mum-friend yesterday, when I was being sad on Faye's behalf that she felt lonely and isolated. The rest of her peer group have organised themselves into giggly girlie-wirlie hair-flicking make-up-donning cliques (most significantly the powerful Alpha hockey 1st team), and they save seats for each other in the dining room and classroom, so that Faye has to wander off and sit alone.

Faye would never stop anybody who wanted to, from sitting next to her. And if she tries giggling she just sounds silly.

Meanwhile the pack leaders - usually pretty, sporty, skinny, clever little minx's (see 'Mean Girls' for ref) - select a particularly under-confident henchman or two, and strutt about mocking their less dominant sisterhood.

Yet put one of these types out of her comfort zone, say, alone at a drinks party full of adults at a strange house, and she will quake. Unlike my Faye, who blooms!

Meanwhile, Will, the male cousins, and sons of close friends, aren't excited by throwing food around, getting drunk/stoned, toilet-humour jokes, being loud in groups, notches on their bedposts, or hurting other children on the rugby field.

Instead, the offspring of those closest to me, are thoughtful, mature, steady, focussed, high achievers. I am confused, disappointed and generally pissed off that whereas in my small world this sensible type of child comprises the norm, in the outside world they appear to be spread so thinly, and life is made so difficult for them by their shallow peers.

University, I think, will prove the melting pot where my sort of minority group will find people of their own ilk; but it is sad, and surprising to me, that there aren't more like-minded children along the way.

Glum
10/03/2016

I'm still glum.

Not enough to do, surrounded by mud.I have closed the B&B til May.

The idea of mixing guests with builders' dust - or worse, putting them in a bedroom with a hole where the window used to be - fills me with dread. I just daren't attempt to co-ordinate the two.

So now I have no family here to make a mess and to look after, no business, no school runs, no income to speak of, plenty of time to look after my home and my horses, yet Sashka is still working twelve hours a week for me.

There wasn't enough for her to do last Friday; I was in London over the weekend, resulting in nothing at all for her to do on Monday.

So we enjoyed a coffee and a fag break, as is our habit. But I've worked out that this little luxury is costing me rather a lot. I left a message on Sashka's answerphone suggesting we discussed what to do about the situation and the next thing I know is she's taken a new Friday job - agh!

Now I'm in a major pickle. I am planning to re-open a spick-spock-sparkling, perfect, immaculate B&B on April 29th, and, a week later, put the house back on the market at £850,000+ to take advantage of the early May Bank Holiday.

I can see that many people would give their right arm to be in my situation right now. But personally I'm feeling in aimless limbo, and I don't like it.

Dead Pheasant
10/03/2016

I returned from my London trip to find a very beautiful dark blue cock pheasant stuck upside down with its tail in the air and its head down the drain outside my back door. Very dead.

Was it a rather ungainly-looking present from Paul, who had just delivered some hay for the horses?

Or a dire symbolic warning of impending doom put there by inbred locals - revenge for being rude about them?

I think the most likely explanation is that it must have found some rat poison and was desperate for water.

Or perhaps it simply flew into a wall.

Whatever. I'm not going to gut and eat it. It's going on the ever expanding horse manure heap, just in case it poisons me. Or casts some wicked spell.

Devoted Dad
16/03/2016

Ex and Will don't believe Faye enjoys riding. They think she only does it to please me. Every time they see her compete, she cries, they say.

So I challenged Ex to come and see for himself how much she loves her weekly lesson - a ten hour round trip from London for him.

And today he came.

Back last September Vegas wouldn't jump anything.

Faye and I both had butterflies, wondering what the crazy horse might do today in front of Ex.

Well blow me down, but they happily jumped a metre together! Their biggest ever. One vast bright yellow horror came right up to my tummy button. Ex was so impressed he took a picture!

Stir Crazy
18/03/2016

I'm wondering whether I am going nuts, living all alone in the middle of remotest Dartmoor, with nothing to do, and no one to talk to except Twiglet.

So I am embracing the rare experience of no deadlines, and no responsibilities - until April 29th.

Yesterday I rode a 20 mile round trip to the second highest pub in England.

Today it was Ready Brek and yesterday's paper in bed; in my 'groom's kit' of white fluffy dressing gown and blue wellies I've fed the horses; still in my pyjamas I've done my osteoporosis-busting disco routine, practised Liszt's Nocturne Number 3, written this...

What shall I do next? It's only 11am!

Roof Of Horror
07/04/2016

Mark and Kay popped round for tea.

"I don't think there's anything particularly wrong with those plastic tiles of yours," commented architect Mark, pausing to check out the already-leaking-again new roof on his way into the kitchen for some lemon drizzle cake. "There's no felt to drain away the water, and the pitch of the roof is so shallow, and so are the valleys, that I think with the colossal amount of water we've had recently the leaves aren't washing away, the water's overflowing out of the valleys under the tiles, and it isn't being wicked away by any membrane underneath."

EEEEEEEEEEEEEKKKK!!!!!!!!!

I'm about to be charged £15,000 to re-tile the entire thing - possibly all for nothing! I nearly drop the teapot! All I'd done was ask my nice neighbours around for a friendly cup of tea and my entire world is spiralling off down some vortex.

I make an urgent call to Peter the builder who has a long chat with my poor architect friend - who thought he was only coming round for a cup of tea; and there's not a lot more we can do before the tile manufacturer man's visit next week, to see if it's the tiles' fault, or the building's design.

Oh - and cancel our order for £15,000 worth of new tiles. Fast!

Standstill
07/04/2016

When your life's at a standstill, you live in the middle of nowhere, you're used to juggling 15,000 balls in the air at once, and the only person you see all day is the postman, you start checking emails, book sales, kindle sales, online dating sites, house rental and B&B sites like some mad thing, to make sure that you still exist. Well at least I do.

And the results are not encouraging. I've sold a grand total of 2 books throughout the whole of March. And no one wants to rent Wydemeet, nor visit as a B&B guest. Nor buy it.

On top of all of this I have now started reading "How To Be Single" and it is so depressing I really should burn it. It's about an American woman researching dating around the world. So far she's checked out New York, Paris, Australia and Rome, and has only found single women making themselves attractive, charming and available to a dearth of uninterested average men who dip in and out for a laugh when the mood takes them. Is it the same the world over - or simply hers and my perception?

But there are stirrings of life yet.

I've got five new windows! Simply fitted with no observable dust nor detritus, and although they're plastic, from the outside they look just the same as the old ones, albeit a bit whiter. From the inside though - oops. In the olden days, as you stood in one of Wydemeet's rooms, sometimes your hair would blow around in the wind shrieking through and round the sides of the original windows. Now you feel as though you are actually sheltered from the incessant gales. But I've made an error. I've only replaced the windows at the front of the house, meaning that when you're inside the rooms concerned, you've got great big plastic windows in front of you, but the old leaky wooden ones to the side. Oh dear. I hope nobody notices that they don't match. Better draw the curtains.

Cheerful?
12/04/2016

Why do I feel so cheerful? I can't imagine. Sometimes I think that our bodies are full of illnesses, some of which we avoid, some of which we submit to a little bit, and some which take over when our immune system is down. So that when we get them just a little bit, we feel tired and a bit sad, but don't really understand why, as there are no other symptoms.

Whereas today I've felt great! For no particular reason. Just a 12 hour kip and that feeling of being at home and knowing who and where everyone and everything is.

Hearing Sashka and Peter Builder chattering away together downstairs this morning, as I savoured my osteoporosis-busting Ready Brek and tinned mandarins in bed, made me want to throw back the covers and join them! So I did. Peter is beginning to get used to seeing me in pyjamas at any old time of day.

And then on to my new health club, that the contract means I've finally been allowed to join, to meet Granny. Well - what a perfect venue for a Granny encounter!

The club appears to have bought a job lot of Stannah stairlifts - everywhere you look there's another, complete with its heavily branded casing, and mechanism to get you up three steps sitting down. There are a whole load of rooms set aside for playing Bridge in upstairs, and Granny, Faye and I met outside on the terrace for two 'afternoon teas' between three.

£22 later, and it was time for a swim in the outdoor pool, presumably where a walled garden used to be, adjoining the beautiful Georgian house that now comprises the Club.

It's April 12th, but really, it could be summer. Life's sunny!

Three Weeks Left!
16/04/2016

The house is surrounded by scaffolding.

Both the insurance people and the tile manufacturers have inspected the 'new' leaking roof, and so also have the original architect and builder responsible for fitting it.

The insurance people have pledged quite a substantial amount for redecorating inside where it has leaked as a result of storm damage, but believe the actual materials it's made of are not fit for purpose, so won't pay to have it replaced.

The manufacturer's man, who came all the way from Cambridge, says it's been installed incorrectly.

And now my lovely original architect and builder have demonstrated that it has been installed correctly, but hasn't coped with the extreme conditions of Dartmoor combined with climate change, or whatever has caused the weird wet weather of recent months. And they are going to put things right for me for nothing.

I really do feel as though I am surrounded by the most decent team of helpers.

The falling-down barn is beginning to look almost nice - newly painted in a fetching shade of grey. Wydemeet's old roof and falling-off leaking chimney stacks look as good as new, the new windows look so stunning that the bloke who fitted them has used a picture of the front of Wydemeet to illustrate his website, and soon the 30 tons of granite chippings will arrive to cover up the disgusting cracked concrete yard. The electric gate will be finished next week because I appear inadvertently to have thrown away an integral part of it - the bit that attaches the new ram to the gate itself. Damn. More expense.

So I've still got to finalise renewal of the oil tank, replacement of the central heating pump, gardener, sewer-empty-er, carpet cleaner and something else that I've already forgotten. And hopefully we will be good to go before I re-open for the summer season, and put the house back on the market, on May Bank Holiday weekend.

Signs Of Life
16/04/2016

I've just remembered.

I really enjoy this B&B lark.

I'd probably do it even if I weren't paid for it, but I am, and quite handsomely.

I've just waved goodbye to my first customer since November. Called Ralph, he is 69 and wears flowery shirts and trainers. He's a repeat, and has been warned about the building works. His chat flows like a ceaseless gentle river and we have spent hours over breakfast - runny scrambled egg, two sausages, large tomato and two rashers of bacon for him; osteoporosis-busting Ready Brek with mandarins and creme fraiche for me - discussing the best restaurants we have visited, and sawmills.

It was probably the easiest, most pleasurable £200 I have ever made. He has departed in his sporty Hyundai with a signed copy of my book under his arm, promising to be back before Wydemeet is sold.

Meanwhile I now have four or so other bookings, received variously direct via my website, through Booking.com (Dutch and German), and, new for me, Airbnb. So I have updated all my websites and am sitting here with bated breath that everything will be ready in time for their arrival. I suspect and hope I am the only central Dartmoor B&B left with any vacancies, so they'll have to book me!

Birthday Party for a 14 year old
16/04/2016

Well what would you do?

To drink or not to drink - that is the question.

I have spent many hours researching low alcohol, but not no alcohol, cider, because Faye doesn't want lager. I have failed to find anything that comes in small cans that contains anything between 0 and 4 degrees.

I drafted a letter of invitation, and sent it to Faye, Will and Ex for their approval. They all said fine, but Ex suggested I just check it with Faye's housemistress at school.

Well.

When my mother summoned me one day to say, sorrowfully, that my old housemistress from school had died, I replied, "GOOD". Whereas Faye's housemistress is like a right arm to me, that I can lean on heavily! She knows everything that her girls get up to, and is immediate to summon them and discuss any issues. I respect her judgement absolutely. And she has said a very clear 'non' to my alcoholic letter of invitation. So Red Bull it is then.

In just a few hours' time, I have ten of Faye's school's most experienced party-goers descending on me for the night, all being delivered by a minibus from Newton Abbot Station. At a cost of £70 return. Agh!

We are going to provide them with an inexhaustible supply of sausages, white rolls, crisps, chocolates, profiteroles, fizzy drinks, fruit juice and pain-au-chocolats, which Faye and I are off to buy in a minute.

But the biggest weapon in our arsenal is my henchman, seventeen-year-old Will - party-goer extraordinaire. I am paying him £25 to stay up all night and oversee the whole thing. He will instinctively laser in on any imported alcohol, and I have instructed him to tell them that he will be keeping it and taking it back to school with him.

He has downloaded appropriate music for the children to dance to all night, and he and Faye have turned the sunroom into a dance-hall, complete with flashing lights and Will's £450 disco speaker; the Bothy into a sort of druggy den, without the drugs (hopefully); and Will will oversee how many children (because that's what they still are, at the end of the day), can leap into the hot-tub all at once.

Meanwhile I shall have a bath and watch telly, shut away in my private little bedroom, and get a good night's sleep.

Alcohol Free?
22/04/2016

Only eight came in the end. Five girls and three boys.

No alcohol.

Thank God.

Because oh my goodness they proved hard to handle! Even for two die-hard, cynical old party-goers like Will and me.

I refused to be a 'Nazi-parent' by searching their bags, or putting a padlock on the drinks cupboard door. I think relationships between children and adults fare best where there's mutual respect and trust. Will told me of a party at which all the children's bags were confiscated, gone through, and actually guarded; yet the party goers still managed to get wasted on drink and drugs somehow.

After supper I hung around in the kitchen, read the paper, and was in bed before midnight, while the music thumped out through PA speakers and a sub-woofer, from the Bothy, across the river, past the sheep, and up the valley to Neighbour.

At 3am, Will rounded up the children and sent them to bed, boys and girls in separate bedrooms.

At 5.30am I discovered them all crammed up tight together in the hot tub for the third time, and sent them back to bed.

At 9.00am I crept into the three boys' Bothy to find five children. One of them, I'm afraid to say, was mine.

After our young visitors had sleepily disappeared off in their minibus to the station, I came across young Faye washing up some titchy plastic cups which smelt strongly of liquorice.

Odd.

I quizzed her about it and finally all came out. Despite Will's and my best efforts, one of the boys had smuggled in a small amount of Sambuca and three cans of beer. Not enough to get anyone pissed, but an indicator that Faye is unlikely ever again to attend a party entirely free of alcohol. Lucky, in the wooden Bothy, none of the children realised that you're supposed to set fire to Sambuca!

It also emerged that one of the boys had put pressure on Faye to steal from my drinks cupboard. Bless her, my darling daughter refused to let him - absolutely point blank. "My Mum and Will will hate you forever if you try doing that," she firmly admonished him.

Eddie The Eagle
22/04/2016

Last week Faye and I went to the cinema twice in two days, having not been at all in two years. We saw The Jungle Book, and Eddie the Eagle. Both proved well worth the 60 mile round trips.

I came out of 'Eddie the Eagle' feeling a bit shaken and sad though. That film could equally well have been the story of Ex becoming the first person in the world to walk from Canada to the North Pole all alone, without any resupplies being flown in to help him. Against all the odds, he succeeded on his fourth attempt, back in 2003. Unlike Eddie though, the ending wasn't a triumph shared, and our marriage failed soon after.

But I've had another idea.

The obvious sequel to 'Eddie the Eagle' ('a semi-biographical sports dramedy', according to Wikipedia) is 'The McVitie's Penguin Polar Relay', which Ex and I organised, back in 1997. It comprised a team of twenty 'ordinary' British women walking in relay format to the North Pole. Their 'baton'? A stuffed penguin - the only penguin ever to reach the Top of the World.

Here is an equally unlikely true-life story of courage, character, and British eccentricity. What's so significant about this adventure is that it opened up the whole idea of 'normal' people actually surviving in the High Arctic, and Antarctica too. Before the Relay, fewer than 100 people had ever actually stood at the North Pole! These days every Tom, Dick and Harriet is on his or her way there - most of them blind, deaf, and pogoing on one leg.

This is Ex's real legacy, which I think deserves to be celebrated.

I must contact the producer, Dexter Fletcher, today.

The Reality of Divorce
09/05/2016

"You can swim in it!" exclaims Lydia proudly.

She is showing me her jacuzzi, which is four times bigger than mine.

Behind us is her family home, which sleeps 17, and in front of us are two horses and several sheep quietly grazing an emerald green field. 900 acres of green valley, fields and woods, stretch out beyond, a backdrop of steep hills leading up to the skyline. All Lydia's. The highest farm on Exmoor.

So here we are. Meet the two mad women of the moors - women of substance; aren't we lucky?

Lydia is my alter-ego. Her children have been at school with mine since they were eight, and now here we both sit, stranded, alone, high up, miles from anywhere, on top of our respected cold, windy, wet, bleak moors, watching our children and our horses from our much-loved, gilded, expensive prisons.

Lydia uses an agent to let out her home for most weeks of the year, while she crouches trapped among the wellies and anoraks of her boot room, on the other side of the door. Every word, every merry peal of laughter from the happy multi-generational families beyond, enjoying themselves on holiday, are clearly audible through the thin pine.

She has no kitchen, sitting room, fridge, nor cooker - nowhere to sit, or store, prepare or clear up food, nor anywhere for her or her family to relax in front of the telly. She keeps popping up and down to turn the boiler on and off, to minimise the oil consumed by her guests in what used to be her comfortable family home.

Often she cries for what used to be.

Her ex, meanwhile, has a new manor house and drives a large car, courtesy their recent divorce.

"Sell!" I urge poor Lydia, as we sip our mugs of PG Tips in the morning, pyjama-clad, shivering beneath our bedcovers.

"But the children love it," she murmurs quietly.

Of Gardeners and Carpet Cleaners
10/05/2016

I've found a gardener from Buckfastleigh, through Google.

He's arrived, with compost and flowers for my pots, looking tall and strong - bearded and with a ponytail as you might expect from a bohemian ex-jeweller who works for £12 per hour.

I have asked him to make the garden and outside the gate look beautiful - it's all about first impressions for potential punters.

"Sticks, sticks, sticks," I mutter, as we walk up the drive together. There are sticks everywhere. Great piles of them gathered over the years. And more scattered all over the 'lawn' as a result of Storms A-H this winter.

Three days and £300 later he has finished his work, leaving for home at 8pm.

The next morning I go out to admire my garden. Sticks, sticks, sticks. They're all still there. The 'lawn' resembles a ploughed field covered in sticks and debris and flattened mud from the scaffolders' Doc Martens. Long, long grass and dead reeds, and more sticks, untouched, all along the bank in front of which my potential purchasers will park their cars.

Not a sign of any weed killing and none at all of the urgent raking required. What has he been doing all this time, at such vast expense?

Ah - here we are. There is a circle where the trampoline used to be at the back of the house. That looks tidy. And some carefully strimmed pretty little paths leading down the part of the garden that nobody sees, which will grow over and need to be strimmed again by somebody else, sooner rather than later. And a lot of pretty pansies in pretty pots, waiting to be watered.

Suddenly three men leap out of a van - they're here to clean the carpets and some windows, to give Wydemeet's insides a cheerful lift.

"Does the job really need three of you?" I enquire. "Might one of you be prepared to pick up sticks?"

They are amenable and friendly, they say 'of course!' and I feed them my B&Bers' left-over croissants. Then I trudge upstairs to my office to discover their carpet cleaning machine has leaked all over my most expensive carpet - so wet that the water has reached the hardboard below the underfelt and a large brown stain is spreading upwards.

Hoping it will go away when it dries out, I turn the corner to find splashes of paint all over the landing walls, as if somebody has been trying out new colours on it. This must be Perfect Peter's idea of 'touching up'. And it really is totally, utterly, unacceptable. The whole landing will have to be redecorated.

I go outside to find him to say so, and bump into Raef, our original builder, who has kindly returned to repair the seven-year-old leaking roof.

And finally I trudge over to the garden shed, pick up something wiry that looks like a rake but which keeps collapsing, and wearily attempt the job of repairing what was once my lawn, in time to a mantra which goes: "Three hundred pounds, three hundred pounds, three hundred pounds..."

Shaking
10/05/2016

I'm sorry to have to admit to you, oh dearly beloved reader, but I am reaching for one of Sashka's very strong fags, while handing her a one pound coin for the privilege. My hands are trembling as I shake another one out of the box, immediately following the first. No vape is up to how I'm feeling right now.

I have just received a casual email from Perfect Peter the builder, saying he will complete the job half way through next week. That is three months, THREE MONTHS, after we agreed what was to be done, and I have now parted with over £20,000 in up front payments.

Meanwhile, Wydemeet went live on Rightmove at midnight last night as planned, ready for viewings to take place this Bank Holiday Weekend.

A total of £30,000 worth of work, including the five new windows, repairing the roof, tarting up the hideous old barn, and covering the cracked discoloured concrete of the yard with granite chippings, was all planned in order to create a favourable first impression to people thinking of buying Wydemeet. The keenest of whom will be visiting this weekend.

"It all happens in the first couple of weeks," the estate agents have said to me.

The house is currently surrounded by scaffolding, there are piles of builders' debris around the dilapidated yard, and holes in the roof stuffed with layers of bright yellow plastic.

Three months they've had, in which to sort everything out. Days and days and days of nobody appearing. The scaffolding's been up for weeks. I haven't nagged because I have placed all my faith in Perfect Peter, and he has developed a heart condition over the past few months so serious that he can scarcely walk up the drive. I really don't want to be the final straw on that one. He has always said I can rely on him and he will look after me. Well bollocks! He hasn't! He's let me down big-time! I might as well never have bothered with all this face-lift lark. And there's not even an apology, an explanation, or even an acknowledgement that he's missed the all-important, agreed deadline.

Perfect Peter sees a new side of Mary of the Moor in my emailed reply.

And then up pops a second email. It says that the electric gate will finally be fixed a week on Wednesday.

"Call yourselves a business????!!!!!!!!!!!!!!" I pound the keyboard furiously, feeling a bit sick with all the nicotine buzzing around my system after Sashka's cigarettes.

I first ordered the replacement ram for my gate at the end of January. Four months ago. Surely my gate company does nothing but replace gates and rams all day every day. Why on earth has it taken four months for them to sort out mine? The gate is the very first thing that potential buyers see! A knackered gate indicates a knackered house. I am helpless, livid, frustrated, despairing.

Viewings
11/05/2016

The hake, as ever, is delicious. It's my favourite dish in the chandeliered, thickly carpeted restaurant of my new club. And not bad value at £12.50 with a 10% discount for members.

I'm with one of my favourite online-date-mates, Little John, having a lovely time and avoiding going home.

Everything at Wydemeet is finally coming together, and it's going to look fantastic, but I don't want to pretend to Perfect Peter that I am pleased with how the job has been done. Nor celebrate with him over a cup of tea and a piece of cake.

And anyway. There's no point. After all that, no viewings are booked for the Bank Holiday Weekend.

I'm going to be stuck in the middle of Dartmoor for ever!

Raking in £1000s
11/05/2016

"If you leave my purse, with over £700 in it, on the car's dashboard again, there will be extremely serious consequences," I admonish Faye.

I don't think it's fair to castigate people when they make a mistake for the first time (although it certainly is if they repeat it).

We are at the local cross country course, and Vegas is due for the Pedigree Chum factory. We whizzed through preparing breakfast for our lovely B&Bers, and here we are at the most beautiful spot on the whole of Dartmoor: Holwell Lawn, just outside Widecombe, along from Hound Tor.

Having pranced around the collecting ring looking like consummate professionals in school colours, the stupid horse has just refused the first titchy jump. And the third. And then a six inch high white dolls house.

This one she refused so many times that the pair was eliminated.

Aaagghhhh!

So they had another go. This time they would have won the whole thing by a twenty second margin - but because it was a second attempt, this round didn't count.

Anyway - I'm actually meant to be writing about my B&B. It's thriving. I've wanted all five couples who've visited this week to become my best friends. They've already given me straight tens on TripAdvisor Reviews. After all the uncertainty of last year, while I let everything run itself down, and sacked all the agents etc, we've slipped to a shocking Number 22 in TripAdvisor's "Best B&Bs on Dartmoor" hit parade.

But we'll soon be back in the Top 5, you'll see! The house is immaculate inside and out, everything works as far as I know, and as well as having my own direct booking arrangements, I have recently re-signed up with Airbnb; Booking.com; and TripAdvisor Instant Booking, all of whom take 15% +VAT commission. But I don't care. I feel like being busy once more. I've started going a bit mad on eBay again, and have ordered some replacement thermal jugs for fresh milk, some new garden chairs, a sack of grass seed, and two lawn rakes.

Open for Business?
19/05/2016

The Tesco man, delivering my B&Bs' breakfast of croissants and piccolo tomatoes-on-the vine this morning, was rather less friendly than normal, avoiding eye contact, spending most of his time looking down at the ground and talking to Twiglet.

I signed the handheld computer-thingy and came upstairs back to bed, coffee and Ready Brek. I peered in the mirror to admire my new spray-on fake tan bought yesterday (£20 at Salon Fish, Ivybridge) only to discover that my pyjamas and dressing gown were open right down to my rather orange naval.

No wonder Mr Tesco couldn't look at me, and I was feeling a bit draughty.

Staying Put?
19/05/2016

There is nowhere I want to move to. Both houses I like, in the area that I like, have been taken off Rightmove, for whatever reason, and no new equivalents put on. All that's currently available are those overpriced 1950s agricultural bungalows with land; or apartments in grand houses.

I think the one with no central heating that I was going to buy is probably now under offer, and I suspect that Famous Rockstar has finally realised he needs to have somewhere in mind to move to, before selling Haldon Brake.

I commented to my nice estate agent my idea of the emotional roller-coaster of buying and selling houses being as bad as online dating.

"Now there's an idea for some PR," he muses.

"I'm up for it!" I chirp.

Meanwhile my house has been on Rightmove for nearly three weeks, and not a single enquiry.

During this time, I've had five sets of B&Bers staying here, gorgeous weather, and my large home now looks so beautiful that I am enjoying moving around in it, just gazing. My guests are like an endless series of best friendss coming to stay. The differences are that they go out and give me some space, I make them a nicer breakfast than I would bother with for my normal mates, and as a result of them my purse is bulging with £20 and £50 notes, enabling me to stay in this wonderful home rather than ending up in a debtors' prison or the workhouse.

And now I've just received notification of my first viewing - for next Tuesday. "They're cash buyers looking for a remote second home with views, enough money to do it up, able to move straight away," says my estate agent, full of excitement and enthusiasm.

Another Beautiful Day
03/06/2016

Twiglet's been sick in Faye's bedroom.

Faye is now old enough to clear it up herself, I think to myself, if she must insist on having the dog sleeping with her every night.

Leaving me free to jump back into bed and carry on tap tap tapping on my laptop - to you, dear reader.

The sun has been shining every day for a month now, and living here is a pleasure.

The viewers came and went, with nothing being heard from them again.

We could be here for years and years and years yet.

But in balmy sunshine, both children home for half-term, living within our means thanks to the B&B, who's complaining?

First Transgender
04/06/2016

I've just had my first transgender booking.

He/she filled in their name as: "David Conway, was Sarah Conway". The room booked for tonight, through Booking.com, at the single person's rate of £85.

At such short notice, I thought I'd better give whoever it was a call, just to firm up details. I got through to someone who sounded like a bloke and explained I was calling to check that I should be expecting a single person to arrive later today, and I was planning to upgrade them to my posher room, Hexworthy, normally £130 a night for a couple. And were they transgender as the form said "David, was Sarah".

The bloke replied rather tetchily that the booking was for him and his wife, Sarah.

"In that case, then, I'm afraid the normal charge for a couple is £115," I said.

"That's not what it says on the Booking.com form. I've had no trouble with Booking.com for three years, and it says £85," he exploded. "You should stick with what's advertised. You can't suddenly change the goalposts now, blah blah blah."

He went completely mental when I suggested he might book directly for two via my direct website if it were simpler, and then I wouldn't have to pay the commission.

In the end he was so obnoxious and rude I lost my temper too, and very nearly hung up on him. I wish I could maintain my sang froid like Maggie Thatcher used to do so effectively on the Today Programme. I didn't really want him and his stupid wife to come anyway. I still have the most terrible cold, can't think straight, and forgot the butter for my B&Bs' breakfast this morning.

After we had both slammed our phones down I composed the sweetest email to him, saying that I was so sorry I could not suddenly accept a couple when the booking had clearly been made for a single person; hoping that at such late notice, in such beautiful weather, at half-term in the summer, he might find space in my dear friends' Prince Hall Hotel, Tor Royal B&B or Archerton B&B (although they are all obviously very popular), and imploring him to be kinder to them than he had been to me, if they were able to accommodate him. And lastly I said that under no circumstances would I dream of charging him a cancellation fee, and that the literally scores of existing reviews raving about Wydemeet and my service are testament to the wonderful experience my guests enjoy here.

I hope the stupid tosser and his poor wife don't even find a bed in a camping barn, and instead are forced to sleep rough, or in a narrow bed with horsehair, nits and lice.

I Don't Want To Go!
25/06/2016

Or do I?

Savills has arranged another viewing.

And suddenly I'm sitting here tapping away at the kitchen table waiting for my two German B&B couples to come down for breakfast, thinking - what if the next people want to buy?

Today is yet another beautiful, warm morning. All four doors to the garden are wide open, letting the sunshine flood in. There's total peace and privacy.

Nothing's broken anymore, since I gave the house the facelift. Except for one kitchen chair where various poles have flown off.

I've had the Mole Catcher in, and he caught three. We lined them up in a row and I took a picture. I must say they looked absolutely yuck with their matted brown fur and disgusting little pink arms. I shrieked and ran when the nice man held the first one up.

"Only been dead for a couple of hours," he said cheerfully. "Still warm. One mole can move a ton of earth in a day you know." And so they can. Because the wrecking of my entire lawn was down to just one of those little bastards. It's all stopped now. Hurray!

The B&B has settled into a calm, extremely profitable, rhythm. I've given up trying to be too keen a Mum at my children's far-away schools. The horses are blooming and so happy you can almost see them smiling, and I watch them grazing amongst the flowers of the six acre pasture, flicking their tails at the few flies that we get.

My once-fifteen-year-old son has now turned seventeen, and has suddenly clocked that by downsizing and moving nearer to Exeter, we will still be miles away from his school, and we won't get another house as nice as this one. And he's not as desperate to live next to a bus-stop and a shop as he was two years ago. Meanwhile, Faye and Vegas are loving leaping over massive obstacles in the horses' massive field just outside the kitchen, and going for burn-ups in every direction across the moor.

And now, possibly most significant and exciting of all, two local families have bought the inn at the end of my lane, and are planning to turn it into a 'destination pub' with the best food on the moor, overseen by a 2* Michelin chef. So we will have a community again, somewhere I can go to on my own, and prop up the bar without being embarrassed. Hell! I've even offered myself to work there one night a week! They will enjoy bossing about Lady Mary and paying me the minimum wage!

I counted them up, and I've realised Ive got nine very good girlfriends living in the middle of the moor. And tonight I am attending the local shoot's dinner of venison, in a barn down the road, and reintroducing myself to everybody again.

Both the houses I wanted are now off the market and there's nothing else that I like the look of.

To move or not to move?

It is still true that the only single males I ever see around here have four legs.

I Know What They'll Say
25/06/2016

That I'm mad.

I've just stumbled across a house that I would really, really love to be able to buy.

It's through three gates, at the end of a mile long single track lane running beside the River Teign, the only other house in the vicinity being half a mile away.

It's got 16 acres and five enormous agricultural barns.

The house is a Victorian square brick thing, with plastic windows, swirly carpets, and silver wallpaper.

It's surrounded by nothing but sheep.

I stood in front of it moved, gloating, insides churning away.

"What's the point?" they'll say. "It's got all the same drawbacks as Wydemeet, and you won't know anybody. What happens if you get ill, or break a leg or something? Nobody will find you."

But it's stunning - the view from the south-facing windows and garden stretches for miles of green hills and trees, reminiscent of the cover of my copy of The Sound of Music LP's cover. And it's five minutes off the A38; just fifteen minutes from Exeter. With a thriving village called Trusham, and its excellent pub, just around the corner. A different climate, sheltered, and riding for miles all around, devoid of bogs, rocks and gorse bushes.

The children would take one look at all those barns and think: party party party! I take a look at them, together with the stream and little pond and space and flowers and privacy and I think: "Wedding Venue £££££".

And this little farm costs £150,000 less than what I hope to get for Wydemeet.

So perhaps I won't bother with the weddings. I'll think "sit about doing nothing in the permanent warm sunshine" instead.

Life's Not Very Fair
02/07/2016

On the face of it. Yes. My children and I are hugely lucky and privileged.

And yet.

Ex told me this afternoon that he got engaged yesterday. At Wimbledon where he was a VIP guest on centre court. He popped the question to his very nice girlfriend in the bar there. I have been expecting this and looking forward to it. It is good for the children that he should be happy and fulfilled.

But.

I don't think it's quite fair. I think that I deserve happiness more than he does. He behaved badly, and I behaved decently and honourably. It is easier for men.

And.

Our 14 year old stunning blonde daughter Faye is the loveliest little person I have ever met. There is not a bad bone, particle even, in her beautiful body. God knows where she came from. She must have got mixed up at the hospital.

Anyway. She did brilliantly, but less well, as ever, than the It Girls, at the schools' horse event today. And the two It Girls went off to have a sleepover together, leaving Faye behind with me, because she does not excite the others, or conform to cool stereotypes.

As a Mum it makes you want to cry even harder than your daughter. She is very brave, while the rest of the girls from her school jostle for position and dismiss her with put-downs just because she isn't sophisticated, super-sporty, super-clever, judgmental, bitchy, shrieky and hysterical, nor prepared to save a seat for a BF over and above anyone else. When she tries to copy the others' behaviour, she simply comes across as idiotic.

When she is relaxed with people who care for her, there is no one who is easier, more delightful, relaxed, enthusiastic, charming company.

I do hope the rest of them grow up and appreciate that.

And I really would like somebody to come along and appreciate me.

Am I Dead?
21/07/2016

The car blows up, and then the brakes fail.

Faye, our two horses, Twiglet, and I cruise to a smooth halt outside our destination - Pine Lodge, a small stable yard with self-catering cottage, 1000ft above sea level, on the top of Exmoor. We are a couple of miles from Dulverton, and have just come up a very, very long, steep hill.

Right now we ought to be at a B&B in the New Forest, which I booked and paid for several months ago, after days of research.

Today is the culmination of the worst two weeks of my life, third only to my Dad dying, and the end of my marriage.

I had always thought I was a lucky person, but over the past fourteen days every possible thing that could go wrong has, and things that shouldn't have gone wrong have gone wrong too.

What's lucky? That we are still alive. I think.

"Get out of the way you stupid f******er!" I screamed. "Stop!! Pull over you t**t!!" But the well dressed lady driver coming down the hill towards us in her immaculate Peugeot estate, her window wide open, our window open too, so that she could hear every profanity, just kept on coming. Clouds of black smoke were billowing out of our hired twenty-five-year-old short-wheelbase Pajero diesel 2.5l, as I jammed on the handbrake.

"I love your road rage," giggled Faye.

An uphill start with 2 1/2 tons of trailer and horse behind us, we resumed our crawl to the top of the hill, and turned left into the B&B's drive. As we cruised down the slope and into the yard I gently put my foot on the brakes. Nothing happened. Harder. Was I going mad? Nothing. Pushed the pedal to the floor. Still nothing. Pulling up smoothly to a halt using just the handbrake, I turned to Faye.

"We should be dead," I said. "I can't believe that happened when it did. We might have been anywhere. And that would have been the end of us."

So here we are, marooned, in one of the most dramatically beautiful places in England, in utterly stunning weather, free to play horses, until my beloved Gold Monstrosity is returned to us, and the Pajero taken away to that 4x4 scrapheap in the sky.

Our problems all began with my car's fuel gauge. It said 'empty' when it wasn't.

"That might be a nuisance, if I run out of diesel in the third lane of the motorway and can't steer," I thought to myself, so on the only free day I could find in my diary, I booked my car into Super Sexy Dick's.

That evening he brought it back, saying he would have to take out the fuel tank to reach a dodgy sensor in order to mend the thing.

I found another vaguely feasible day for this to take place, and was drumming my fingers by 4.30pm because the car hadn't come back, and if I didn't get the B&Bers' clean bedlinen back from the launderette I would be in Big Trouble.

I called Dick who said he'd sorted out the fuel gauge but the car had started juddering during the drive back to me, so he'd driven it back to his garage.

"Use my Subaru, but don't take it as far as Exeter, or it'll fall to bits," he cautioned me.

4.30pm the next day and the car had still not been returned. I called Dick.

"I don't know what's wrong with it, you won't get it back today," he informed me.

"Faye!" I yelled. "Quick! Grab Vegas, chuck on the saddle! You're going to have to ride to the Pony Club Show Jumping Rally!" (Ten miles away.)

Two hours later I pull up in the knackered Subaru to find her popping happily over the jumps. And then it was time to come home, darkness closing in. But how? Nobody else was coming back our way.

So Faye rode on to a friend's field a further 30 minutes from home, and left Vegas there for the night. And the next night. And the next.

Meanwhile, in desperation I found an estate car to hire to get to West London for my friend Nicola's 'Party of the Year' at the Hurlingham Club, and on to Will's School Speech day in Dorset, followed by bringing home the Huge School Trunk.

During all this, Twiglet had started hopping.

An expensive visit to the vet who said "Could be arthritis or hip dysplasia."

Eh? In a six year old cross-bred?

"You need an X-ray. That will be £150."

I duly booked an appointment for the dog, got there (just) in the ancient Subaru, to be faced with an actual bill of £350. The prognosis was a probable cruciate ligament, and the treatment recommended: restricted exercise and Metacam. Just what everybody else had already anticipated, £350 ago.

Somehow the Subaru continued on to Plymouth Station to collect Will from his latest party, but by now I was becoming increasingly nervous that I would have no 4x4 to get the horses to our New Forest week's holiday.

Meanwhile Wydemeet was to be rented out for the week, to a party of ten. (From Malaysia. They'd tracked us down via Airbnb.)

With all this car-stuff I had done absolutely nothing whatsoever to help Sashka clear up for the rental, to be immediately followed by the arrival of four B&Bers.

I googled Newton Abbot, Totnes and Exeter 4x4 hire, and there was nothing available.

Finally I stumbled across 'Earth Off Road' in Totnes, which had only been going for six months. Their normal fleet was already booked, but they kindly offered to put their old Pajero back on the road especially for me, for as long as I needed it, for £150.

"It's not pretty," they warned me.

"I really could not care about that," I replied, desperate.

Dick meanwhile had been up for four days and nights with only four hours sleep, trying to sort out the Gold Monstrosity. The strain was beginning to affect his and Sashka's relationship. She had tried asking him a question, which turned out to be a bad idea.

And then one morning, for no apparent reason, it having been checked by three diagnostic computers, Dick texted to let me know that finally the car seemed to be working! I went to collect it, and set off for home, but after about four miles, it reverted to 'limp mode', barely managing to summit our hill.

Somehow I managed to get myself and the truck to 'Edge Off Road', to swap my embattled car for the tiny little Pajero.

When I saw it, my spirits, which by now weren't all that great in the first place, sank even lower. Short wheel base. Nowhere to put equipment for two people, two horses and a dog to last a week. And not enough oooomph or weight, in my opinion, to pull a couple of tons of trailer and horses. On top of which, it wasn't ready to take away because a brake caliper hadn't arrived, despite the hire company having spent £27 on a 24hr courier to get it there.

Pear shaped? Banana shaped? Prickly pear shaped.

I hired a titchy Citreon for the day, just to get me home, and the next morning (the morning we were supposed to be heading for the New Forest) I headed back to Totnes to swap the runabout for the Pajero.

But the Pajero turned out to be even worse than I had anticipated.

Bouncing all over the road, wobbly steering, the engine screaming every time we came across a small hill, I popped into a garage for some diesel, and tried opening the fuel cap. Couldn't do it. And collapsed in tears.

When I finally reached home, I started calling tow-hire companies anew. Finally. A Ford Tipper - whatever that is. But I would need to collect it by 5.30pm. I leaped back into the Pajero and tore up the A38 at 60mph max. I got there at 5.45pm and they wouldn't let me take the Tipper.

I found myself sitting in their customers' chair rocking backwards and forwards screaming, "I have to have it today! You can't do this to me! Please! Please! I am so, so tired! I have to! I just have to!" I was sobbing. I couldn't breathe. I've never lost it like that in my life before. They threw me out.

I sat in the Pajero wondering what to do next, and eventually limped into the only cheap hotel I could find in Exeter. Still in my riding clothes of this morning, I lay on the bed, thinking, doing, saying, nothing.

At 8.30 in the morning I was back at the Ford Tipper place - dirty teeth, hair, who cared?

While the man was completing the paperwork, I went round to look at my purchase. Well that was no good. It was a bloody lorry! Far too wide for the Dartmoor bridges!

Close to tears yet again, I asked the man to refund my money and to call the last-ditch final 4x4 place in Exeter.

Hey?! Things were looking up! A Toyota HiLux? Yes perleese!!! £30 per day? Is that all? Whooppee Shit! Why wouldnt they let me have that before?

I raced across Exeter to the other trading estate where the HiLux place was, to find a sour faced woman in reception.

"It'll be ready for you in 30 minutes," she informed me in her ugly foreign accent.

"So shall we sort out the paying?" I suggested.

"Aren't you on account? If not, you can't have it," she said with relish.

"Can I buy something?" I gasped in desperation. The entire trading estate was simply drowning in gleaming 4x4s, every direction I looked. And they had the perfect thing. Another Gold Monstrosity, except in bright white, with flashing lights on its roof.

"£13,000 + VAT? I'll have it!" I exclaimed.

"We'll have it ready for you this afternoon," said the charming salesman. Well that was no good. No time to hang around that long. My house rental people would have arrived by then. It was going to have to be the Pajero, after all that.

I 'raced' back to Wydemeet, to discover that Twiglet had had diarrhea all over Sashka's clean kitchen floor. The rental people were due in 45 minutes time. Panda was dressed and ready for the 120 mile journey in the baking sun. Vegas needed collecting, still in her field the other side of Dartmoor, we chucked all the baggage we needed for the next week into the tiny boot area, and off we set.

We went up the first hill. "This is going to be OK!" I exclaimed in surprise.

The second hill. The overheating needle started moving ominously. Phew! We made it to the top at 5mph.

No worries. We reached Vegas' field and into the trailer she trustingly trotted. Up and down, up and down, right and left, the tiny Dartmoor lanes, and finally we were onto the relatively straight, flat road of the A38. I put my foot to the floor, and the speedometer inched up to 35mph. We were never going to get to the New Forest.

Deja Vu
21/07/2016

So there we were, in the car park of Haldon Hill Garage, on a boiling hot day, all our belongings for a week in the boot, homeless, two horses in a trailer behind us, wondering what to do, where to go, and how.

Just like two years ago.

Will was so far from being amused this time, that I think he was verging on being ill.

And then I had my epiphany brainwave! To just give up on trying to get to the New Forest B&B, and stay right where we were for the week - in Haldon Hill, where we want to live eventually - instead!

More frantic googling and phone calls, but the best we could find was a field several miles from the good riding area; and a hotel near the Club which was so hot we spent all night draping wet towels over ourselves.

Things seemed to be looking up a little though, until.

After our sleepless sweaty night we went to check on Twiglet, who wasn't allowed in the hotel and who had had to sleep in the car.

Splatters and pools of stinking diarrhea all over the Pajero's driver's seat, gearbox, and boot. Wretching and gagging, Faye borrowed the hotel's equipment to clean the thing out.

Meanwhile I was becoming increasingly discontented with our current situation. Time to move on.
Another epiphany moment. Why not Exmoor! We'd always wanted to go on a riding holiday there, and it's half the distance of the New Forest. In fact I drive almost there and back every Tuesday for Faye's riding lessons.

That day we spent sunbathing by the Club pool, de-traumatising, investigating Exmoor's horsey B&Bs, hoping things might be better tomorrow.

A slither of luck - I finally found a B&B which was prepared to have us and the horses at a moment's notice! So now it was just a matter of getting there.

Optimistically greeting Twiglet in the car the next morning - yuck! More diarrhea all over the driver's seat, and Twiglet wandering around the carpark unhappily excreting water and blood.

Sunny Exmoor
22/07/2016

"We look after your animals properly," said the vet's receptionist, looking at me accusingly.

"Oh - well I don't," I replied - something about her made me cross.

Lovely Bibby of our B&B had put the horses in her beautiful field overlooking the whole of Exmoor, and driven us down to do our jobs - the local vet, the car maintenance man, the Co-op, and a tea shoppe. Breathe.. and... relax.

It turned out that Twiglet had picked up an infection while enduring his expensive morning of unhelpful x-rays at the vets, and a course of antibiotics, chicken and rice were prescribed.

A gentle evening ride around the River Barle in the sunset, and happiness, finally, began to be restored.

It Just Won't Stop!
22/07/2016

Oh how embarrassing.

"There's not much wrong with this car. The brakes are just a bit spongy, that's all," says Bibby's kind friend who has come to move the erstwhile death-trap Pajero out of everybody's way.

I must have been imagining it then, being such a nuisance to everyone, and all for no reason! I am such a moron!

So Faye and I decide to take a little drive around Exmoor to buy a map, and to have lunch at the renowned Tarr Steps, one of the noted beauty spots of the moor. It has a long, long clapper bridge, and a ford too deep for most cars to cross the river, and there's a very pretty inn half-way up the steep bank.

Full of anticipation, I hop into the old banger, drive ten yards, and. Uh Oh.

I've put my foot on the brake pedal and nothing's happened. Oh well. Let's see if we can get to Dulverton, a couple of miles away down that steep hill, in the low gear of the lowest range of four wheel drive available, combined with the handbrake. A one in twenty-five drop is ahead of us. I yank on the handbrake. I can't do this. I ease the car into a side-road and hail the next vehicle going past.

One guess what it is.

A Ford Tipper! Agh! And the little lorry is perfectly small enough for this Exmoor lane. Perhaps we should have taken the one on offer when we had the chance!

We spend the day sunbathing, in and out of the river in Dulverton, and as evening approaches, start making our way up the steep hill again, back to our stranded car.

My way of hitching is to leap in front of approaching cars shouting "Stop!" and waving my arms about. Finally my fourth victim does as asked, and takes us back to where I had originally parked the Pajero.

Eh? It's moved! About twenty feet backwards! As I stand in the middle of the road gaping, a tractor approaches and the driver pops his head out of the side.

"It was in the way so I picked it up and moved it," he explained. "I spotted the keys from under the back tyre, so I've put them back where they were."

Returning uphill to our B&B is not much of a problem.

But how are we going to get back to Dartmoor?

Three Leaks
25/07/2016

"We towed a Freelander from your car, up the hill behind Totnes, then we loaded it with all the people we could find and put a ton of steel in the boot, and finally I thrashed it for twenty miles at 3,500 revs," Jo from Edge Off Road reassures me over the phone.

He's on his way to Faye and me, as we wait for him at our B&B in Exmoor's back of beyond, in the vain hope that today we will be able to exchange his clapped out blown-up Pajero for my Gold Monstrosity, and that it will get Faye, me, Twiglet, Panda and Vegas the 70 miles home, including Haldon and Holne hills - the two longest, steepest hills that I know of in Southern England.

My concern is that Jo doesn't appear to have found anything actually wrong with the car, apart from three fuel leaks. So why should it suddenly start working now?

"Will's just texted wondering whether I'd like a lift home!" says Faye out of the blue.

Eh?

Well, it seems that Will is practising driving Ex's car, and they're both on their way from East Dorset to Wydemeet, to collect their boards for an afternoon's surfing in north Cornwall.

By the time they hear full details of our predicament, they've nearly arrived at Wydemeet. And guess what? They turn round, and sweetly fly 70 miles backwards, to our rescue.

"I am so glad that I've brought up such a kind, decent, thoughtful boy," I text Will. I am charmed and warmed that Ex, too, is doing something so unselfish, making such a big sacrifice on what must be one of the best surfing days of the summer.

Warmed up pizza is served all round when they arrive, and a bit later Jo turns up safely and swaps the Gold Monstrosity for his Pajero. Its brakes seem to work for boys, but not me. Why?

Off sets my little family in convoy, and happily, by supper time, we reach Wydemeet; no mishaps. Not even the smallest splutter. How odd. I text Jo to let him know we've arrived home safely, but he's beaten me to it. He's messaged:

"Am in hospital. Can't speak. Did you get home OK?"

Cracking B&B Gromit!
16/08/2016

Throwing everything at the marketing of Wydemeet B&B appears to be working!

We are full almost every night of July and August. We are becoming like a well-oiled machine and the money is rolling in! Over July alone, total income, including the week's rental, was approaching £6000!

What's interesting is how much of a racket the agents are. All their boasts of 'lowest price guaranteed!' are basically, simply, lies! Always call any accommodation provider direct, as it is very much worth their while to strike (sometimes a seemingly ridiculous) deal to ensure an otherwise empty room is occupied. At the very least they will save 15% + VAT by taking a direct booking rather than one that comes in via the agents, and a cash payment is always particularly attractive.

My TripAdvisor comments continue to be flattering in the extreme, and brighten up my day. I will be utterly gutted if all of a sudden I get a 4 blobber, but the whole system keeps up the pressure to provide a really good service and avoid complacency. Every time a new guest arrives, it's like taking another exam, and I still get butterflies!

We are so well stocked up on everything we need in terms of bedlinen, toiletries, frozen sausages etc, that we are able to be far more flexible these days. We are now sufficiently light on our feet to accommodate same-day bookings, single people, single nights, and even the occasional children and/or dog.

I have finally worked out my 'dog policy' (it has taken three years) which is that they are not allowed in guests' bedrooms but must stay in the comfortable 'dog area' by the back door. I think the idea of endless different dogs sleeping on the same patch of bedroom carpet every night is really a bit disgusting, actually. Every time I agree to a dog coming, I subsequently regret it, as they barge through the dog-gate, eat Twiglet, whine through the night and through breakfast; and the other day I came down to a very weird smell, and the stupid puppy had shat in the wash room.

Take out the overheads, and running the B&B represents good money for what amounts to half a day's work every day. But it does mean no days off, and no lie-ins for weeks on end; no privacy, and a sort of low-level stress/grind of being on permanent good behaviour, everything in and around the house consistently looking its best, and not much private use of the piano nor hot tub - as I think greeting your guests in a wet swimming costume would look stupid, and you never quite know when they're going to appear.

So for once the overall context of my life is relatively calm, never mind the daily hiccups which continue to drive me to drink and fags. Oh no. I mean my vape-thing.

PS: Jo got home safely in his clapped-out Pajero. On arrival, he had subsequently driven (in a proper car) to hospital to visit his mother-in-law.

Sex and Puke In Ibiza
17/08/2016

Faye and I are swimming around the outdoor pool at the Club, on a miserable grey August afternoon.

"Let's book a cheapie to the sun," I suddenly say.

So that evening I plug 'Spain anywhere' into Sky Scanner, and up pops Ibiza as the cheapest destination, flying Wednesday to Wednesday from Bristol, peak season, convenient midday flights, at £60 return each. I immediately book - seems churlish not to. So cheap it doesn't matter too much if we change our minds.

So then I turn to Airbnb to book some accommodation, and discover the catch. There isn't any. None, on the entire island. Nothing cheaper than £300 a night, unless you rent a camper-van for two. We're talking Babington House prices here! Film star levels! Agh!

I search and search for a twin room with access to a swimming pool. Too late I realise that cheap lodgings are far more significant to one's bank balance than are cheap flights. Finally, up pops something belonging to a Brazilian mathematician called 'Flavio', with a kidney-shaped pool, 'beautiful sunsets', small kitchen and bathroom with shower, and a little balcony. I book it. Then check out where in Ibiza it is. Using Google Earth I discover it is next to a motorway in the heart of an industrial estate.

Whenever there's a spare moment during the next couple of weeks I check out Airbnb, Booking.com, Trivago, Ibiza Rural Villas etc etc etc for a viable alternative. Absolutely nothing. I am no longer looking forward to this holiday, but am actually beginning to rather dread it. And what's worse, the UK appears to be heading for a heatwave that week. We could have stayed on enjoying our Club after all!

So with trepidation we board the flight, and simply cannot find Flavio's place because there's no address listed on Airbnb. We drive into a slum with a few filthy children playing around in a muddy pool, huge ruts in the road, and some oiks covered in tattoos playing around with the wreckage of a rusty old car; while thin stray cats weave around them. We ask for Flavio and nobody has heard of him.

"Thank God it's not there, Faye. I would be so sorry if I had brought you to that place," I mutter to my sweet daughter, who is now looking rather nervous.

We thrash around on the wrong side of the road in a manual car with the gear stick on the right, until finally there's a call on my mobile, and it's from delightful-sounding Flavio.

"My place is just behind the Go-Kart track," he says. Dread seizes me. Yes. I was right the first time. The slum.

And here he is: lean and beautiful, warm and smiling, putting down his beloved rescue-cat and embracing us, and leading us into his tiny apartment, with shared miniscule kitchen, balcony, shower room and telly, his bedroom door eerily a foot across the narrow dark passage from our own, the whole place smelling of hippy bean sprouts.

Guide to Ibiza
17/08/2016

A current online date called Adrian has been kind enough to supply me with an "Idiots Guide to Ibiza", which I am going to follow. It goes like this:

Ibiza .. A local map in English is obviously a must ..

A novices guide ..

Ibiza town (The Capital) .. An absolute must .. Excellent pavement cafes around the Marina with superb iced coffee & a top place to people watch ..

Dalt Vila in the 'higher town', the ancient part of Ibiza town & another must visit .. I rode a scooter to here in 1976!

There is a very busy road connecting Ibiza Town to San Antonio on the other side of the island (the home of sex & puke) ..

If it's S&P you are really after, you need not go anywhere else! .. It's all here & It's disgusting ..

Close to SA there are two beaches that have become notorious with sub 30 years of age Brits, Cala Basa & Cala Conta .. Again. I feel you will have to be brave to visit ..

There are eateries of all types in SA & I have to say that last time I was there, there were a couple of half decent Thai Restaurants, just on the outskirts ..

If you draw a line all around the south coast of the Island to Ibiza Town, I have to say that I do not know this area at all, so cannot comment ..

Heading north from SA you will eventually arrive at Portinax .. An ex fishing village now given to tourism, but pretty much unspoilt ..
Directly to the west of Portinax is a lovely beach called El Port de Sant Miquel .. I have been here a couple of times, quite beautiful ..

infact, the whole of the north western coast is littered with small coves & beaches .. It would be good to explore .

Near San Miguel is the hippy beach of Benirras .. Follow the signs from SM .. Only one road in & out, go early in order to park ..

If you go on Sunday, you will see & hear the Hippy bongos .. Well worth it for the atmosphere & superb sun sets .. There are beach bars etc .. Thinking about it & casting my mind back, it's quite a magical place ..

Wherever you go on Ibiza, you will be handed colourful fly sheets & pieces of card advertising & giving details of the open markets & night clubs .. These are what you need as they also give directions ..

Some of the main clubs are on the main road between Ibiza Town & San Antonio, others are in or just south of Ibiza Town, the main one being Pacha near the Marina & one I have attended ..

Space is just south of Ibiza Town & is pretty famous .. Eden in San Antonio is well known ..

I cannot remember the name of any of the outdoor markets, but look out for the fly sheets .. The Hippy ones are superb, also with excellent laid back music .. I bet you come home with more than one CD! Again, if I remember correctly, the Hippy markets may also be sign posted ..

Cas Pla
17/08/2016

"We've got to cut our losses and waste the whole of tomorrow trying to find a last-minute place to stay," I whisper in despair to Faye, over our delicious supper of mussels.

So in the morning we pack up our Ryanair hand luggage and scarper, relieved that dear Flavio isn't there, so we don't have to explain to him that we don't like his much loved home.

We don't see any further accommodation advertised until a couple of miles from the port of St Miguel.

"Rural Hotel Cas Pla" reads the sign. We turn off the main drag and head up, up, up, up - I'm in first gear all the way and am dreading an uphill stop/start.

"Shall we give up? It's hopeless!" I wail. But then finally, in front of us, are the signs for the hotel. Four Star. No way are we going to be able to afford this. But we've come so far... We walk in and there's total silence. The place must be shut. Eventually, having walked through beautiful gardens, bars, outside reclining places, sitting rooms, dining rooms, a pool table, weight room and two swimming pools, we chance upon Reception. But there's nobody about.

"Shall we give up? This place is for millionaires!" I exclaim. We accost a maid, but she doesn't speak English.

"Rafaella," she says. "Ten minute."

We recline in an enormous white leather sofa, one of four, in the shade, while around us two couples help themselves to a sumptuous looking breakfast. Our eyes are agog. We have eaten nothing so far today.

A beautiful wisp of a woman floats up. She has long ringlets and a short white dress, above lean tanned legs, and she's welcoming us with a warm smile. We explain the situation, and what? Am I hearing correctly? She has a spare double room and we are bartering. Down from 270 euros to 170 euros. That's hardly more than I charge for a room in Wydemeet! She is so sorry for us that she changes her mind and turns the double room into a suite fit for a prince, on two floors, emperor sized bed, huge telly, patio, bath, biggest shower head I have ever seen... all in tranquil grey and white. We are breathless! Ours for two nights!

And after that, for 180 euros a night, a private twin apartment with its own sitting room and little garden, for the six nights until we have to leave this paradise.

My luck has turned. For what must be the first time in seven years. Eh? I don't remember cracking any mirrors back in 2009.

My 60th
31/08/2016

Faye's and my Ibizan days of paradise quickly assume some kind of order.

I rise at 9.15am and read my Dawn French book, "According to Yes", lounging next to one of the two pools in the sunshine for an hour. Then I wake Faye and we have main course of cheese, eggs and ham, and pudding of croissants and pastries, for brunch til 11am.

We return to the poolside to do screens and read, in the peace (there are more sunbeds than people here - the whole place feels deserted), til 4ish, with drinks and crisps at around 2pm and a 30 minute swim at 3.30pm.

Then we gather our things and go beach-crawling (there appear to be hundreds of stunning little coves all around the island); ending up at a cafe for a one course dinner at around 8.30pm.

In this way, over six days we circumnavigate the whole of Ibiza - on just one tank of fuel, in our jolly little Fiat. Ibiza is even smaller than Dartmoor! 221 square miles, to Dartmoor's 368! No wonder it's a bit short of accommodation during peak season!

I haven't been this happy for literally years. I am so happy I can't really believe it. I absolutely love this place. I am really, really loving being here. I simply don't want to go home at all! Everything about it is so very beautiful.

We visit the beaches and cafes of the North; the hippy market which is so colourful and so expensive, and so short of the cheap tatt that we're after for presents; the main town with its £300m superyachts which are listed on Google; the beautiful thin Eurotrash of the neighbouring island: Formentera; and the concrete jungle that we have been warned is the Clubland of San Antonio.

We find that the clubs look neat and tidy during the middle of the day when we go to take pictures of ourselves outside them. The beaches are immaculate. We don't see anybody sleeping on them, let alone any 18-30s vomming, or having sex. We make a special trip to the gay nudist beach - and there aren't any. It's full of normally dressed families! 'San An' looks perfectly respectable and the naff beaches nearby prove extremely attractive.

Something very odd has happened to Ibiza's PR. It's nothing like the way it's normally portrayed.

I'm swimming round and round our hotel's pool for my mandatory half-hour, mulling over all of this, and I have a Eureka! moment. The hotel has 25 bedrooms. Will, Faye and I will celebrate our 21st, 18th and 60th birthdays here in 2019! Hurray! We can come back!

Might it be economical to charter a private plane?

Will I Ever Sell My House?
20/9/2016

I've dropped the price by £75,000.

Why not? I only had three viewings during May, June and July. Pathetic. Especially after so much work has gone into making sure that everything now looks nice and works - for the time being anyway.

And yet there's still not really any action going on. A couple who really like it say it's too long a daily commute to Torquay hospital (he's a consultant there, and I agree with them). And another couple is coming from Berkshire to see it on Friday. But really - don't hold your breath.

I am convinced that what's critical in this sale is the extraordinary location, rather than the price. Marmite. A lot of people would actually want paying to be made to live right out here!

Meanwhile, however, the B&B is thundering along with lovely guests after lovely guests.

I have just waved off my 'Fourth Timers' - the first time they came here they had just met, and Olivia rode Panda. Now they have both learned to ski, both learned to ride; got engaged, married, pregnant, and finally produced little Bartholomew. I love them so much that I wanted to give them supper all of the four days that they were here. This paying thing is becoming embarrassing!

And my most recent pair have returned beaming from wild swimming in the East Dart in their wetsuits, after a game of ping-pong, all ready now for the hot tub. They are wedding photographers and have promised to put up lots of pics and a link to their wild swimming YouTube vid on TripAdvisor. And the mandatory 5 blobs.

I have had over 25 room nights booked every month during the summer, and have settled into something of a routine, the pre-visit nerves having mostly subsided. It is a highly pleasurable and efficient way of making money as a self-employed person on the moor, working the hours you choose with no travel. I'm reckoning on about £40 per hour. I get such a buzz from seeing everybody who comes here looking so happy, too. And now the children are back at school, I have to admit that the endless stream of B&B guests prevents loneliness and boredom setting in.
What pisses me off though, is that when they all seem to think that I'm so nice, why don't I have better luck in the romance stakes?

Change of Life
11/10/2016

"I am devoted to Christ."

This is how Larry from Bristol, who has just 'viewed' me on match.com, describes himself.

I don't know whether to giggle or to sigh.

This is hopeless. Everything I try is hopeless. Everywhere I turn seems to end with me facing a brick wall.

I just don't appear to be able to move on. I can't sell my house so I can't relocate. I can't find a bloke. I can't sell my book. I am stuck. And then I will die. And it will all be over. And I will have simply stagnated since my marriage ended seven years ago. Meanwhile, Ex is now happily engaged to his very nice girlfriend, and my anger is growing.

Because after all this time and effort trying to make things happen, I have finally given up. Up until now, I have been fuelled with optimism, and hope, for a new life, which might have ameliorated the intense pain and frustration of the bust-up all those years ago. After all, initially I believed I was going to come out of the calamity best! But I've come out of it worst. And recently I have begun to lose all hope for change.

So, instead, I have come up with a cunning plan. I am going to misappropriate my children's school fees, and spend £3000 on going through 'The Hoffman Process'. My goal is to emerge the other side, after a week's intensive therapy, as a calm, centred, serene, poised and comfortable person, as I have seen three of my friends do before me.

I am certain that by undergoing The Process, they have saved their marriages.

One of them has transformed from a person so desperate to be loved that she was in danger of being bullied. Last week I saw her dancing slowly with her husband on the terrace by their pool, and they looked so very much in love. "Yuck! Not fair!" I yelled at them.

Another suffered unspeakable humiliation when his business failed very publicly, and the family seat was sold. He enrolled on the course and has emerged a gently confident person. Happy in himself - in a way he never was before. His wife has fallen in love with him all over again.

A couple of days ago I returned from five days in Cyprus with my very best friends, alarmed at how sharp I have become; and how often I found myself saying, "What really pisses me off..."

Last night I found myself talking with a specialist farming counsellor who annoyed me, so I became strident, in order to shock him out of his complacency.

"Rarely have I come across anybody so bitter," he remarked.

Outrageous of me, really, as people would kill to experience the day-to-day life that I enjoy. Relative financial security, surrounded by love and friendship, balanced children (so far), large comfortable home in a beautiful place with nothing to do all day except organise my B&Bers, chat, swim and ride my horses.

This new aggressive and negative attitude of mine must surely be damaging to my children. And not helpful to me either. But The Course is going to make me become nicer. It will even put a stop to my endless barbed comments to Ex. Perhaps I might manage to kiss him hello and goodbye, and send him birthday and Christmas cards!

Maybe I will contentedly stay put; or perhaps the nicer new me will find everything starts to happen after all, and on we go.

But £3000 for a week. Ooo-errr. A price worth paying, I hope (less than what I sometimes turn over in a month of B&Bing) if it's to change my life for the better, and the lives of those closest to me?

The one problem is that I don't have a week spare to do it in, until January 21st 2017. Perhaps something will have changed by then and I can move on again without having to invest in the pricey Hoffman people. Otherwise goodbye £500! I will send them their deposit in a few weeks' time, and then I believe they will interview me, to ascertain whether I am 'ready' for them to work their magic on.

Epiphany Moment
26/10/2016

"You're the boy on the bike!" I exclaimed, glancing again in my rear view mirror at the young hitch-hiker sitting in the back of The Thug - my new and already much loved black and gold 'John Player Special' three litre diesel truck, brought back from a tiny town in the middle of Wales, after the Gold Monstrosity eventually gave up the will to live.

Faye and I had become used to grinning at this good-looking young man, as he cycled in one direction across the moors of a Saturday evening, and we drove home from Faye's school in the other.

"Who are your parents?"

"Do you know the Morrison-Princes?" he replied.

"Oh wow! You're Alistair!" I blurted.

The last time I saw him, he was ten - the year my children left their lovely village primary school for the posh prep.

Grown up, charming and eloquent, Alistair is now in his gap year, prior to starting university. He told me that he was working at Badgers Holt in Dartmeet, and hoping to move on to the Forest Inn at the end of my lane, when it finally re-opens.

Well, a couple of hours later, as I was driving along the road to Totnes (as opposed to Damascus), I had an Epiphany Moment.
"Why am I selling my home?"

Over the past two years so much has changed.

Will, who originally suggested the move, is no longer 15 wanting to live next to a bus-stop, Costa's and cinema. These days he appreciates the solitude - he can play his music as loud as he likes. And the grotty old gaffiti'd Bothy breathes character when compared to his rich friends' luxurious purpose-built party barns. Wydemeet is a cool home after all!

The B&B's ticking along highly efficiently and it's fun. I have absolutely loved every single one of my guests throughout the entire summer. Why stop? I can just about afford to live here like this.

The house is much nicer to live in, since I have had it 'done' - especially with its draft-free new windows, and smart gravel outside.

It's become clear that I'm never going to build a new social life through my Club, nor through Faye's new school, even if I move much nearer to them both.

I won't be able to afford anywhere close to Exeter with big bedrooms and party-space for the children, huge field and stables, and fabulous riding outside the gate, as I have here.

But more significantly, I've realised that when the Forest Inn opens, it will become the centre for all local yoof to congregate - just as it was for their parents thirty years ago. It's probably too late for Will, but Faye is already part of that gang.

And then there's me. Having the Forest Inn throbbing with life at the end of the road could change everything! Like a permanent party almost in my sitting room! I should be able to go there on my own and not feel too much like a slapper, sitting at the bar on my own, sipping Spritzers.

Bugger all the shitty weather and the endless driving that I have to do.

I'm going to test my theory. Big Decision. If I feel welcome, happy and relaxed on Forest Inn Opening Night, I shall take my house off the market. For ever.

I open the familiar door and walk in.

Eh? It's heaving, yet I don't know a soul! After living here for 21 years!

Except, suddenly, there are Adam and Sarah - two of my favourite people in the entire universe - who were drawn back by the moor after a decade of living on a Dutch barge in St Katherine's Dock. And gradually, through the merry throng, I recognise more and more welcoming, smiling faces - so many friends I've made since moving here in 1995. How could I possibly find anything like this somewhere else?

So. That's it. Decision made.

I am staying put. I can't think of anywhere I would rather live.

I've taken my house off the market. It's deleted from Rightmove. The Savills signs are gone.

They will have to carry me out in a box.

The Forest Grim
8/11/2016

"I feel like a posh twat," remarked Will, as he regarded his game pie suspiciously, perched on a chair facing a pillar, in the main thoroughfare used by the waiters and waitresses of the pub.

I hope that in time he will get used to the new ambiance of his once beloved Forest Inn, now that every lunchtime and evening since its re-opening a couple of weeks ago, it's bursting with happy customers.

What he remembers with such sentiment is scampi and chips fresh from the freezer, slammed down in front of him in an empty room, by a dour landlady who appeared to resent most of her clientele.

I've visited the pub five times in eight days, and posted up its first TripAdvisor review, titled "Best Food In Devon!" There have been plenty more five blobbers on their site since then - the entire community being absolutely thrilled to have our pub back, delighted with the exquisite food, ridiculously low prices, and enthusiastic warm welcomes by its new owners.

What intrigues me is the decor. It's not somewhere you would take a romantic date to. We all recognise the light green patterny carpet that has been there longer than we have - pre-1995. The rooms are large, square and bright. The furniture - plastic tables, lightweight stainless steel cutlery and upholstered chairs were bought as a job lot from a place that had understandably gone bust in Tavistock.

The thick new curtains are bunched on the rail and don't appear to fit the drafty windows.They look as if they have been ready-made to fit some rather different-sized ones.

But worst of all, in one corner of the room there's a purple pool table, a darts board, and an electronic score board with flashing red lights! Agh!

So - who is the target market? The local young? Or picky posh people like me?

Party Time!
8/11/2016

"The downside is that you're going to have to take part in the carol service," I warned the children, now that we've decided to stay put, so are able to discuss ideas for parties this Christmas. "I've offered the organisers sax players, a flute, readers, and even myself for the organ if they're completely desperate."

The children's faces fell, but we already have Will's 18th planned for early December (a sit-down dinner for 20, Great Gatsby theme), so all is not too disastrous in his world.

I looked up the port that he was given by his kind godfather at his Christening, which would probably be about the right age to serve at his party by now. Wow! I'm glad I did! One bottle of 1994, and a case of 1997. Apparently the 1994 vintage is 'Classic' - ie one of the best vintages of the centenary. And 1997 is 'Excellent'. Neither is yet ready for drinking though. Eh? It's already been waiting for 23 years! The website neglected to say when we can finally crack it open, but I'm sure that for Will's 18th, pinching one of the bottles out of the case won't hurt.

Will's friends are 'hardcore' party-goers apparently, which means they did all the stupid stuff when they were about 15, and are no longer interested in getting ridiculously drunk or high, or having casual sex all over the place and being sick a lot. I hope he's right! Will is currently rebelling against his avant-garde school by dressing really smartly. After a recent rugby match, I spotted an immaculately groomed young man in a smart slimline suit that I can't imagine ever fitted his father, complete with tie and cufflinks. My son! Wow! Where had his grungy black hoodie and low-slung skinnies gone?

Once we've knocked the 18th on the head, we're going to hold our huge 'annual' Christmas party again - something I've neglected to do since I got cross with the rubbish local community who never asked me back to anything, nor looked after me when Ex went off. Traditionally we would just ask everybody we knew for Cava with a raspberry in it, lager, elderflower with a raspberry in it, and cocktail sausages covered in mustard and honey, served by young waitresses, so that I could enjoy myself instead of having to be a good host. In previous years, we have had up to 150 people attending, from every background and of every age, their cars getting stuck in the mud outside our house, parked all the way up to the cattle grid. But this time we're going to call it a 'House Re-Warming Party'. Just like in the olden days, except that Ex won't be here to make it go with a swing. Wydemeet works perfectly for such a throng, as all the rooms interconnect so that you can walk around the whole ground floor of the house in a circle.

We'll have Christmas here for the first time in years, and some friends have already invited themselves over for New Year's Eve. I have always been a bit shy of asking people to come all the way out here for not very good cooking and no male host. So I'm dead chuffed that they want to come. Watch out December - we're gonna party!

Happiness
8/11/2016

How often do you feel more than content - actually happy?

"You've made the right decision, girl," shouted the whipper-in, as I galloped across the open moor on my beautiful mare, surrounded by innumerable similarly mounted friends going back twenty years. There was one bloke out who drives 200 miles from Worcestershire twice a week, just to enjoy the riding right outside my gate. When for me it's 20 yards. I hung my head in shame. Why did I ever want to sell?

I had run out of excuses. I was no longer trying to get pregnant. Faye's riding lessons are now on Thursdays, not Tuesdays when the hunt meets around here. I'm no longer planning to move. The first year's subscription has halved. So at long last this morning I finally coughed up the £275 Dartmoor Hunt subscription. "Let's crack open some champagne!" exclaimed the master.

There were about thirty horses out today. I knew almost all of the riders, and even those I didn't recognise welcomed me. I found myself introducing people to each other. I am part of it, in a way I have never felt before. I belong at last. And I had been ready to throw it all away.

I'm Falling to Bits
27/11/2016

Ouch! Some bugger of a horse fly appears to have bitten me on the opposite side to where my appendix probably is.

It's left a nasty red mark about an inch long.

Agh! I think some bitey bug must have been living in my vest-thing, which has been hanging up unused in my cupboard for months, and is now very hungry. As the bloody insect's attacked me again - a bit higher up.

Eh? Now I can't sleep because the bites are so painful it's as if my whole left torso is swollen!

I make myself scramble up on Panda and lead Vegas around the block, and I almost enjoy myself as today is so beautiful. But I can't quite. It's just such an effort to do anything.

This is odd. The unsightly two red patches are still here a week later! And looking more closely they appear to have little red specks in them. Hmmmmmm.

Tap tap tap. 'Mild shingles'. Afflicts people over 50 suffering from low immunity and stress. Lasts two to six weeks. Well who would have thought.

And so it does - lasts three weeks. Three weeks of sneaking back to bed every day, the minute I've finished with my B&Bers. And then getting up again to drive somewhere to socialise. I can sit and eat and drink and chat - no problem at all!

And now - post 18 year old Will's half-term, complete with endless parties and driving and getting lost and 50 point turns in tight places with people hooting at me, and not being able to see out of my muddy back window properly and sweating and hurling my truck around - both my arms seem to have gone out of order.

On top of which I appear to have developed such a bad cold that I feel really, really ill.

What a bummer - when everything else is such fun!

Not Moving On
15/12/2016

All the self-help books tell you that you have to 'move on' after the end of a relationship.

So I have been trying, obediently, to do so, for seven years.

I've practically bust a gut trying to move house, to find a new job, a new position in life, a new social world through the Club and Faye's new school, a new man - you name it. And I've failed on every single front.

Well. Good. Because I haven't been this happy for years.

The experts' stupid advice is just that - stupid. What they actually should be saying is "Stay Put". Encouraging the broken hearted and lonely to build on what they have already created, rather than running away from the familiar, just when they need it most. Honestly. Silly idiots.

I've lived in Wydemeet now for 21 years, and have built up a wide network of friends - both on, and all around the moor. I would be dead before I could achieve that again. While living at Wydemeet, I've made the house just how I want it. I would never be able to find anything else that would suit me better that I could afford. How mad to even think of starting again.

Murder They Wrote
3/1/2017

I appreciate that she tried to kill him, which I suppose is a bit drastic. But nevertheless, I think the Kate/Rob BBC Radio 4's Archers storyline of subtle control emerging within a marriage has proved a bit of a turning point in the nation's consciousness.

It's not something that ever crossed my mind before, but post the Archers thing I'm guessing that several of my closest, most able and intelligent girlfriends are/have been suffering from various degrees of spousal control, verging on abuse, for years. Probably each party remaining totally oblivious to the fact. A couple of the wives have recently finally cracked, doing things that were completely mad, wrecking their lives still further, possibly forever.

We knew Kate would be exonerated, of course, because it's the BBC, which needs to be responsible about giving hope and support to the many women (and indeed a few men) who find themselves in an abusive relationship.

I think there's a lot to be pleased about in modern day life, and one thing is this opening up of issues which were once either not recognised, or taboo.

Our little family has recently been involved in a bullying incident at school. It's been an uncomfortable, but very interesting and ultimately rewarding experience. I can see now why it is so difficult for the victim to report what's happening to them. They have been so undermined already, yet if they complain to the authorities, they have to be quizzed, questioned and further tested, the perpetrator given a chance to put their side of the story, and witnesses, who may not have a full grasp of what has happened and who are in thrall to the perpetrator, questioned.

In our case the issue was dealt with 150% satisfactorily, but it was scary going through the long, very structured process. Previously I couldn't understand why all those celebrity paedophiles' victims didn't come forward straight away, but now I can.

I am also a great fan of this growing trend for labelling. Take 'the spectrum' for instance. I recently commented to a friend's 24 year old son, who had always struggled with making friends, and who had been an unhappy handful throughout his young life:

"You're very clever, aren't you?"

He replied without hesitation, proud as punch: "Yes I am. I'm Aspergers you know." He was only recently diagnosed, and thrilled about it. Suddenly everything made sense and he could finally relax into being the real him. He's just emerged from Plymouth University with a First, he's become an expert street dancer, and has loads of new friends.

I've got a couple more extremely clever mates who aren't great on the old empathy front. When I suggest that they might be 'on the spectrum', they happily concur. In fact I reckon about 10% of everybody I come across is somewhere on it. Perhaps we all are!

Narcissim - there's another. I wonder if around 95% of men are a bit narcissistic. Just as I am! Just flatter us and give us a bit of a stroke - and you'll have us all purring.

Hot and Wet
3/1/2017

"Oi! Over here young man!" I yelled, leaning my heavy frame in its size 16 M&S black and white swimming costume out over the side of the hot tub, and beckoning to the teenager who was attempting to close our electric gate after his parents' car had come in through it.

"Sorry - don't know your name," I called, "but do drive around to the back, and Faye will greet you with tea and Christmas cake!"

I sank back into the 40C churning water of the jacuzzi, and Matron, Mrs Watson (the children's old art teacher) and I resumed our contemplation of how to handle our friend's imploded marriage. Every aspect of it. Beneath my newly arrived guests' bedroom window.

Well I had asked them not twice, but three times, when they planned to arrive. And with no reply it was impossible for Matron, Mrs Watson and me to time our monthly tub session around them. Now that my two friends had driven all the way over here and we were immersed, I was loathe to get out. So I didn't. I thought, instead, I'd time it so that Faye would have finished giving our guests tea before I was running past their door, upstairs, dripping in my swimming costume, all over the carpet, to get dressed.

Forty-five minutes later and rather hot and wrinkly, the three of us heaved ourselves up, and tottered with our towels wrapped around us, towards the stairs. Just as my guests emerged from tea in the kitchen with Faye.

"Oh hello! Have you had a nice journey? Has Faye been looking after you OK? Was the Christmas cake nice? Have you found everything you need? blah blah blah standard guest-talk" babbled I, standing in the middle of the hall, bedraggled old towel scarcely hiding my white whale-like physique, mascara blearily running down my face, wet hair hardening soaked in chlorine and sticking to my neck, the carpet at my feet stained dark brown with running water.

Dignified I turned and walked up the stairs. Dressed in five minutes and raced back to Faye

"How embarrassing from nought to ten was that?" I gasped.

"Nought," she replied.

This Year
9/1/2017

Every morning I would tiptoe downstairs, turn on six switches to power up 100m of fairy lights twinkling and flashing all around the house; feed the horses (in dressing gown and wellies); and return to bed with my Ready Brek and mandarins; ready to re-emerge as other signs of life were heard around the house, shortly before lunchtime.

My little family has enjoyed four weeks of indulgent, loving, relaxation and celebration. I can't remember such a prolonged stretch of time when I have been happier, actually. If you were ever wondering whether or not to have children - do it! But now both of them are back to school, while 2017 stretches blankly and meaninglessly ahead.

I'm back to that sad old routine of swimming, riding, being a lady who breakfasts, elevenses's, lunches, teas and dinners, and watching children's sports matches and school concerts.

How else shall I occupy myself, resisting the ever-present temptation of pressing that button of the devil's - Daytime TV - 'On'?

I know! I will re-edit my failure-book into six parts, and make myself into a famous author!

Oh - and begin that oh-so-necessary calorie-busting diet.

Floreat Etona!
9/1/2017

Friday 13th. Probably most apposite. This Friday heralds a dinner to celebrate my school peer group's forty years of leaving our alma mater, Eton College. The end of the Autumn term of 1977 - our Oxbridge term. Now we're all 57 or 58. What on earth will everybody look like?

I attended the last 1977 Leavers' Dinner a decade ago. I was quaking with fear. I had suffered some mild bullying at school, mostly because I was more or less the only girl being educated there (my father was a house master and subsequently Vice Provost) and I had arrived in the sixth form, as an object of fascination, rather than being part of the furniture from the beginning. I think that some of the boys with the bigger egos resented what they perceived as my undeserved notoriety.

So here I was, the first time, aged 47, ready to face my demons. I was one of the last to arrive at the chapel service, having missed the group photograph because I was busy getting a bit pissed with some old friends I'd bumped into, at the pub where we were all staying.

In Eton College Chapel the pews face each other, and the aisle comprises very uneven flagstones.

"Agh! I am going to trip over in front of everybody, as I walk between 200 men all interested to see how fat and wrinkly I have become!" I thought to myself, as I shuffled in.

The service began with a hymn, and I was the only one present with a silly high voice.

"Why on earth have I put myself through this?" I silently questioned myself, over and over again, as I could see people peering over their service sheets, and squinting down our row, to get a really good view of me. I spent most of the service gazing hard at the floor.

Afterwards we made our way to one of the school's beautiful huge old rooms for drinks, and all of a sudden I was surrounded by smiling friendly interested faces. On we went to dinner, and it was the welcoming speech.

"My Lords, Lady and Gentlemen," began the Provost...

Tables were banged; legs beneath were thumped. I blushed with embarrassment. I was touched and moved. It was as if I was their little mascot. My shoulders felt lighter, as my demons of thirty years flew away. And now I'm putting myself through it again.

This time I am sitting next to a chap who was one of the most unkind to me of all. Some time ago he made the most abject apology and we have since become very good friends. He is just so funny!

Anyhow, he has sent me the seating plan for our dinner this Friday. Eeeek! It comprises all the coolest boys of our year, including a couple who were Lords then, so they must be Earls now; and one who I have enjoyed hating nearly as much as I hate Her, for my entire life.

I have just googled this thoroughly horrid boy, to discover that he has lost all his hair, become an artist specialising in dull clashing colours, previously living in New York but now back at his family farm in Oxfordshire, who is married to one of America's leading socialites, people like Christian Louboutin having attended their wedding back in 2002.

The thing is that even if these people are now penniless incontinent alcoholic vagrants, at reunions somehow everybody automatically reverts to their original school status.

"Should I be scared?" I asked Faye. She burst into loud peals of laughter. "You will tell them all to Fuck Right Off!" she howled.

Well I am sincerely hoping that they are all pot-bellied and bald now. Lucky I found that fat-camouflaging dress in the sales last week!

Dreaming
15/1/2017

"Love him, hate him, don't know him..." Tim and I went through the list of 100+ Old Etonians, astonished that there were so many names that we didn't recognise.

"OMG! Obviousleeeeee - they've all become Lords and Earls since our day, and are called something different!" I exclaimed. That would be about 25% of the entire list!

As I round Ascot Racecourse, cruise past Legoland and up the Windsor

Relief Road, my nerves are really beginning to kick in. Windsor Castle - oh so familiar, serene, like something from a fairy tale, welcoming me, reddy-orange as the sun sets, and five minutes later I'm squeezing through that familiar narrow archway into the carpark of The Christopher, 110 Eton High Street, behind the wheel of my filthy John Player Special truck, two sacks of horse food in the boot, and "also available in black and gold" scrawled into the thick mud of the rear window by hilarious Faye.

"I used to work here," I inform the receptionist of the Guest House. "Must have changed a bit," he replies. True - it was sticky and smelt, forty years ago.

I am relieved that I don't bump into anybody I know as I sign in, because I haven't washed my hair for eight days.

Just as I emerge from the shower, the phone in my room bleeps.

"We're here!" cries Chris, one of the few OEs who has remained a close friend throughout the past four decades, and who has volunteered to look after me this evening, alongside Tim, our other mate.

In the end, rather than a fat-camouflaging dress, I have opted to wear a nylon Wallis black flowery top and some sparkly leggings - the most important thing, in my opinion, being to look as thin as possible, rather than appropriate. Competition is fierce, as the most handsome boy in the entire year has brought along a picture of me aged 15 - the best photo ever taken of me. How am I going to stand up against that, now weighing half as much again and covered with wrinkles? Heck!

Quickly I smear on a face, and race to the bar to be greeted by eight warm smiles. Yikes! I don't know who half these people are!

We stroll past a new Budgens where the garage used to be; and my old primary school: The Eton Porney School - which still displays the same sign outside of its founder, CE Porney. I'm not making that up.

And our little groups now moves into the anti-hall of Eton College Chapel.

A roaring sea of animated black and white. I fail to recognise a single bloke. And then all of a sudden I am besieged - one chap interrupting the next, and me trying to remain polite and interested to all...

"Do you remember getting pissed at Windsor Castle - I had to sit next to the queen at dinner straight afterwards!" reminisces Jimmy.

"Oh yes! I drove home on my motorbike to meet my boyfriend, who had personally mined some gold in Alaska to make into a wedding ring for me!" I reply. "My Mum said, 'I don't like tight girls in my house' and I kept singing, 'Tonsils in a bottle' and nearly wetting myself laughing."

"Do you remember trying to snog me behind the marquee at that party?" I ask another.

"I think about you every day - I have called my website 'Yram - Mary spelled backwards - because you used to recite the whole of Mary Had A Little Lamb backwards," - this is to the most lovely gentle person called Fabrice.

"I drove past your old home this morning, where you had that Christmas drinks party, and you had all been hunting, and I was so, so jealous; and now that could have been me!"

On and on it goes, until we're summoned into the Chapel proper for 'The Photo' - taken from the organ loft.

"How much are you looking forward to zee drinks, gentlemen?" yells the French photographer; snap snap snap. Tim had rushed over and grabbed me and put me under his arm to ensure that I am happy and safe, swapping places to put himself in the horrid, lonely, end pew seat.

"I was the only one banned from singing in my whole prep school because I'm so bad," my other neighbour shouts over me, as I attempt 'Praise Him Praise Him' in my weedy high voice.

We meander through the school yard, dropping in on a classroom dating back to 1422, with the poet, Shelley's, name carved into one of the desks.

Agggghhhhhh! There is my most hated boy, right in front of me!

"How are you, Mary?" his eyes twinkle and crinkle in the most warm, affectionate and friendly way. I melt. He is no longer even the slightest bit scary.

Real champagne, imbibed in a deep carpeted golden reception room lined with grand portraits, and one chap after another makes his way over especially to say hello. It's weird - a bit as if there is a blanket over the head of each one, the blanket gradually slips off as he talks, to reveal underneath the image of the younger person I had once known so well.

Dinner, and I find myself at top table, on a stage, opposite the provost and new headmaster; everyone on the table apart from me is titled. They are so funny, they were so thick at school.

"I was with you for Ancient Greek in Division 14 - could hardly read or write!" they shout at each other. I just avoid doing the nose trick with the most exquisite chateau something; the chef has somehow succeeded in serving fillet steak for 100 in ultimate moist, juicy, tender, tasty perfection. Heavy silver candlesticks, gleaming cutlery, millions of glasses. Wow! Wow! Wow!

"My Lords, Ladies and Gentlemen," begins Lord Waldegrave. "It's particularly nice, this evening, to have the best balance of sexes ever at such a gathering..." queue much table and feet banging and stamping and thumping. "Especially as she's the daughter of my favourite rowing coach.. etc etc"

Next it's the headmaster, and thirdly the boys' representative speaker - a chap who was particularly friendly and kind to me, when we were both at school. Back in the early eighties he was featured in an illustrated article in Saturday's Daily Mail magazine, called "Oxford Bright Young Things". His reported behaviour had been so bad that a merchant bank withdrew its job offer to him, so he became a DJ instead. Now he's the CEO of not one, but two Footsie companies. He must earn several million a year.

"Ahem..." he begins. "I am more astonished than most, to find myself standing here, talking to you all (in the absence of Hugh Laurie); having been the most unpopular boy in our entire year group."

'Intelligence and a good sense humour are ten times more sexy than looks,' flashes across my mind. I've just been informed that this chap is married to the sister of the best looking Etonian of all time.

And then he begins to talk about me.

"Blah blah blah blah blah blah and carried it all off with dignity. And then, showing us exactly what she thought of us all, she chose to marry an Old Harrovian," he concludes.

"Big mistake," I murmur, but my neighbour elbows me and hisses "shusshhhhhhhhh!" as the whole room explodes with more bangs, hoorahs and whistles.

It can't just be the flowing wine responsible for this whole experience beginning to morph into a sort of ethereal feeling for me, can it? This is beyond anything I could ever have dreamed of.
A few days later, and the evening is still living with me, different images and conversations going round and round in my head. I just can't believe that any of it really actually happened at all.

Gentle Swim
26/1/2017

... for'Referrals and Over 50s'

I park in the Disabled car parking space right in front of the entrance to my children's old school's new pool. It's 50 metres long and was apparently once the 'warm up' pool, located in the basement, for the London Olympics. Princess Anne opened it two days ago. I've never seen a pool this big before. I think it's one of the only ones in the West Country, yet it's just across the moor from me!

Anyhow. Shock horror! I am utterly appalled to discover that nobody in this swimming slot, which is meant to be for doctors' 'referrals' and ancient people, looks particularly old, or swims much more slowly than I do! Agh! I have become one of them!

Leggings for £1.99
2/2/2017

My best mate Alice came to stay at the weekend.

She looked stunning, in layers and layers of floaty black and a bit of grey.

Underneath though, she's even fatter than I am, she insisted.

Well you'd never guess, and she looks miles more elegant than I do, so I decided to copy all her clothes.

We went through my wardrobe together and threw out 75% of everything I owned, leaving just a few things for when/if I ever get thinner again, stuffed right at the back of the cupboard.

And since then I've gone completely bonkers on eBay. Clothes are so cheap these days, compared with when I was young, hundreds and hundreds of years ago. Especially black stretchy ones. I've gone so mad that I've now got just as many clothes as I had before, but this time they're all huge!

So I'm wondering now whether I might have accepted my great big new size, and am cheating by camouflaging my rolls, rather than going down the cheaper, more constructive, less enjoyable route of cutting down on what I eat and drink.

We folded all my unwanted clothes into neat piles and put them in a wheelie binbag for Sashka to take her pick. She used to be larger than me, and now she is smaller. Annoyiiiiing! It is always a bit nerve-wracking offering your clothes to friends - for two reasons. One, that it's such a patronising grandiose Lady-Muck thing to do; and two, that it's so hurtful when they don't want any of them, because you have such execrable taste.

Well Sashka took alarmingly little, and I will have to deliver the rest to any charity shop who will take it, other than the Mare & Foal Sanctuary one. I hate them. They told me that I wasn't looking after their grotty little Dartmoor Hill Pony properly, when in fact it was that very pony that put Will off riding for the rest of his life. And I also hate them because their Company Accounts show that the 400 horses they own (many of which are so old and stiff that they can hardly stand up, according to my farrier) are supported by over £4m of public funds every year. That's over £10,000 per grotty equine!!

Meanwhile my other ruse is to sell my better quality garments via eBay. We dressed Faye up in each item and took a pic of her wearing it on my phone. I hadn't stopped to think that all our silver was displayed on a table in the background. Silly moi. Anyhow, I've just finished putting all my 'good clothes' up on the site, and nobody's interested in any of them. What an effort all for nothing. The only success I've had is a bid of £1.99 for a pair of faux leather leggings.

Never mind. I've got something to take my mind off such frustrations. Another meal out tonight at The Forest Inn. Last time I went there I think Alan, the chef, put two pints of cream in my moules mariniere!

Best First Line Ever!
2/2/2017

When I was nine, I used to busk on my sax to the sheep outside our garden gate in remotest Dartmoor. I didn't make much money, but loved the thrill of playing alone, outside in the wind.

"That's the best opening line of a Personal Statement I have ever read," announced the lady who was interviewing Will for a place at Leeds University, to read Music With Enterprise.

Well. He got the offer. Two As and a B.

Meanwhile, I am preening myself. So obviously I'm good for something. I wrote his Personal Statement in 1 1/2hrs flat. Because that's what I do. Write. And sell things. And people. Myself mostly. Over and over again I experiment with my profile on the Encounters internet dating site to make it as attractive as it can possibly be. So even though my 'Online Dating Profile Writer' business has proved to be such a spectacular failure, and the sales of my first book are pathetic, it would seem that I do get some things right sometimes.

Then the lady caught Will out. "What type of sheep were they?" she continued.

"Oh, errrmmm, weeeeeeeellll - sort of ..... white," replied Will.

Well for God's sake he's lived in the middle of Dartmoor for his entire life and doesn't even know that most of the sheep that gather outside our gate, and jump over walls and cattle grids into our garden, are Scotties. Scottish Blackfaces. Delicious!

Terrifying!
8/2/2017

"If you cancel your card before Monday we'll kill your family," growled the drug-addled, crazed crackhead; his blank, staring eyes rolling, threatening Will, mouthing at him just an inch from his eyes.

It was 6.30 in the morning on a dark Brixton street, the last of the late night revellers emerging from the nightclub behind Will and his two school friends.

The mugger claimed to belong to the Brixton-based gang, GAS (standing for Guns And Shanks), which has been responsible for the deaths of several people over the past decade. Shanks means knives. GAS has a long-standing feud with a rival gang across the road from their housing estate, called ABM (All Bout the Money), and most of the killings have been between the two.

"Did he smell?" I asked Will, who had phoned me from school, clearly sinking into shock, ten hours after the ordeal which had lasted an hour and a half. He was only now becoming properly frightened and slightly tearful.

Will and his friends had been accosted by two black men, and had been marched individually to AGMs down small dark alleyways, and told to withdraw a total of £500. But their card limits meant they could only manage £320. So they were then relieved of their provisional driving licences which, of course, have their families' home addresses on the back.

"Who's going to buy a train ticket for £100, catch a taxi from Newton Abbot and get sent to the middle of nowhere by the bossy woman on the sat nav, eventually arriving at Neighbour's farmyard, only to get bitten by their dog?" I laughed, in an attempt at cheering up my shaken favourite son. "What would be the point of that?"

Then I went to bed. Where I didn't sleep. Not because I thought I was about to get murdered by some Sarf London junkie. I was much more worried for Will. He has always been nervous of getting mugged in London, just as he was always worried about flying. I scoffed at his fears - but this encounter was nothing like being relieved of your mobile by some ad hoc hoodlum scoundrel. Just as the Ryanair emergency landing we experienced some years ago really did happen, the chance of which was one in millions! Why do these things always happen to Will? As a result he has a genuine and understandable fear of flying. How will he feel about backstreets in London now?

Pre-Twiglet days, I was always more frightened of spiders than of rapists and burglars because I thought you could reason with a human. But if they're off their heads on drugs, I suppose you can't. I hadn't included that situation in the equation.

The mugging happened a couple of days ago now. The boys have reported it to the police and will be meeting with the victim support people shortly.

Will's godfather happens to be CEO of a charity which supports the children of prisoners, and one of his colleagues works in that part of Brixton and knows the leaders of GAS, which has actually largely dispersed now. They believe Will and his friends were probably deliberately targetted, and the GAS link made up to inspire fear.

Huh
12/2/2017

"This is one of my favourite B&Bs in the U.K. The remoteness, the warmth of welcome, the willingness to help, the size and comfort of the bedroom and facilities. For me, it ticks all the boxes. This is the first time we have visited in the winter and I think it is even better than summer. I would travel down to Dartmoor every time I visited the U.K. Just to stay here."

And then what? He gives me 7.5 for 'Cleanliness', and 7.5 for 'Value For Money'!! What????? That brings my average for Reviews on Booking.com down to only 9.6, whereas one B&B nearby scores 10! I am not a happy bunny.

So this one review, out of 84 x 5 blobs, has got me thinking. And spending. A Lot.

I have researched how much my friends and family spend on their children's university education, and as a result of my conversations, have decided that I am going to now blow quite a significant proportion of my savings on my house instead.

I mean - I charge my punters through the nose and have been getting away with murder (not literally, except of mice, moles and spiders).

Such as: the leg always falls off the dressing table, the side table has a bit missing and wobbles, the dressing table chair has a bit missing, the chair for clothes has cracks in the woodwork, the bedside cupboard only shuts if you stick a wodge of loo-paper in the door, the bed's upholstery is stained, faded and dusty, the curtains haven't ever been washed in twenty-five years and are mouldy, the window seat cushions are marked with Twiglet and toothpaste, the carpets have spills of coffee and wine on them, the paintwork is cracked, mildewed and peeling, the windows leak so much that the room isn't warm enough, the blind has a broken string, is discoloured and hanging wonkily, and there are wires trailing everywhere to all the various appliances.

I am having to work too hard, prostituting my personality to make up for all of this in order to earn my 10/10s, and am beginning to think that possibly I am slightly ripping off my customers, which doesn't sit comfortably with me.

So every spare moment of the past week, I have been studying the internet to see what to do about the above. Blimey - it's going to cost me £10,000s to upgrade. But because I am no longer planning to move, I will also reap the benefits of making everything nicer - not just my guests. I am going to turn my two B&B rooms boutique!!!! And rack the prices up even higher! And when I don't have any bookings, I am going to sink into the sumptuousness of it all myself!

The first question is: Farrow & Ball or Dulux?

I have spent hours and hours and hours on researching dusky pinks for my bigger bedroom,"Hexworthy", and checking out mumsnet etc on their views of the various posh paints available. Dusky pinks are clearly not nearly as in vogue as grey, as there's a desperately small range to choose from. Except for Dulux, of course, where you can make up whatever colour you want into 'flat matt'. At half the price. The decision is made. I've sent off for some testers, and Peter is working on a quote. Meanwhile new windows are ordered, and now I am checking out beds.

Not being a natural interior designer, I am studying the websites of all the most expensive luxurious B&Bs and hotels in the area, and am copying what they do. Agh! One new bedroom chair: £400!!!! This is going to be painful!!!

Brown Teeth

20/2/2017

They've both got brown teeth! What teeth they've got left, that is. In fact one of them has even got a black tooth!

And they're wearing grubby ill-fitting, baggy, too-short jeans and trainers.

"Are they gypsies who want me to pay them to tarmac the drive?" I think to myself.
But no. Eeeek! It turns out they're the first B&B guests I've had for ages. They've booked in to the poshest B&B in the area, and they're going to be sharing a bedroom on the other side of a thin plywood wall to mine! And tomorrow night I'm going to be all alone with them in the house! Agh!

Will has already greeted them and given them tea and cake. "Were you scared?" I whisper.

"Nah - good bant," he replies and retreats to a re-run of Dexter, now I've just invested in a new Smart Telly complete with Netflix, our celebration present to ourselves for Staying Put.

Tommy, the smaller, really really skinny one, with the shaven head and bobble hat, prefers sitting smoking in his large van, parked in the drive with its generator on, to being in my house.

He asks for sliced white bread for breakfast. "Urrmmmmm - I've got 'Bit of Both" I stammer. I cut it into triangles and he uses it to dip into the yolk of Neighbour's fried free range egg. Looks delicious!

I am a hopeless B&B proprietor that day, as my children and I bask in front of the new telly and the lovely log fire in the sitting room, which is supposed to be set aside for guests, while my brown toothed boys are yomping across the moor in the fog, searching for a crashed aeroplane in some old tin mines that everybody walks to; one of them, Ivan, carrying several bottles of pills for high blood pressure, testing out his new hip.

When they return, I offer them the use of the sitting room and the fire, waving at it merrily, well aware that the flames are fading fast and there's no wood nor coal left anywhere near, and I'm not planning to replenish stocks as I race off with my children back to their schools, after the most glorious half term.

Late that night, as I bring the horses in, Tommy is still sitting smoking in his van. I can see the 'cherry' - the glowing red spot of his fag, through the window. I settle down to episodes 5 & 6 of Breaking Bad and finally retire, close to midnight. But this is just all too close, and too weird. I quietly pick up my dressing gown and alarm clock, and retreat to Bellever - the little bedroom at the other end of the house which has a door you can lock.

The next day, Tommy says, "Can I not have any of that poncy stuff with my breakfast?" (parsley garnish, and triangular sourdough toast). And he demands tinned tomatoes, not real. I happen to have a can of Tesco's Savers chopped ones in the larder, which only cost 13p, so yes of course! Why not?

"This is our solid silver teapot which I'm serving you from, on purpose," I greet him, grinning.

"You might find that disappears," he responds.

"Have you ever watched Four In A Bed? We were in it," I venture.

"Bet you didn't do very well - too forthright," says Tommy.

I don't put out the Visitors' Book because I'm a bit worried about what they might put in there. They're going to hate what I plan to do to those two B&B rooms even more!

They're both psychiatric nurses - I've always thought psychiatric nurses were often more bonkers than their patients. They've both been married for 25+ years to wives they adore, and both have children in their twenties who are at university and/or pursuing responsible careers. They have kept their room very clean and tidy.

I am surprised, and rather delighted that, when the time comes for them finally to leave, it's big hugs all round.

"That was my first ever B&B visit," says Ivan, who booked the stay and paid up front. "It was great! I'll write you something nice on the website-thing and will probably come back in the summer!"

In With The In Crowd
22/2/2017

I'm not in the least interested in chasing foxes around the place, and anyway, these days it isn't foxes, it's trails.

Nevertheless, I had always hankered after being part of a hunt - for my whole life. As a child I would attend meets in Dorset from time to time. To me they were like something out of the most beautiful, glamorous fairy tale, full of rich posh people - the county set - whose families had all known each other for generations. Utterly inaccessible. I never imagined for a moment that I would ever become a part of it all.

I thought that owning a horse probably cost even more than owning a car, and never even considered that I might be able to have one. Until I was well over thirty years old. What an error! While yes, horses are frantically expensive - shoes alone cost £65 every six weeks - far more than I spend on my own feet; it turned out that actually I could have kept one the whole time I was a yuppie in London in my twenties. What a wasted opportunity!

Anyway, soon after eventually acquiring my first horse, I found myself actually living the dream. Only it wasn't quite what I had expected. I found that the mounted followers tended to go round and round in circles and stand still in lanes a lot. The 'field' comprised largely terrifying, wrinkly middle-aged women yelling at me to get out of the way of the hounds, or hunstmen, or whatever, using jargon that I didn't understand. Apart from that, nobody spoke to me, and I felt like a wallflower at a party. And if I tried to make conversation, all the horses would suddenly move off mid-sentence, leaving me gawping foolishly. I never saw anything like the scenes of 100s of horses flying over enormous hedges and ditches that you see in old books and paintings.

But I was with the wrong hunt. Things are very different here.

What I love more than most things is meandering around large tracts of beautiful moorland, surrounded by friends all chatting away, on my horse who is enjoying herself even more than I am. To me, there is nothing more stunning than the sight of lots of horses galloping over Dartmoor, hounds streaming ahead of them in full cry, the fit and handsome young hunt servants in their scarlet jackets, and the rest of the field all smart in navy or black, bright white stocks pinned at their necks, hair neatly kept in place by a hairnet, looking like something straight out of a 200 yr old Snaffles print.

Now that I have finally become a full subscriber to our local hunt, at last, after 21 years, all of a sudden I find myself nurtured in the arms of a warm and friendly cliquey club.

I have just returned from four hours of charging around the high moor, in horizontal rain, gale force winds and fog; chatting away without pause. Today's was the most important meet of the year, as it brought together all four Dartmoor packs. I've been out with each of them over the years, and I found I knew almost everybody. I don't think my verbal diarrhea had much to do with the meagre amounts of port supplied by the hotel where we met, though. I think I was just, simply, happy.

So this joining the local hunt properly lark has turned out to be another very significant benefit of staying put. They ride all around my house every Tuesday and Wydemeet is located centrally in their 'country'. Their favourite pub is the Forest Inn, where they meet regularly at the end of my lane - a long haul for most of them, but I can walk there! I've been good friends with several of the members for a couple of decades. I feel that I am now part of the 'in' crowd. At last! For the first time in my life I have been made to feel special in a social grouping! How I have always yearned for that, and finally, here I am! Oh what fun it is!

Next Tuesday, for the first time, I have offered to hold the meet at Wydemeet. I really do owe so much hospitality to so many, after all the meets I've attended over the past twenty years, and all the port and smoked salmon sandwiches that I've consumed. This meet-thing feels as challenging as throwing our Christmas drinks party! I'm slightly panicking as to where to start, and wondering if anyone's going to help me, and if so, who will do what exactly.

Sashka, who's done millions of these things in the past, says I've got to supply roast potatoes as well as sausages and sausage rolls, and that the horses have to stand on the grass and not on my new gravel, because they will all poo on it.

Hunt Meet
1/3/2017

Why do tramps drink cider when they could have port?

Shopping for the hunt meet last week, I discovered that a bottle of ruby or tawny (no idea what the difference is) port from Tesco costs only £7 a bottle, yet it's 19% proof! A lot more alcohol for your pound than wine; and much handier to carry around than cider. What a nice surprise! I bought seven bottles.

Shortly before the horses and foot followers were due to arrive, I was given a briefing in Hunt Meet Etiquette:

The 'hunt servants' - the 'master' and the 'whipper in' - have to be served their drinks in proper glasses, not plastic cups.

No drink nor food to be served until the hounds arrive...

.. and a whole load of other things that I've already forgotten.

Well, on the night prior to the meet, as well as the port I'd bought cocktail sausages, mini sausage rolls, spiced potato wedges, two tray bakes, bags and bags of fun-sized chocolate bars (because they were on special offer), and plastic tumblers for fifty; got out the Baby Belling, turned up the Aga, put out some baking trays and bingo - all ready.

Five friends turned up at 10.15am to help, but there was nothing for them to do except enjoy a cup of coffee, a fag, and a plastic tumbler-full of port.

The oddest thing was seeing all the horses and hounds and people gathered in my drive. Sashka made me go out and 'meet and greet' them, in my striped apron, rather than hiding away cooking 250 sausages in the kitchen.

The most surprising thing was to discover that everybody else is as greedy as I am! I only just had enough of everything! Payback time after I've been stuffing my face at hunt meets since 1992.

Organising the whole thing turned out to be quite straightforward and rather fun. Now we've just got to clean up all the poo. I think I might offer to do it again next year!

The hunt itself was a bit hideous, with my normal chat carried away on the gale-force winds, the horses sinking up to their chests in bog. When, at 1pm precisely, just as predicted by BBC Online Weather, the horizontal snow and hail storms hit us, while the trail seemed to be heading for the wild and woolly wilderness that comprises Fox Tor Mire, I decided that I'd had enough, and turned for home.

Meanwhile, my heart went out to dear, dear Faye, who I'd had to collect from school the day before, because she was suffering from exhaustion, having battled through these conditions on top of the moor for two days, as part of her 'Ten Tors' training.

"I hated it, I'm pulling out," she had wailed down the phone to me.

"When we were organising the McVitie's Penguin Polar Relay, and had 100 women out on the moor in conditions which weren't as bad as this, we had to take five of them off the moor as they were suffering from hypothermia," I reassured Faye. I will have to come up with some further tactics to tempt her to keep going for their next training session: two nights and three days in the Brecon Beacons in April.

One is the reward I gave her this time. The opportunity to lie on the sofa, fire lit, and catch up with six episodes of Breaking Bad..

Spending Money Is Stressful
12/3/2017

Farrow & Ball or Dulux Flat Matt?

Oak or bamboo?

Wood or upholstery?

Wool or polypropylene?

I've splurged a dusky pink Dulux trade flat matt tester behind the curtains in Hexworthy, and 'lavender grey' in Dartmeet. Both look horrible.

In despair, I speak to my sister, who says I must use "Paint and Paper Library's Temple" dusky pink. Agh!

I google the company, and discover some interior designers in Ashburton are suppliers of their paint, so I call them.

"Paint and Paper Library" is a range of colours made by Little Greene, only more expensive, they advise me.

I give up. We agree an hour's visit for a 'colour consultation' at £100 + VAT so they can tell me what to do, and here they are.

"All your personal things and clutter must go. All the watercolours and photos, and china bits and pieces, and display shelves. Clear the mantelpieces. Get rid of all the books. Anything in that horrible lilac colour - dye it. We will create a 'Romantic Jane Austen Feel'. Just a few pieces of nice, dark furniture, one or two oil paintings and some antique dark wood mirrors," I am instructed. "Visit the antique shop in Ashburton for a couple of pretty, single wardrobes with mirrors on the front."

I feel like crying, but can't, because I'm seeing an electrician and a window-fitter at the same time, before racing off to collect Faye from school on our way to a horse competition 100 miles away; both of us, as well as the horse, booked into a B&B for the night.

I have made a chart, with times and dates for a new kitchen floor, new hall/stairs/passage carpet, new windows, tidying up of wires, new shower, refurbished macerator, carpet cleaning, curtain cleaning, house clearance, chippie and decorators; all interspersed with various B&B bookings.

I have been on eBay buying posh clocks, mugs, oil paintings, beds, mattresses, headboards, and chairs; and tomorrow I'm going shopping for new duvets, pillows, valances and throws.

I have opted for an oak kitchen floor (because, unlike bamboo, it has knots in it, so doesn't look like laminate); Paint and Paper Library and Little Greene in 'Leather I, II and III' and 'Stock I, II and III' which are 'tonal' with 'pink and yellow hues' respectively (because the paint and its cleaning qualities are better than F&B these days apparently); polypropylene (because it comes in 'gold', is cheaper than wool, and you can clean it easily - plastic carpeting is much improved, I'm told); and a new superking rattan sleigh bed, (because it's less masculine than mahogany, and if you get one stain on an incorporated, upholstered headboard, that's the end of your new, rather chi-chi, bed frame.)

Meanwhile I am re-writing my first book into three separate volumes, to be called the 'Surviving Solo Series', at the same time as constant driving, and eating out. Last week I drove the 100 miles, there and back to Faye's school, five days running; and also ate out with mates five days running. I am getting really fat with all this stuffing my face, and sitting in a car all day. Swimming and riding twice a week don't seem to be making much difference.

With all of this self-inflicted activity, my 'life of leisure' is actually beginning to feel marginally stressful.

Tears
1/4/2017

I've always thought of having children as a hobby. You get the crap things of the day done, and then you are left free to enjoy the fun - which in my opinion is the children. Over the past couple of decades, mine have brought me almost nothing but joy. They have never been rude, they have always been loving, they try to please at all times, they are such a pleasure to have around.

They make me cry.

"City of Stars...." the crystal clear voice swept lilting, from my mobile phone out through the speaker, and all around the truck.

"What the fuck????????????!!!!!!!!!!!!!!!" exploded Will, whom I was collecting from school at the end of his Spring term. "Is... that.... Faye????????"

"Yup," I nodded, my eyes wet. "Last week, at 'Blundells Unplugged', duetting with Greg, whom she's known since she was born. Just imagine how good she could be by the Upper Sixth!"

"Your son behaves with grace," Will's housemaster had written about him, amongst many other compliments, in his Spring Term report which I'd read earlier that morning. Blinking back more tears.

Going Going Gone
1/4/2017

Last week, I went along to our local auction house, Rendells in Ashburton, and found nine things that I wanted, including a pair of butler trays, as required by my interior designers. They were valued at £70 for the pair. I had recently seen one, not a pair, for sale in an antique shop for £495!

I went round the showroom with my list and, under 'maximum bid' put £201 in the relevant box for the trays.

There was a massive oil painting on display, valued at £10. I put £51 in the box. Two Victorian 'over stuffed chairs' valued at £25. My maximum bid was £95.

Because after spending days and nights on eBay, with several deliveries of this and that arriving every morning, I know how difficult these things are to find.

By the day of the actual auction I was hugely excited and desperate to know how I'd got on. I gather you can actually watch the auction happening live online, but I was far too busy to sit about doing that.

Anyway, I rang Rendells first thing the next morning, to discover that I've become the proud owner of everything I wanted. For the grand total of £396.50. That's £3.50 less than just one new 'Swoon Editions' pared-back interpretation of "French rococo style hand-carved Lille armchair" (which I would rather like for my Dartmeet room, but it costs as much as a bed!)

I hitched up the horse trailer and raced off to the sales room, and threw all my new purchases into it, nestling amongst the straw and horse poo. My two B&B rooms are going to be transformed!

Crash!
1/4/2017

My nice B&Ber, a strapping marine called Mike, who helped me put up a wall map of Wydemeet and its environs, has just gone through one of the lovely overstuffed Victorian chairs I have bought.

"You can see it's been repaired before," he says.

"Don't worry - I broke its predecessor three weeks ago," I reply. "Leaned forward to speak to Faye and the leg broke in half.

"The main thing is that no one has been hurt - have they?" I query, nervously, all too aware that as a result of my last home insurance claim, my annual premium has risen from £890 to £2010.

Bugger. I'm just going to have to bite the bullet and buy new things instead of second hand ones.

Bed Linen
1/4/2017

"That's fine - he is most welcome if he stays in the kitchen," said Alison, owner of the B&B I'd booked for £75 through Airbnb, for the night before Faye took part in the horse competition. I'd forgotten I'd got a dog, so hadn't checked whether this B&B was dog friendly and instead, had just turned up with Twiglet, ready to leave him in the back of the car with a bowl of water.

I sank into the deep and sumptuous double bed with its massive pillows, deep mattress, crinkly duvet, smart box pleated valance, and, the final trick of it all - silky smooth mattress topper.

Days later I am sitting at the bar of The Forest Inn, chatting to one of the owners (who is also an indigenous cattle farmer) about bed linen. He has completely refitted the pub's B&B rooms with new beds, mattresses that cost £800 each, and bed linen, including mattress toppers, from Dunelm, where I am about to have to spend a small fortune. Rooms at The Forest Inn are £80 a night. At Wydemeet they are about to be £160 and £180, if we are to include a 30% single night supplement.

You can see the horsehair coming out in chunks from one my 80 year old beds, which makes Sashka and I giggle. I am becoming increasingly alarmed that I really am ripping off my customers.

Undressed
3/4/2017

Neither of my children appears to have got dressed today.

Chips off the old block.

I managed to get some kit on because I had to greet the electrician who came round this morning; but the lady who was due to collect the curtains to clean them for the first time in twenty-five years was ill, so didn't get here after all that.

I finally got round to washing my hair at the swimming pool. It's been a week.

Faye, it turns out, did actually achieve a bit of a walk on the moor with the dog, so she must have donned some sort of a trackie at some point, but post jacuzzi and soak in the bath, she was back in her jimjams by tea time.

Meanwhile Will stuck to his daily timetable of six hours' of A'level revision, interspersed with sax practice of 'Hit The Road Jack' (Grade 3, even though he recently achieved a high distinction in his Grade 8 exam), to ensure he plays it perfectly at a wedding he's been booked to perform at, during his summer half term; right in the middle of A'levels. Possibly a bit of an error time-wise that - but it's worth fifty quid.

So there was no point at all in his wasting time changing into proper clothes.

6.30am
5/4/2017

"It's a quarter to nine," announces Claire Balding, between earnest, holy, has-been popstar interviewees, on her Sunday Radio 2 Show.

"Hah hah - you got the hour wrong," I sneer at her, snuggling down deeper into my pillows.

Quarter to nine??!!!! AAAAGGGGHHHHH!!!!!!! The clocks have changed! And my B&Bers like an early breakfast!! AGGGHHH!!!

Somehow I succeed in throwing on some clothes, slapping on a face, and having breakfast laid in minus fifteen minutes.

"Had you realised the clocks have changed?" I query, leaning casually against the wall, as my guests pop their heads around the dining room door.

Bloody Hell - in last year's time, to be properly ready for an 8.30am breakfast, I should actually have got up at 6.30am! On a Sunday!

Sometimes I think I'm worth the ridiculous amounts of money I make in this job.

Personality Disorder
9/4/2017

"He chatted away perfectly nicely over the gate to Jane's little chestnut shetland mare, and then when we put them in the field together, he picked her up by the scruff of her neck and shook her," warns my great mate Richard, about his horse, 'Cranky' who he is kindly lending to me and Faye.

My darling beautiful gorgeous mare, Perfect Panda (19) hasn't been sound now, for nearly two months, and I don't quite know what to do about her. I have the best specialist equine vet in the county coming to visit on Wednesday, to carry out all possible tests and to tell me whether it might be a good or bad idea to put her in foal.

If she's too lame for that. Bang!

I have two other friends with crocked old mares. I thought we should have a joint funeral, cremation and communal sob into our wine if the worst comes to the worst for us all. A fourth friend is looking at having to kill her horse too, after it got tangled up in some wire and lost both its heels. But hers is a gelding and she doesn't love him like we love our mares. When I had to put down my first ever horse, after he developed a strangulated aorta, aged 26 and hunting fit, I cried for four years.

So we've now had Cranky for 36 hours and he has been wonderful in every way, grazing away quietly just by the garden, in a patch that he could easily escape from if he felt like it. Faye and I went for a ride together yesterday, and he and she looked utterly stunning together. Richard says he won't jump, but we have a feeling that we might be able to change all that. We are both seething with excitement about this. It is all just too good to be true! Something is bound to go wrong! But otherwise we will have to buy him quickly, at a rock bottom price, before we turn him into an extremely valuable eventer!

Multi-Tasking
9/4/2017

I am juggling floor man, carpet man, curtain woman, window man, house clearance, electrician, plumber, decorator, wood turner, chippie, mattress deliverer, wardrobe deliverer, telly deliverer, bed deliverer, auction house deliverer, bed linen deliverer, amongst an ever-increasing number of B&B bookings, and soon the wheels are going to come off.

I double booked an Airbnb person yesterday - they will have to go into Dartmeet instead of Hexworthy; I pissed off my great mate George who has looked after me for years by making him feel a second class citizen amongst all these other people; and I have only left one day for the refurbished hall wood floor to be unusable as its new coating dries, despite lovely Tom and his daughter Willow putting aside their Easter Monday to do it on.

I only just noticed that I'd been sent the wrong mattresses, once they'd been lugged upstairs and the couriers had returned to Hull. The small label said 1400 pocket springs instead of 3000. So somehow they've got to be changed or I can't advertise '3000 pocket springs' on my B&B website, which is my plan.

Immediately Faye's new flatpack bed arrived, she and Will sorted out getting her old Vispring up to his attic room, and his babies' bunk beds and mattresses down to the horses' field to be erected into a furiously burning funeral pyre laced with half a gallon of the lawn mower's petrol. Faye put together her new bed and also a flatpack chair, and both children are ecstatically re-jigging their rooms.

Wonder-Cathy, my house-clearing friend, made short work of taking away a pile of unburnable junk; a wardrobe, and all Faye's beautiful girly children's furniture (boo hoo), and two Nespresso machines to sell; and dismantling Ex's glorious 80 year old mahogany beds, with their horsehair falling out from the mattresses. "I sold a couple like that last week," said Cathy. "I could only get £50 for them."

She has to pay £36 each to dispose of mattresses, so these have to be burnt, and we will hide the old small telly in a wheelie bin, or that will apparently cost us a fiver at the dump.

My final bill for house clearance is -£200, taking into account the profits Cathy will make from selling my stuff. "You're too cheap," I say. So we agree she will only pay me £175 to get rid of everything for me. Bargain!

The wardrobe, superking bed and telly seller have all messed up on delivery dates, so none of these have appeared as yet, despite being paid for on eBay a fortnight ago. I am never buying anything 'collection only' again, unless I can collect it myself.

I don't suppose for a moment this mega refurb will ever pay for itself - the paint alone is costing nearly £1,000! But hopefully it will look really nice when it's done. And anyway - now that everything is finally coming together, it's beginning to turn into fun!

That Mad F*er**
14/4/2017

Cranky has a new name.

He's now kicked the s***out of my mad mare Vegas twice, as well as taking a chunk out of the stable. He's escaped from his solitary confinement so I had to lead him back in my dressing gown in the dark with a torch at 3am. And he was so lazy getting to and from his riding lesson, as well as in it, and couldn't jump, so Faye's gone off him and is back on Vegas.

I summoned up my courage and got on him yesterday - he was fine. When we got home I said to Faye - "what do you think about having a little go around our jumps in the field?"

She nodded with enthusiasm and trotted on him towards a cross-pole, one foot high. TMF stopped.

A little perseverance and ten minutes later we had a horse that was looking like a proper show-jumper, cantering towards the jumps with no need for kicking, taking off in the right place, and making a nice shape over them. He loves it, but is terrified. He could be good! We are really excited about this project - all over again!

Everybody's Ill or Dying
14/4/2017

My nice curtain lady's husband rang from A&E to say she'd suddenly developed a very fast heart-rate and high blood pressure so they wouldn't be coming in to collect the curtains and window seat cushions for cleaning today. The decorator's father has died so he's missed two days. The bed lady's father has died so she hasn't got round to organising the delivery of the bed. The wardrobe courier is ill so delivery of that has been delayed. The correct mattresses finally arrived at 7am yesterday morning. The electrician says that there's no earth, so he can't fit either of the new chandeliers, nor the (wooden) light switch that didn't arrive until he was actually here. I have now exchanged 56 messages (I'm not exaggerating, it really is 56) with the seller, to arrange re-collection of the telly.

We've got six hours before our B&Bers arrive, and the bed's not ready for them to sleep in, I've got 18yr old Tessa and her friend manning the fort for the weekend, hoping to spend time revising for their IB and A'levels, and Sashka has a wonky knee.

While I'm playing away.

Colour of Poo
14/4/2017

"LLLLLLLLLLLLLL. Yuck," is my reaction, having stolen upstairs to take a peak at the decorating of Hexworthy, my poshest B&B room.

"That door being the colour of diarrhea, opening onto the pink carpet, looks completely disgusting! Hey - come and see what you think!" I entreat my guests who are staying in Dartmeet, the other room, and who it turns out I know, from when our children were at prep school together. There is so much of mutual interest to discuss, we can't stop chatting - and now it turns out she is a frustrated interior designer and uses cool words to describes different colours, such as 'accents'.

"The navy cushions might pull it all together," she suggests doubtfully.

"Hmmm, it's not to my taste" says tactful Nick, the angelic painter of the sad life who, it turns out, has just met a very frisky lady through an online dating site called 'Muddy Matches', when a friend of his signed him up without consulting him.

I lie awake through the night, deciding that I must call the interior designers and warn them that, in their hasty colour consultation, they may have made a terrible mistake.

But I forbear, and now it's all done we're beginning to quite like it, even very fussy Will. "Get rid of that nasty cheap chandelier and put in a proper lampshade," he says.

And Nick, at the paintshop yesterday, heard everybody there discussing 'leather' as the colour of today. Apparently I am absolutely 'on trend'!

A Good Girl
15/4/2017

"Buck's Fizz anybody?" I offered, as Faye blew out the seven candles on her Cyril the Caterpillar 15th birthday cake.

"It's so old I daren't serve it to my guests, but it seems alright to me. We can keep the sparkly cover for a bottle of Prosecco another day," I said.

Faye, and her two girlfriends who had come for a sleepover, shook their heads, content with pink pop from Shloer.

After an Easter Egg hunt, they set off for the pub, for hamburgers, coke, darts and a few games of pool.

All finished off with a hot tub and netflix, and then they took themselves to bed.
It only struck me the following day that at no point was there a moment's concern regarding fags or booze.

£30,000 Later...
25/4/2017

7.5 Facilities; 7.5 Value For Money
Not enough hanging space

How very dare they?

This from the first couple to stay in Hexworthy, arriving four hours after we had finally finished it at such vast expense and trouble.

The couple who, in their review description of the place, professed to love everything about their stay at Wydemeet.

The only couple in three years, to ask for, and receive, breakfast in bed.

The couple who spent so many hours at the recently refurbished Forest Inn, commenting that Ray, the bartender, was 'very dry'.

"And they were very drunk," he countered.

The couple who say they can't wait to come back.

Who have now pulled me down again from 9.7 to 9.6 in Booking.com's rankings, after I've spent thousands and thousands and thousands of pounds turning Hexworthy into the ultimate boutique B&B room. Just because I like the useless dressing table and have refused to swap it for a wardrobe.

Agh! I give in. Luckily it's the local auction on again this week, so I'll troll down there and get one.

Weeping Guest
26/4/2017

Tears were coursing down Edna's cheeks.

She and her husband and 13 year old son had spent two nights at Wydemeet.

They had been riding at my mate Daphne's trekking centre up the road, and enjoyed it so much that Edna, a strapping Swiss language teacher, had gone back again for another ride in the afternoon.

"Your home is paradise!" she sobbed. "I don't want to leave!"

Her delightful family couldn't have cared less about the lack of wardrobe.

Nevertheless - I've sworn a £175 bid at Rendells the Auctioneers, for rather a nice Edwardian one in walnut.

I've also bid up to £156 for an elm linen box, even though it's got woodworm. I've just been visited by an old schoolfriend, who finally got married last week, aged 59. She and her new husband have stayed at three hotels in the past few days, and commented that I really need something for people to put their suitcases on.

It Looked Nicer Before...
10/5/2017

"It's exactly the same colour as it was before," I comment to Nick, as he applies the second coat of Little Greene's "Stock Deep" to the walls of the Dartmeet Room.

".. only a little darker," he says carefully.

Excitedly I run upstairs to view the completed experience, having spent the weekend at Badminton Horse Trials while Sashka prepared the house for an invasion of six women who are going to take it over at vast expense this Friday.

I flick on the ugly white plastic light switch - the one that my electrician refused to replace; and, oh no! I really am going to have to contact the interior designers this time.

We've got jolly yellow sheets and light tourqoisey blue bedspreads against my newly painted mustard walls. Mustard! I hate mustard! It's horrendous! What an utter disaster!

I spend a sleepless night - round and round my head I am wondering how I'm going to broach all this to the designers: "Do you seriously want to put your name to this?" I will say.

I can't bear even to look in the bedroom the next day.

But two days later I must hang the mirror and pictures to get them off the floor ready for the carpet cleaners. I open the door nervously. It doesn't look quite so bad today. Bang bang bang goes the hammer onto my thumb more often than onto the picture hook pins.

Maybe, once I've sorted out the lighting, it might be OK after all?

Wretched Wardrobes
10/5/2017

It's happened again!

"Perfect in every way," he'd written. And scored me 7.5 for value for money; bringing my Booking.com average back down from our reinstated 9.7, to 9.6 yet again; meaning that Wydemeet has slipped several places down the pecking order, if you press the button on Booking.com which selects your B&B accommodation according to 'Review Rankings'.

The reason being, it would appear from what he said, that there is 'not enough hanging space' in Hexworthy. Grrrrrrrrr.

Anyway. So I've bitten the bullet.

I didn't win the walnut wardrobe at the Rendells auction, despite bidding £80 over the valuation price. So I've bought a beautiful inlaid mahogany wardrobe for Hexworthy; and a pretty mirrored Victorian one in 'satinwood', whatever that is, for Dartmeet. Each cost £100 off eBay (a lot cheaper than a new white MDF one from IKEA I would imagine); and £80 to deliver.

The only trouble is that the front door of the Victorian one has already fallen off.

B&B Bore
10/5/2017

I've got a new oak kitchen floor, a re-vamped oak hall floor, pristine thoroughly cleaned old carpets in all the rooms, new carpet on the stairs and landing, two new beds, two new mattresses, new pillows, valances, duvets, mattress toppers, two new wardrobes, a new bedlinen press, a new chair (I paid £79 for it on eBay, and now see that they normally sell for £200!), two large FreeSat TVs, two Victorian chairs, a new tub chair, new chandeliers, lights, glasses, cups, sugar bowls, bed spreads, throw cushions, and eventually I will sort out the window seat cushions. We've redecorated, tidied up all the floating wires, I dread to think how much I have spent. And how boring about it all that I have become.

If any future guests give me less than 10/10 (if they come at all, as I am now charging so much) they will be shot.

Poo and Wee
20/5/201

"The lavatory's exploding and there's poo and wee and bog roll and water coming out and pouring through the ceiling and it won't stop!" screeched Karen down my mobile, as I attempted to negotiate the M4/M5 junction complete with a ton of horse and trailer behind me, en route to Faye's most important competition of the year, 150 miles away from home.

"Look him up, and him up, and him up!" I yelled at poor Faye, shoving my address book full of plumbers' numbers at her, while she was innocently attempting a bit of shut-eye in the seat next to me, after a hard week at school.

"Tell that one I'll even pull the bailiffs off him if he comes to help!" I yelled as I called Sashka - imploring her to join the hunt for a plumber - any plumber - anywhere - able and willing to drop everything and fly over to Wydemeet to stop the stinking flood from washing away the six ladies staying there overnight.

Nothing but answerphones.

In despair I called my friend Malcolm, who had fitted the macerator and most of the other plumbing when I created the B&B nearly four years ago, who lives in Totnes and is normally to be found two hours away, lecturing on fine art in Falmouth. His mobile no longer takes calls, it told me. So I ordered Faye to text him.

Five minutes later, and goodness knows how many gallons of water sloshing through the ceiling of my house, a text came back informing us that Malcolm happened to be down the road in Ashburton and would be at the house in twenty minutes' time.

I felt sick. I'd probably lost at least a decade off my life. I really must find out where the stop cock or whatever it's called, lives.

The end result has turned out as follows:

1) It would seem that the macerator had inadvertently been flicked off at the wall. Its switch is at floor level on the landing at the top of the stairs, and must have got knocked as the new carpet was being put down, the day before the ladies' arrival.

2) Malcolm did a bit of cleaning up, had tea with my six ladies, only to discover that he knew one of them from thirty years ago.

3) My ladies loved their stay, didn't think they'd been ripped off, wouldn't accept a rebate, would like to return, and saw the whole episode as adding to their experience.

4) The carpet shop has replaced the carpet and is reimbursing me £350 for expenses and out of goodwill

5) Vegas refused the third jump at the Important Competition, and was eliminated, meaning that after a year's preparation, she wasn't permitted to take part in the cross-country section. We all cried and I dropped her off at Faye's riding teacher's place on the way home, to be sold.

6) I have added notes to my 'house gizmos' information document about where all the stop cocks are.

Bad Guests
4/6/2017

"Here! Quick! GO!" I cried, and thrust all the cash I could find in my handbag - £50 - at the Austrian man standing, bemused, in my drive.

He had said on the form that he would be arriving at Wydemeet 'late evening'. When's that? To me, it's about 11pm. So I'd left out a note (thank God) and departed to collect the children for half term - a six hour round trip.

And there my late evening guests were, as we drew up the drive at about 8.45pm. Him wandering around, and his partner sitting on a rock looking black, and smoking a fag. They'd arrived at 3pm, the ATM wouldn't give them any money, and so they hadn't booked anywhere for supper.

I couldn't bear the thought of them having nothing to eat on the first night of their holiday, and I didn't really feel like rustling up something for them myself, so off to the Forest Inn I sent them - its kitchens close at 9pm.

"Breakfast at 8pm?" they queried on their return.

"Sorry - my only rule. Breakfast is served any time after 8.30pm. You can come down in your pyjamas at 5pm for it if you like?" I smiled, grimly, thinking to myself "it says that all over all my websites".

At 8.30am they appeared as Radio 2 bleeped its half-hourly news headlines, and I brightly enquired, "Sleep well?"

"No," they replied. "The bed is too hard. We didn't sleep at all."

"Ah - that will be my brand new 3000 pocket sprung mattress," I said. "That's what beds seem to be like these days. The one in the other room is softer," (as it says on the website). "Did you hear that incredible thunderstorm last night, with crashing thunder and masses of lightning? You can see out of the window the devastation that the wind and lashing rain have caused!"

They were totally unaware of it. Clearly slept right through it on their 'horrid, hard' expensive new bed.

So bollocks to them.

Music Everywhere
4/6/2017

Like almost every other sixth-former across the nation, Will has spent all day every day of half-term continuing to revise for his A'levels, which start on Wednesday; getting up early so that his teenage body-clock is ready and prepared to be wide awake and refreshed for each exam's 9am kick-off next week.

Between revision sessions he's been practising his sax - a repertoire of 1 1/2 hours' worth of recent and current classic pop hits, now including Duffy, Kate Perry etc, for his second ever paid 'gig': the wedding, which took place yesterday.

When he leaves school, Will has chosen Leeds, because it's the most happening place for music after London and Bristol, he says, and it offers the only course which mixes music with business, which has high entrance requirements and therefore attracts committed intelligent students, but doesn't insist on a maths or music A'level for entry. Will's goal is to become the next Phil Harvey (manager of Coldplay), and I have every confidence that he will succeed.

Apart from horrid foreigners who only come through Booking.com and simply don't 'get' our unique offering here, this year I have had the best guests ever out of this world! I have wanted to join almost all of them at the pub for supper, get them to stay for lunch with me, and I simply didn't want any of them to leave!

Caroline is one, who has a son who plays his guitar to himself all day, every day, even sitting on the loo, and who now plays in a successful band in LA. Tim, who works as a pastoral carer for 12 year-olds at a school in Hackney, is friends with the manager for Jay Z. He's having lunch with her this week, and says he'll make enquiries re a possible internship for Will.

Anyway.

Yesterday, Will and I arrived in very good time to set up for the wedding, and found ourselves driving around the grand estate where it was being held, looking for the right place to unload his gear. Round the corner came a Land Rover with a scruffy old bloke in it. He was so rude, arrogant and unwelcoming that an already very nervous Will was thrown.

"Are you the owner of this beautiful house?" I queried, cheerfully, smiling. "I do this sort of thing too - I know what it's like!" and we obediently turned the truck around to retrace our path, as we had been ordered to do in no uncertain terms.

Thirty minutes later, having been moved on three times, and with all Will's sheets of music blowing away in the gale, the unsmiling old codger turned up again.

Sweetly I twittered, "I thought I recognised you! This sax player you've booked was head boy of your son's school!"

For the first time ever, Will forgave me for showing off about him.

After a wobbly and slightly uncertain start, as the jolly ushers chattered away in front of us, warm and friendly in their grey suits and shiny brown shoes, Will gradually began to settle.

The end came as, in the warm spring sunshine, the stunning blonde bride, in her beautiful white lacy flouncy gown, and her handsome new husband paraded slowly towards the entrance of the gracious old mansion, down an aisle made up of all their best friends blowing bubbles all over them, while Will blasted out 'Happy' on his sax; his crescendos and high register impro echoing backwards and forwards around the courtyard. Just like the finale of some wonderful romantic musical.

I felt a bit funny. So this is what it has all been about.

On the way home, Will ripped open the brown envelope that one of the bridesmaids had handed over to him.

"20, 40, 60 EIGHTY POUNDS!!!!" he cried. "I wouldn't have paid that much for me!!"

My son has finally, finally appreciated that he is already capable of commanding a far higher hourly rate than either of his parents.

More Bad Guests
4/6/2017

One person for one night costs me about the same to look after as do two people for two nights, and blocks out the possibility of people coming for longer, especially significant over weekends.

So I have now decided to add a 30% single night supplement; or 12.5% single person reduction, which I thought would suit everybody. They don't have to come, but at least the offer is made, so that there is somewhere available for them to stay that accommodates their needs in central Dartmoor. Other providers simply don't do single nights because it's not worth their while at standard rates.

The result is, however, that the cost of my extremely expensive 'Hexworthy Room' becomes stratospheric, at £180 for one night. Well they don't have to come.

The trouble is that they do come, and then compare it with somewhere else that they have stayed at for two nights or more. And they're not here long enough to make the most of the location, the hot tub, and, most importantly of all, My Chat.

Which means that I continue to get marked down in Booking.com's reviews, despite my beautiful new old wardrobes. And also despite the current state of the pound.

But any more of this and I shall withdraw my kind and generous offer of making my rooms available for one night only.

I have just said goodbye to a pair of silent Swedes who had spent the previous couple of nights at Mitchelcroft - the best B&B in the area, boasting straight 10s on Booking.com's reviews, something that I'm not aware of any other guest houses ever having achieved. At Mitchelcroft they provide proper home-made cake and compote (cooked by themselves, not purloined from the WI at fetes, like all my fare). They have chairs on decking outside each room, overlooking a stunning view across Dartmoor, as the sun sets. And they only charge £100 a night.

The Swedes looked grim as they handed me my £180 in readies in the morning. I don't suppose they slept either.

I keep checking in to Booking.com, full of dread, to see what they've said.

Never mind. Whatever happens, it seems fairly clear to me that life at Wydemeet has settled into a really rather blissful routine, and I haven't regretted my decision not to sell after all - not for a single second!

It would also appear that my future career as Rich and Famous Author, despite my best efforts, is looking challenging – at best. Meanwhile my role as World's Best Hostess ain't going half badly; despite my reluctance to serve breakfast at a normal time. So perhaps I should just settle down on that front too. Relax and enjoy what I have created over all these years.

Which leaves one more thing. Love. What am I going to do about that?

3 LOVE IN THE COUNTRYSIDE

One and a Half Minutes of Fame
6/6/2017

Kate's lower lip trembles and her eyes well up.

"I can't do this, I keep on crying!" she wails.

We're sitting in the kitchen, surrounded by lights and cameras, and Kate's supposed to be describing what I'm like as a friend, to a telly programme called 'Country Loving', which is going to feature MOI!

This is the London-based TV crew's second visit, and they've already spent six hours filming me, my animals, and my home, for a new BBC2 reality TV show, in which city-dwelling viewers are supposed to look at my video-profile online, and request that they get to meet me with a view to joining my idyllic, romantic country life.

What could be better PR to bring on my future career as Famous Author?

The trouble is, unusually for Reality TV, this is supposed to be an upbeat positive jolly sort of programme, so for once they don't want tears.

"She's such a good friend," sobs Kate.

I help myself to another piece of cake.

We seem to have been filming forever, and I am astonished and touched that Kate volunteered to take part in the first place.

"I've got millions of friends, and I can't think of a single one who would want to go on telly just for the sake of it," I said to the producers, when they sprung the need to get someone to talk about me on air. But when I mentioned this to Kate the other day, she immediately offered herself for the role.

And anyway, it's turning out to be fun! For both of us! Between tears, we're howling with laughter, looking at all my current potential online suitors.

The telly people wanted to film me in the most romantic spot of all around here - at the confluence of the Swincombe and the West Dart; and also get some footage of me riding the horses; but we've had some hurricane wildly raging outside all day, with no sign of abating, so that's out of the question after all. I can't allow my hair to get wet or I look like Esther Rantzen, and I want to keep my high heels on, to make my legs look longer.

"What do you most miss about not having a man?" they pry gently.

"Ummm, errrrrr, weeeeell, I don't think that would be suitable to say on a family show," I end up lamely.

What I have only recently realised is that this could become really, really big. To find potential dates for me, they plan to promote Country Loving on other BBC programmes, such as The One Show. There will be ten lonely hearts, or 'contributors', altogether, with our video'd profiles up on the BBC website. I can't believe that after all this mega-effort, each profile will be cut down to just 90 seconds!

But I think these other BBC programmes will want to parade us live; the 'romantic encounters' will presumably be filmed - and if all goes well, I anticipate papers like the Daily Mail doing features on us, researching our family backgrounds etc, like they do with I'm a Celebrity and Big Brother contestants. We could become national characters - like the people on Gogglebox!

Ooo-errrr. I wonder whether the other participants have realised all this, and whether they're brave enough to go through with it?

While I'm at it, who ARE the other participants?

"Have you got an OAP?" I query. "What about a proper ooo-arrrrr Devonian farrrrrrrmer? How do you get someone like that to come up with endless soundbites? Have you got people of loads of different ages and backgrounds? What happens if the plan goes slightly wrong and the contributors start going off with each other, like Lance Gerrard-Wright went off with Ulrika Jonsson in 'Mr Right' back in 2002?"

Well I am braced. I am bored. It's time for a new adventure. If I am to become a household name - good.

We are drained, and it's time to wrap.

"What Mary really needs is somebody with an equal lust for life," concludes Kate, pulling herself together and giving the camera a broad grin.

Ben
9/6/2017

Yesterday, a largish bloke called Ben turned up in a black Skoda estate. We'd come across each other via 'Muddy Matches'. We'd already enjoyed a two hour telephone conversation, and, by now being pretty jaded by online dating after years and years of it, I was anticipating a typically pleasant, but rather unmemorable encounter. In fact the phone had been going so mental that morning that I'd been so busy answering it I hadn't even bothered to have a bath - and I hadn't washed my hair for two days.

Anyhow, Ben got out of his car and he was just my type. Smiley, stocky, slightly unkempt, ex-rugby player. He arrived on the dot of 12.30 as promised. We shared a cafetiere of coffee. Chat chat chat. Then we drove to the pub, rather than walking, because we're still in the middle of some hurricane. Chat chat chat; including me admitting that I'm actually 57 (he's 51); and that I'm due to be on this lonely hearts telly programme thingy. I had two Spritzers and he had two pints of beer, and finally Ray asked us to leave.

More coffee back home in the kitchen? I cant remember. Then he made me put on some wellies and go for a walk, returning in time for my next B&Bers' arrival.

Agh! They were early!!! So we all sat around the kitchen table tucking into rather nasty Tesco lemon drizzle cake, because both home-made-cake stalls at Tavistock Market had been shut the two days I tried them. Finally, at nearly 7pm, Ben said it was time for him to leave.

I stood an arms length away as he sorted out getting into his car. I knew we could have gone into a full snog right out there in my drive, under the guests' noses, on our first meeting. But this is all far too much for me to compute. Nobody has touched me for years! Why should Ben be 'the one', out of the 50+ dates I have met over the past eight years?

Because he's easy to be with, and smiley, and clearly gentle and kind and chatty and a bit of a maverick, and writes, and refuses to be employed by anybody else, and ran a B&B in his 20s, and went to the same school as Stephen Fry and is six years younger than me?

Well who knows. And what happens about the telly thing? Bloody hell what do I do now?

Overnight Stay?
29/6/2017

"Don't feel you need to come back from his house tonight - we can manage on our own in the name of lurve," offer my kind B&Bers.

Ben and I are sitting on a bench together, not touching, on top of a cliff, gazing out across Lyme Bay, a clear blue sky above us; a runner with a perfect body racing up and down the long steep hill from our vantage point to the beach below and back again, as she trains for the Three Peaks Race.

We return for tea at Ben's neat home on the outskirts of Sidmouth. And move on to supper of ready-meal lasagne. He's bought a bottle of Sauvignon for me in case I decide to stay, but clearly not gone the whole hog! He says he would like to kiss me. We sit on the sofa gazing out into the garden, and hold hands.

"I'd better get back to my B&Bers," I mutter. "Might you come to my house tomorrow?" One more kiss and I struggle up to leave.

Prepared
29/6/2017

He's brought the remains of the cake he had bought for me specially yesterday.

He's also brought his swimming trunks in case we decide to use the hot tub.

And his toothbrush.

Ruined
29/6/2017

"You have just ruined the rest of my life."

I look up at him, with a wide grin, as he emerges through the kitchen door for breakfast.

"I have done the deed."

By which I mean that I have said goodbye to all my hopes and dreams and excitement at the idea of becoming a famous and successful author, using the TV lonely hearts route.

After two visits and ten hours of filming by them. Having met Ben only three times. What a decision! But they had left a message asking me to call them, and I cannot live a lie. Agh! Perhaps if the programme's successful, and my new romance goes belly up like all the others, I can have another go in Series 2.

Life on Hold
29/6/2017

Five days of uninterrupted total pleasure with this new man who has popped out of nowhere. We have used Wydemeet as it's supposed to be used, in daily temperatures of 80+F. We've developed our own little routine of admin in the morning, lunch in the garden, and sitting in various parts of the river in the afternoon, followed by the hot tub and supper, and even more chat; testing out each of the refurbed luxury B&B rooms which, now they are so very newly redecorated, and de-cluttered of any personal effects, feel like going on a luxury holiday in my own home. But, extraordinarily for late June, with no B&Bers to cater for. It is all so surreal and sheer bliss.

Seasons in the Sun
19/7/2017

My life is brilliant. My love is pure.

Oh wouldn't it be great if I could write lyrics like that to describe the past couple of weeks.

Every one of all my dreams of eight years has come true.

And yet. And yet.

I haven't been entirely well for a single day of it. Nor have I achieved a proper night's sleep. They say sleep deprivation is torture. I think it is -

judging by how I felt when Faye was a baby and it negatively affected every aspect of my life.

Two sets of antibiotics, paracetamol, ibuprofen, naproxen, omeprazol - for several days over the past couple of weeks I have been taking 11 pills a day.

I am not really with it and can't get my head around what's happening to me. I am in constant pain from a thousand different areas, and can only just manage to serve breakfast without fainting in front of my guests.

A couple of weeks ago, disaster happened. Cranky threw me. An hour before I was going to pay for him. We were walking along outside our gate; he was on his toes, having spied a group of walkers with grey knapsacks; and the next thing I knew I was hurtling towards the ground - hard and fast; Cranky presumably having dropped his shoulder, spun around and galloped off back home.

Before that I had not fallen from a horse for over ten years.

My immediate instinct was to haul myself to my feet, get back on, and thrash the living daylights out of him. But the walkers' teachers came over to talk to me; I sat in the mud; and gradually the world began to spin, slowly.

We hobbled back to my kitchen where I called '111'; and soon the nice paramedics were dispensing advice and prescriptions. Bruises started to develop down my left side - black as a thundery sky; and I couldn't breathe properly, let alone laugh, cough nor sneeze, as I was damaged where my ribs attach to my sternum.

Breakfast for four the next day, and Faye's school speech day. I managed it all somehow; but Henley planned for Sunday was too much. Ex kindly drove me both ways to Faye's school - 100 miles altogether out of his way.

By the next day I was also suffering from cold sores and a cyst, besides which the pain of the bruising and cracked ribs paled into insignificance.

Somehow I continued with breakfasts and dragged myself to a "Double Date at the Double Locks on a Twosday" with Faye, to meet Ben (who was by now iller from some virus than he'd ever felt in twenty years), and Faye's new boyfriend(!), Henry; her senior by two whole cool years. Neither Ben nor I should have been driving at all, meanwhile The Young Ones had eyes and ears only for each other.

I dragged myself to Exeter A&E where they arranged an appointment to deal with my cyst for the following day; but that was no good - breakfast to prepare!

The next morning, crying hysterically repeatedly down the phone at various representatives of the NHS, in between frying sausages and tossing omelettes, the necessary antibiotics were procured from Boots in Tavistock, and a modicum of peace resumed.

With no prognosis as to how long my riding injuries would haunt me, I managed a 20 minute scramble down to Weston Beach, just east of Sidmouth - the most beautiful, long, deserted British beach that I have ever seen, with crystal clear water and cloudless blue blue sky. My dream of 'just being', with somebody who was totally into me, realised at last - after 57 years! The most romantic day of my life was completed with drinks and walks, arms around each other, sun setting across the river and fishing boats of Topsham.

Ben arrived for another few days of surreal Mediterranean Wydemeet weather, as life geared up for Faye's and my return trip to Ibiza; and for the final demise of my beloved Panda - the most wonderful horse that I have ever met, let alone had the privilege to own. I had thought long and hard as to how this should best be carried out, and when.

"We are just prolonging the inevitable," Sashka and I agreed sadly one morning, over coffee and fag. So I arranged for the kind hunt master to come over to shoot her quickly and painlessly; just by a grave dug by a local farmer used to these things. I couldn't cope with the idea of her being torn to bits by hounds, and anyway, she was too full of painkillers for that to be an option. And the idea of carting off and incinerating an entire horse seemed verging on the ludicrous.

Panda is lucky enough to have lived a life free from any kind of unkindness or exploitation. But now she was in pain and no longer the friendly enthusiast that I used to know. The time had definitely come.

I spent the evening in the Forest Inn with Faye, Malcolm's girlfriend, and Sarah, another empathetic friend, while the sad deed was done. Faye tells me that there is now a flat bit of earth where Panda is laid to rest, but I can't bear to go and look. Meanwhile Vegas walks incessantly around the field, neighing forlornly for her best friend of the last three years.

And then I got shirty with Ben.

Why? After all that? I don't really know.

Is it because I have been exhausted, drugged up, and in pain for the past month? Or, more sinisterly, because I have grown so used to my own company, independence, and space over the past eight years, that I find the presence of someone new invading my home a source of irritation?

Does this mean that I am doomed to be a single mother, alone, for the rest of my life, out of choice? That over all these years, I have moved on, become set in my ways, learning to love my empty, directionless, lonely life, my endless quest for love having become self-defeating?

I am now lying on a sunbed in my favourite place in the world, back again at the wonderful Cas Pla; typing away under stormy skies - a healthy tan already acquired on Dartmoor - still not recovered from my fall; now suffering from acute tonsillitis, wondering about all these things.

What next will my poor knackered body fall victim to?

How will I feel on my return? Revitalised? Refreshed? Full of apology for my unkindness to Ben? Or resigned to the fact that I shall be forever on my own?

Sulky Teenagers
24/7/2017

You're not allowed breakfast, at our posh hotel in Ibiza, til 9am.

That makes me feel better. I always mumble apologetically a bit, when I letting my guests know that they can't have breakfast til after 8.30am.

You can see that the Germans and Dutch don't like my rule, but tough - if they make me get up at 7am every day, seven days a week, for three months, I shall no longer be the charming hostess that I hope I currently am.

In the event, as last year, Faye, and a couple of her friends who are also staying, and I don't have breakfast til 10.45am, just before the staff start clearing up, as my teenagers want to squeeze the last possible zzzzzzzz's out of every morning.

Which means that every day I have a couple of quiet hours to myself, in which to reflect.

I have to say, having visiting friends for Faye has changed the holiday for me. Last year, I so loved having my woman-child daughter to myself, who one minute is jumping off rocks, scuba-diving, hiring 'slippy boats' (pedallos with slides), eating hamburgers off the Kids Menu, and politely asking for a 'Coke Lite'; while the next she is carrying bags for me, locking up the room, navigating, and showing me how the car works.
Faye smiles without stopping, exuding sweetness, gratitude and enthusiasm from every pore.

Whereas I have no idea whether her friends are enjoying themselves or not. We show them our favourite coves and restaurants, yet getting them to chat and smile is a bit like pushing water uphill.

I'm finding it tiring and slightly lonely. I'm missing the exclusive company of my lovely daughter.

My reflection time is resulting in a strong wish to communicate with Ben. So I am. Several times a day, particularly last thing at night with a glass of rose and a fag; while the girls chatter and go to sleep.

He carefully considers everything I say, often replying to me at length, in the early hours of the morning. He is measured and fair and sensible, and I think he must care very much.

Yesterday I read 103 pages of the diary he wrote during his gap-year visit to New Zealand. Clearly during those five months he grew from boy to man. I could feel that he was very like my son Will's less worldlywise, less organised friends, landing in a new country 12,000 miles away from home, with no plans, and nowhere to stay; frightened, overwhelmed, and being rather a nuisance to everybody. Five months later and he was centre of the party!

He also sent some pictures of himself aged 20.

"Woah! Get out the tin of hair dye and a treadmill!" yelled Faye when I showed them to her.

We have been debating how and where next to meet, which was proving so complicated that finally I whatsapped him in order to actually speak to each other. I'm still learning how to use this service - I tried to video the bongo drumming on Benirass Beach for him, but ended up sending pictures of myself filming instead! Our plan is that he will take me out to dinner on Friday at the Peter Tavy Inn - my favourite. He will drive me there too, and basically totally look after me, and treat me like a woman rather than a mate, which is one of the issues that I've been moaning about.

Physically I am still a bit of a mess - I have just started lying on my bruised side, but my ribs hurt too much to swim or sunbathe comfortably, and I am keeping Faye awake from loud snoring due to tonsillitis which I cannot shift. I am hoping that I might finally be feeling myself by Friday!

Hang on to your Fat Tummies!
24/7/2017

I whatsapped my mate, Lindsey, from the Ushuaia Ibiza Beach Hotel, where the plastic stools are too small for our large English bums, the cocktails cost £15 each, there are more waiters than guests, and the music's too loud and doesn't have a tune.

Faye didn't like her £12 banana milkshake which was a bit of waste, because it was made using trendy almond milk and protein powders. Meanwhile my Pina Colada was rather more ice than substance but still - an experience to remember.

I was calling Lindsey because the last time I'd seen her was in a social media'd picture sent to all her friends, of her lying in a hospital bed next to a vast bunch of flowers, looking very happy. I needed to know what this was all about.

It turns out that she's had (non-cancerous she now knows) growths in her stomach and intestine; they operated and ruptured her stomach lining. She's been on a drip for five days but is already up and about organising renting out her coastal Spanish home for £25,000 over the next five weeks.

Our conversation threw up many questions which I couldn't ask over the blaring house music, crashing of the sea waves, and constant aeroplanes coming in and out of Ibiza Airport less than five miles away.

One question is whether these lumps are caused by excessive healthy eating, and/or by no outlets for stress. On the surface, at least, it would Lindsey's is a life remarkably free of stress, as far as I can see. She has the ultimate husband whom all us Exeter girls have known and loved for nearly forty years; two gorgeous, charming children in their twenties, she's solvent, and she doesn't have to do a job, or actually anything much at all. It was her choice to buy various different properties that the two of them can use for urban or rural lifestyles, skiing or sunbathing, according to the season and what they feel like at the time.

Her beautiful, clever, charming daughter, 29 (my goddaughter) has just split up from her boyfriend - a successful, intelligent, responsible man of 30; and gone off treading grapes, backpacking in Thailand, with a 21 year-old spiritualist called Jesus. Instinctively I am appalled. But she was miserable before, losing her confidence and sense of self, feeling that she was letting down the boyfriend by not sticking to a career; and now she is happy. Which means that I am in a muddle.

What is the definition of 'doing nothing'? Is it really 'doing nothing' lying on a beach watching the sun set red, where the sky touches the sea?

Yesterday I completed a quiz in 'Psychologies' magazine, about ambition and what you should be doing with your life. I ticked all the circles, as opposed to the diamonds or triangles, and guess what it said.

"You need a role in which you are constantly befriending new people." Hah!

Perhaps I can put an end to this navel gazing and look forward to greeting my next set of guests with breakfast tomorrow at 8.30am geting back from Ibiza late tonight? I really don't have the answers for everybody else, but B&B-ing is so obviously the perfect role for me!

Weird Ones
1/8/2017

"Why do I always get the weird ones?" whispers Will. "I'll just shut the door."

He had been giving our latest guests tea, earlier, while Faye and I were on our way home from Ibiza.

"One speaks like a man and can't walk, and the other needs a motor to breathe," he continues, "but they're really, really nice."

Faye and I have arrived home at midnight, to discover the house reeking of oil. We have to leave the kitchen door open all night so that the fumes can escape. The Aga has not been mended throughout the week that we have been away, piling through fuel, stinking, meaning we have no hot water in the kitchen or my bedroom; and cooking breakfast for four at once on the Baby Belling is almost impossible.

A £300 new control box is required, apparently, and they 'didn't want to disturb me' to get the go-ahead to buy one during my holiday. Eh? To return to this?! I need the Aga no matter how much it costs! Just a simple text would have sufficed!

Our two guests are utterly delightful. They met during a white rafting holiday and have booked a trip on a rib in Salcombe for tomorrow.

One missed the polio jab by a month, back in 1957, contracted the disease as a child, nearly kicked it into touch and now the polio has returned, so she has to use what she describes as a 'crip-chair', in which she is learning to do wheelies; the other has had three sessions of chemo for a problem with the cartilage in her throat. She used to be a professional singer, and now she can hardly breathe, and suffers from an embarrassing, incessant and exhausting cough more typical of an emphysema sufferer.

Meg is mortified because her biro has left a small stain on one of the Victorian balloon chairs. So what? These two are are so friendly, positive, active and determined to enjoy life as far as possible, that I can only smile, and encourage them to experiment with all the stain-removing lotions and potions that they've brought back from their visit to Tavistock.

I am still suffering health and pain-wise, so preparing breakfast remains a challenge. I work in an automated daze.

Meanwhile Ben is staying in Teddington for the week - a trip that was planned ages ago. I am immensely curious as to how our next meeting will turn out, after all our frenzied communications. Hopefully both of us will have recovered our full health by then, and meet each other, finally the real us, firing on all cylinders for the first time almost ever, after a full two week break.

Weirder Ones
1/8/2017

"Have you got another room where I can stay and lock out my daughter?" enquires the little old lady sitting at my kitchen table at midnight, contemplating a cup of tea and piece of shortbread.

Ben and I have just returned from our dinner at the Peter Tavy, during which he made me feel spoiled and loved and cherished. They put us in a dark little corner, and we were the last to leave. We are both very happy.

The little lady retires gratefully to the tip that is Faye's room, and I give her a huge hug. I cannot imagine anything worse than being afraid of your own daughter.

Ben and I are about to go up ourselves when a head pops around the kitchen door. It's the daughter.

"Is there a key so I can lock out my mother?" she asks. I give her the key and the next thing I know she is yelling at her mother at the top her voice through Faye's door.

"Do you realise we're all walking around on eggshells trying to please you? I have other guests here!" I hiss at her. She threatens to leave. Let her. I don't really care one way or another.

I hardly sleep and get cramp in my thigh as I worry that she might be armed. Then I think of a friend of mine who is classified Aspergers, who has thrown heavy things at her lovely mother from time to time. She would be most unlikely to attack me.

Added to which, I am most unused to sharing my titchy room with a big bloke; but I am particularly glad that he is here in the circumstances!

In the morning the mad daughter's car is gone, and, with some relief, I prepare breakfast for two. And then I spy it - she has moved her Mini Cooper so that it's hidden behind some trees, just outside my gate! She and her mother are still here! Oh no! I warn my lovely existing guests - they're from Essex, most of my favourite guests have been from Essex - of what they might be about to encounter over their Double Full English.

In the event, however, all is calm, and the daughter gives me a very humble and sincere apology.

Clearing her room that day and the next, I find her bin is full of tissues; and her face and eyes swollen. Both mother and daughter appear settled when the time comes for them to leave, and I hug them both. "You need a big dose of TLC, you two," I murmur. I wonder what has caused such intense sadness, and hope that we have managed to make both of their lives a little happier over their 48-hour Wydemeet sojourn.

Apparently the weather over the weekend has been terrible, but I have been having just such the most wonderful time with Ben that I didn't notice. We spent a couple of hours in the pouring rain in the hot tub at midnight on Saturday, I seem to remember. And today he has reprised his own B&B bed-making skills, helping me prepare rooms for tomorrow, so that I can get off to Kent to buy a replacement-horse for Cranky. It is very difficult to imagine how I would have managed this on my own, as I hobble around, half-dead from lack of sleep and a thick, unrelenting cold.

Sleepless in Hexworthy
1/8/2017

I am dead. How can a mere cold take one so low? Combine it with recurrent cystitis and I am a walking zombie attempting to buy a new horse in Kent. Ouch!

We came by train, so that I didn't crash our car by literally passing out at the wheel.

Riding the various horses on offer wasn't as uncomfortable as I had feared, although I felt it afterwards. We found the perfect one almost straightaway though, I think/hope. It is that rarest of beasts: a normal Irish mare.

A bit common, a bit lazy, a bit bland, but does the job, safely. Well that's the idea anyway! Bringing a new four-legged member into the family is the most enormous decision and commitment.

Meanwhile, trying to cook breakfast on the still broken Aga (what do I do? It's been 2 1/2 weeks now and lovely Gary appears to have stopped answering my desperate calls, and the other local Aga man is on holiday until the end of the week) when I'm coughing, sneezing and blowing my nose without pause, walking around in a daze of sleeplessness, is horrendous, and must be utterly disgusting for my lovely young guests (both aged just 19).

I am beginning to long for a day when I finally feel properly healthy. My ears are so blocked up that I can hear my pulse beating against the wax! I have gone back to bed before my next guests arrive, due teatime. Thank Sashka for having already prepared their bedroom!

Little by Little
6/8/2017

Why had I been so horrid to Ben, those three weeks ago?

He wanted to know, and I tried to explain. My email to him had gone for the jugular. Everything always sounds worse when you see it in writing. I was expecting a "Well Just Go Fuck Yourself" as a reply, not a long, respectful, thoughtful and considered one.

Ever since then, though, things between us have been wonderful. A couple of days ago he drove my Mum, Faye and me to the pub for lunch, ordered it and paid for us all, and I finally began to feel properly looked after by a real bloke, for about the first time in my life. I think he is enjoying opening doors for me and generally assuming the manly role. His quiet help with the B&B has halved the time it has been taking me, thereby doubling how long we can spend together; and the other night, shock horror! He beat me at Boggle! Nobody ever beats me at Boggle! Faye (15) beat me too! Am I suffering from early onset dementia?

Then Faye read the instructions and we discovered we had been using the wrong egg-timer. The genuine proper Boggle-one takes three minutes. Ours took only one.

Time for a re-run. Four games later, and Faye and I have scored 21 1/2; and Ben 20 1/2. He is so horrified at being outdone by the girls that he can't sleep!

Can it really go on like this? I think when they make you promise to love honour and obey til death do you part, it's nonsense. You can't control what you think and whether you will love someone forever. So I'm not promising anything.

He's coming back on Tuesday, when he'll meet Will, and only after that will I dare invite him to Sunday lunch at my sister's; and to join Faye and me for a couple of days, during a re-run of the week we planned last year, in The New Forest.

The most frightening date is September 9th - the day of my sister's grand party for 350 guests, celebrating: her 60th; her husband's 50th; their 25th wedding anniversary; and both of their children's 21st's. Should Ben come with me? It would be almost like announcing our engagement to all the people I've known since I was born!

Back to Normality
6/8/2017

I might have to mow the lawn today.

I have now been under the weather for two months - since early June when I first met Ben. He, meanwhile, suffered four weeks of some totally debilitating extreme virus, leaving him feeling ill and unable to swallow. Only now am I getting a real sense of how serious it was, because recently, upon recovery, he has changed into a very different, jolly, chatty, happy, smiley, energetic person.

I am still gurgling and spluttering snot throughout breakfast preparation, and retiring to bed the minute I get the chance to sneak off; but my body has announced that I can no longer expect everybody else around me to mow my 'lawn' for me. My ribs appear mended, and although my hip is still bruised, I cannot claim that it is really stopping me from doing anything.

So perhaps a glimpse of good health is glimmering around the corner? Will Ben like the upbeat, irreverent, bossy, opinionated, and strident me, as much as the quieter, gentler, sweeter, more subdued and vulnerable version?

Poisoned
21/8/2017

It would appear that I have been being slowly poisoned since early June.

But now I've finally sussed out how and why - hah! Watch out world! Ben is about to meet the real me!

I've been feeling normal again, now, for four whole days!

The little room I use when B&Bers are here is above the Aga, which has been splurging out fumes all summer. Returning from a magical week in The New Forest, and no longer inured to the the pong, I discover that the entire house reeks of oil! I am not terribly grateful to my old friend Gary for simply leaving me in this predicament ad infinitum.

That, combined with some slow-release antibiotic called 'Nitrofurantoin', which I've been on for a month, and which should be taken in the evening, not the morning, according to the accompanying little leaflet that I've finally actually read. It would appear I've been suffering from every possible side-effect listed in the thing: itchiness, drowsiness, permanent cough, permanent cold etc etc etc. I wonder why it makes such a difference what time of day you take the tiny little tablet? I couldn't understand why my horrible cold just wouldn't shift! But now I'm taking my daily pill in the evening, I'm feeling great at last!

So I'm sitting here, with every door and window open, feeling really quite good. Although I've got a juddery eyelid, just thinking about all the things that I've got to do today to get the house back to normal after a week's rental.

Tonight is the first night I've been on my own that I can remember.

Yesterday, en route home, I dropped each child off for various parties, the five hour journey, complete with two horses and a dog, taking in a B-road which winds all the way from Ringwood to Wincanton. We dropped Will off at a garage in Shaftesbury which offers both Subway and KFC, where he was being collected by his mate on a tandem bicycle; and Faye was picked up by Angela's Mum from the coach park in Exeter Services.

Faye is going to her first festival today, for which I've made her pay the £97 entry fee out of her earnings from working in the Forest Inn over Christmas. I wonder which her drug of choice will be? My niece defended her haul of alcohol spotted by her parents as she set off for Boomtown with: "You should be glad I don't take drugs, so I get drunk instead."

Uninterrupted croissant in bed in the morning, and the option to watch whatever I like on telly. "The Lady In A Van" as it turns out. I have warmed to Alan Bennett.

I'm mentally doing the sums as to whether it's really worth renting out the whole house, with all the upheaval involved, or whether we should just continue B&Bing throughout the summer. My conclusion, as ever, is to raise the price. So next year it will be £2,950 for a week; and I will richly reward Sashka for doing all the work, and the children for doing their bit, so that hopefully everybody is pleased with the arrangement.

Meanwhile at last I have some energy back, to face a pile of washing the height of Everest; and to lug down Tesco crate after crate of old bottles and tins and potions that Sashka deems too grotty to be left in cupboards and seen even by Airbnb guests - whose expectations of clinically clean rental accommodation appear to be so much lower than people coming via the normal rental agents. Yet the unique Airbnb arrangement of both guest and host contributing to the commission charged, means they probably end up paying more, rather than less, for the same thing! Clever old Airbnb!

Happy Days
26/8/2017

Is it the ibuprofen, Cava, massage machine, hot tub, or simply the warmth of the sunshine on my face? Or maybe it's my new bloke?

Whatever - I'm feeling unusually happy today. Even though, as has been the case almost every day this summer, I'm suffering from yet another physical complaint.

Today's niggle is a cricked neck. I've managed breakfast and clearing up very slowly (so that's £265 earned just this morning, who's complaining?), but afterwards doing anything else has felt impossible.

And now the sun has emerged. On an August Bank Holiday Saturday! Eh? What's going on? It always rains on Bank Holidays!

I struggle with lying in bed doing nothing, but sunbathing doing nothing is quite different!

So here I am, sitting in a deckchair, tap tap tapping away on my laptop, sweat dripping onto the keyboard, having enjoyed a hot, hot tub with Faye, while all my guests are out for the rest of the day.

This month I have made the most ridiculous amount of money - turnover probably roughly equates to the salary of an MD of a small company; yet I've been on holiday for eight days, and spent much of the rest of the time sitting on my arse.

'Wilf's Cabin', in remotest New Forest, is about as far from a pint of milk as is Wydemeet. Nestled in a glade, in deepest forest, any noise you make echoes around its pristine little paddock. The place is a private, windless, peaceful sun trap and I love it.

I had forgotten how much time it takes to look after a horse properly. During our week away, we had to give our mares food, hay and water every day - mountains of the stuff! And pick up their poo off the field as well as grooming them and changing their rugs and everything. Two horses do nearly twenty poos every day - more than an entire (extremely heavy) wheelbarrow-full!

We had a night's break at my sister's to be sure of finding out Will's A'level results at 7am sharp on August 17th; via her reliable internet connection, with her landline to hand in case of emergency.

I had a sleepless night worrying that if my beloved son failed to achieve his demanding offer from Leeds, his entire life would be changed.

My bedroom door creaked open at 7.20am, he put his head around it, and announced gloomily, "I got a B.

"And an A

"And an A*!!!!!"

So, jubilant, we went back to sleep, and ultimately back to the Cabin, where our little family celebrated the future success of Will's life with Tesco's Cava and some pink Shloer.

On a B&B note I was dead chuffed to receive an email from the Cabin's owners on our return home, thanking us for leaving it so clean and tidy. Moi? Lady Muck? How did I achieve that?!

Prior to our New Forest week, Ben did come to my sister's holiday cottage/mansion for lunch. It's tricky introducing a new partner to friends and family when you're as old as we are. What's really of interest to my lot is cramming as much shared gossip/familial updating as possible into a precious few shared hours, as opposed to making polite small-talk with somebody you may well never see again.

Ben didn't obviously fit in - he wouldn't be seen dead in beige chinos and blazer. He prefers sloppy old maroon t-shirt, and ill-fitting trousers hanging from his slightly large tum; finished off with not very clean black leather lace-up shoes that, at school, we used to refer to as 'foreskins'.

Am I over-sensitive and self-conscious? Should I try to change him in order to work better with my familiar world, or simply accept that he is a lovely, kind, smiley friendly bloke, and my gang will appreciate him as they find him?

I have decided that I will attend my sister's forthcoming party for 350 dearest oldest friends alone.

And have invited Ben to join me for the second half of a week's holiday I've got planned in Cyprus with a large group of very best mates, once we've all had a chance to chew the cud and are anxious and hungry to discuss something fresh.

I'd go potty if I had to spend all day every day for weeks on end with my closest friends chosen over fifty years, so why would I want to with someone new?

Perhaps I have spent too long on my own. How lucky that Sidmouth, where Ben lives, is less than an hour away! We have such lovely times together! And then we go back to our separate homes to recover.

Vom
12/9/2017

A stark naked strange man stood in front of me.

"Excuse me, I need the bathroom rather urgently," I stammered.

The man vanished into the small bedroom behind him, while I ran across the landing and into our shared bathroom, with its narrow, latched wooden door and - oh no - no air freshener! Worse still (my mission accomplished), I couldn't open the window!

Whoever he was would have heard that I'd finished through our thin, ill-fitting doors, and immediately re-emerged from his room, this time with a towel wrapped around his waist.

He was dark and tall, still in the excellent body that I had glimpsed previously.

"Sorry - I haven't left it very nice for you," I muttered.

"Doesn't matter, I just need a quick shower as I'm off to Hyde Park for Take That, Blondie and James Blunt, in the rain," he explained, and whizzed into the bathroom through the door behind me.

A couple of hours later and urgh!! Three times, pink, with yellow bits in, tasting of sweet cranberry. A very cleverly designed bathroom where you could be sick into a basin with the plug out, while still sitting on the loo.

What a relief!

This was the result of dancing til 4.30am at my sister's party, refreshing myself between numbers with pink cocktails made with gin.

I returned to my car when 'September' came around the second time (ie the dance tape was obviously on a re-run – but now through silent disco headphones) to check my alcohol levels. Bleep bleep bleep! warned my breathalyser. 0.09. Oh dear. Mustn't drive. I hailed one of the fleet of minibuses which successfully poured me back to my lovely cosy squeaky-clean Airbnb cottage up the road.

Back to the 'tented village' of the previous night's festivities, this time to attend lunch for 80 long-suffering neighbours, and older and younger relations who hadn't been invited to the dance.
Ah ha! A new party game! Pass the breathalyser!

"Guess who's still the most pissed?" I demanded of my sister when she came to visit our table. My niece, who hadn't drunk a drop since 6am, was still 0.06; Will, who was also on the pear juice by now, measured 0.05;

Faye (my darling good little daughter) measured 0; my sister - the perfect hostess - also measured 0; after three glasses of wine over lunch, assisted by my earlier activities I came in at 0.02; and then, oddest of all, the breathalyser started bleeping furiously as my civilised, thin, fit girlfriend Ann measured 0.09; followed by her big strong husband, who had just downed a further two glasses of wine, measuring 0. So the moral of the story is - everybody processes alcohol at very, very different rates! Beware!

Early Onset
12/9/2017

"So sorry to disturb you - I've just got back from a party," I said, bursting into my B&B guests' room at about 10pm, hoping that they would be wanting to order a late breakfast the next day.

"Oh - we got married today," they replied.

"Wow! Was it a good party?" I replied. "Mine was amazing! It was in this huge marquee blah blah blah..."

AAAAAAAAAAAAGGGGGGGGGGGHHHHHHHHHHHHHHHH!!!!!

If only I could re-live those five minutes! What was I thinking of? I had completely forgotten they were spending their first night of married bliss at my home! Having been away from Wydemeet for three days, before leaving I had failed to read my notes on this couple, and entirely neglected to give them an appropriate romantic Wydemeet Well Done Welcome! I wondered why their car, parked outside the house, was covered in sawdust!

Sometimes I could kill myself. I hardly slept later that night, despite being utterly exhausted after the party, the vomming, the special lunch and a three hour drive home in the rain, accompanied by a rather elderly Blondie singing live, quite badly on Radio 2. She is past it if you ask me.

My inspiration, to make up for my poor behaviour, was to present the happy couple with a bottle of champagne, complete with ribbon around its neck, over breakfast, and to talk a lot about their ceremony, and beg to see the pictures, the wedding dress, the wedding wellies and to help carry all their pressies still in beautiful gift bags, down to their car.

Did I get away with it? I don't think so. They didn't write in the Visitors' Book.

Shitty 50
21/9/2017

Shit happens at 50.

Marriages appear to be falling apart all around me, as quickly as are my kitchen chairs. Mostly affecting people turning 50 (my chairs are turning 10).

On first impressions, you might not feel so sad for my girl-friends. Two of them are sitting on assets running into a couple of million or more - big houses, children at private school, estates, 4x4s, horses etc, while a third owns a hotel.

But.

None of them has any cash.

All of their husbands, who remain resolutely in denial that everything will get split 50:50 in the end, were immediately gobbled up by younger versions of their erstwhile wives, and have turned the children against their Mums, while taking a stranglehold on the family finances.

My mates, meanwhile, are distraught, living in limbo-land, hand-to-mouth, taking out terrifying loans with which to pay their solicitors, and being forced into expensive and very upsetting court-proceedings to ensure things get sorted out. As a result their legal bills are heading for many unnecessary tens of thousands.

My suspicion is that, unacknowledged by anybody, these women have endured years of mild abuse within their marriages, and at 50 they've finally flipped and done something really stupid. Resulting in a very bleak future.

I hope I can help a bit, as I feel I'm finally emerging into the light, on the other side.

Lucky Moi
2/10/2017

I'm lying in bed naked, sipping chilled champagne, in a five star hotel, looking out over three miles of deserted sandy beach and surf. It's my birthday, and I'm being 58. I don't think I'll forget this one in a hurry!

Ben has booked us in for two luxurious nights. He's been planning this for weeks and has thought of everything - even down to smuggling in my favourite salt'n'vinegar Hula Hoops!

I had really thought nothing like this would ever happen to me again - yet here I am!

Meanwhile my B&B is running highly efficiently and profitably, and I am beginning to worry that I don't have enough to worry about.

Four months of almost non-stop breakfasts behind me, and now only the weekends are booked. I can enjoy my posh rooms myself, and with nothing to get up for, I can stay the whole day in bed if I feel like it.

Don't take all this for granted. Don't take all this for granted. Don't take all this for granted. That is my mantra of today.

He's Getting Re-married on Friday!
2/10/2017

"I think you should invite me to the wedding, and I'll make sure I'm busy, preferably abroad," I responded, when he told me he was getting married again.

Well he hasn't asked me, but I have made sure that I'm busy abroad.

"Christabel - can I visit you on October 6th?" I called up my best mate with her beautiful massive great villa in Cyprus, on top of the next door hill to one owned by Roman Abramovich's nephew (only Christabel's is bigger). I fled to her five days after my marital bust-up eight years ago, and after my return last year, she is becoming used to taking me under her protective wing.

"Aida and Frank will be there then, I'll just have to check that's OK with them," Christabel replied.

Well the upshot is that next Friday, twelve of my favourite people in the world, including Ben, will all be staying at Christabel's, and we'll probably be toasting Ex and his new bride. I doubt I will be feeling particularly sad.

Big big big big Mistake
14/10/2017

"Enjoy married life with him," I spat; and roared off in a cloud of fumes and dust, in my John Player Special truck.

I don't remember being so angry for literally years. I hardly ever get really angry anymore. I was still raging an hour later when I reached the kitchen and checked the map.

Ah. Perhaps his suggestions for where we should meet and where he should take Faye out for dinner before returning her to school weren't quite so stupid as I'd thought. Even though he still hadn't been 100% sensible.

Time to eat humble pie. I emailed him an 80% apology straight away. And sat. And waited. One week... two weeks - no acknowledgement.

"Dear Mary

Thank you so much for taking the trouble to write and apologise for your unwarranted outburst. I know how difficult it is for you to admit you might be wrong sometimes; and I, of course, could have thought a bit harder about how to minimise the inconvenience I was putting you to.

Love from Ex"

Well I thought of sending the above to him in my sarcastic way; but forced myself to remember that such an action would be childish, so instead I sent:

"Dear Ex

I am very sad that you haven't taken the trouble even to acknowledge my apology, blah blah blah.."

Still no response. So I asked Faye for Ex's fiancee's email address and wrote:

"I am so sorry re my outburst. I should never ever have said it. Wash my mouth out with soap.

"The one thing to come out of this is that Faye, who has never seen me lose my temper in all of her 15 years, has now found out for herself, first hand, that her Dad is much better suited to you than to me."

Fiancee responded immediately with a charming and generous reply. The results of all of the above are:

- when best friends say he and I weren't suited I finally understand them. Nobody at all anywhere in the world exasperates me like he always has and still does

- she can now easily understand why he couldn't stand living with me, even though I am really nice

- any friendship I thought I may have had with him is entirely false, as my two emails to him continue unaddressed

- her family will have some justification to perceive me as some kind of a monster

- there will be a shadow over the happiness of their marriage, as the part I play within it continues unresolved

- Faye can finally understand why her Dad felt he had to leave her much-loved Mum

I am kicking myself.

Struck Dumb
14/10/2017

"So what's your relationship with the bride and groom?" Audrey's next door dining companion politely enquired.

"I'm his ex's best mate," she sniggered.

The bloke was so surprised that he couldn't think of a response. If the monster ex is so bad as to drive away this lovely husband and father, how come her best mate could remain friends enough with both, to make it onto the wedding invitation list? And be allowed, by the horrible ex, to accept? And still remain best friends?

He pulled himself together and asked,

"So what's he really like - this new bloke that we're letting into our family?"

Well-trained by me, Audrey replied, smooth as 3 in 1 bicycle oil, "Oh didn't you know? He's world class."

Restful Holiday
14/10/2017

"It was lovely, wasn't it, to see them looking so very much in love together, just as you said in your speech," continued the Voice Text on my answerphone; as Will's godfather sent him an enthusiastic and congratulatory long message, oblivious to the fact that the number he had sent it to was actually my personal BT landline.

So this was the answerphone message I received on my return home from my Cyprus get-away-from-it-all little holiday.

I had been away for nine days, during which time Ex had re-married; Sashka had suffered the 'Week from Hell' whilst overseeing Wydemeet and its B&B customers; and National Express had gone off with my suitcase.

The lady at the National Express's deepest darkest Heathrow depot uncharmingly insisted that 'friends and family' should, at some stage, collect my 23kg suitcase, full of my entire life, and bring it to me personally – the coach driver having driven off with it, straight past me screaming and shouting and jumping up and down in front of him in the middle of the carpark of Woking Railway Station, 12 hrs earlier at midnight Cyprus-time.

The lack of my suitcase meant the lack of laptop charger, which meant I missed Dr Foster on catch-up, because my newly installed Smart TV doesn't appear to have any internet connection, and without the laptop I can't use 'chromecast'; and I couldn't use chromecast off my mobile as it doesn't seem to have sufficient memory to carry the programme, or the app, or whatever it's called.

So here I am, back from the most blissful holiday of doing nothing but eat, drink, sit in the sun and chat to my best friends of 35 years; sleep deprived, with a line of cold sores along my lower lip; and a throbbing headache.

Week from Hell
19/10/2017

"Can you ring me NOW!!" screamed the text from Sashka. She'd sent it at lunchtime. Now the sun was just about over the yardarm (whatever that means). "South West Power has turned the electricity off all day, and we can't open the gate!"

Oh dear. I had been warned about the power cut, but hadn't been too concerned about it because Sashka could cook the B&Bers breakfasts on the oil-fueled Aga, and then they would be out for the rest of the day, while the second lot weren't due to arrive til the power was turned back on.

Well - too late for me to do anything about it now. I expect she got Neighbour to take the gate off its hinges.

"I have had the Week From Hell!" texted Sashka, as I was due to return.

"Now you know that it's not all roses, being Lady Muck of Wydemeet," I smugly and cheerfully replied.

Over coffee and a fag, a couple of days later and just about recovered, Sashka is laughingly recounting her ordeals.

The day I left for Cyprus, edible John the new plumber had arrived to replace the neutraliser in the water system. A pipe burst, nobody knew where to turn the water off, and the entire ground floor was flooded, just as the first set of B&Bers was due to arrive.

Three days later, the power now turned off for the day, not only can't our guests get out through the gate to their riding lesson, they aren't able to lift their enormous young Rhodesian Ridgeback over the gate.

And then - utter disasaster: THE MACERATOR!!!! Of course! I had totally overlooked that! If I had remembered the likely consequences of a power cut on the macerator, I would probably have flown straight home and collapsed in a nervous breakdown.

The water is pouring out over the top of the loo, recounts Sashka, flooding through the brand new carpet, and snaking its way through the ceiling and down the flex of the hallway's main light-fitting.

Ever-resourceful, Sashka removes the dripping lightbulb, before the power comes back on again and there's an explosion; erects table lamps throughout the hallway instead, and together with her ever-patient Rhodesian-Ridgeback-owning guests, mops up the mess.

Neighbour unscrews the electric arm of the gate, and Sashka flees home to her parents and partner for a cry and a couple of very stiff gins.

Two days later, and the vet is due to arrive, to give our new horse, Diamond, a booster tetanus jab, while Sashka is preparing breakfast for her fourth set of guests,

Just as the eggs are white and orange and soft and ready to be served, there's a cacophony raging outside. The horses have escaped into one another's stables and Vegas is kicking the crap out of Diamond, who has smashed through my grooming kit, and is covered in blood running from her neck, chest and head.

Hmmm. Perhaps "Week From Hell" just about sums it up. Whatever - it is quite clear from all subsequent comments that my B&Bers have just loved their stays! Very well done and thank you Sashka! Phew!

Pedantic Grammar
19/10/2017

"I have been seeing the same bloke for four months now. He is very kind and nice, and seems to fit in with my life and mates very well," I inform Sir James - my charming, funny, clever conman online date, with whom I'm still in touch despite the fact that he appears to struggle with the difference between truth and fiction.

"Can you please clarify that sentence. Which is it, or is it both ?!!!" is his response.

Slurp!
19/10/2017

It's nearly midnight. I'm in dressing gown and pyjamas. The light still glows under the bedroom door of the good-looking 16 year-old German boy who is staying in my Dartmeet Room tonight.

Tentatively, I tap.

"Yah?" I hear. I ease open the door and whisper,

"Would you like an adventure?"

"Hmmmmm?" he says.

"How do you feel about spiders?" I continue.

"I'm scared of them," he responds.

"How would you like to see Twiglet eat one?" I persevere. "It's in my bedroom..."

Well - what else was I supposed to do? I couldn't possibly sleep in there, with a six inch brown spider glaring at me from on top of the curtain rail. I had already tried perching Twiglet on the dressing table below to jump up at it, but all he did was slide around and scratch the mahogany surface, like 'Dancing On Ice'.

I arm Armin with a pink feather duster attached to the end of a bamboo stick, while I stand on the other end of my double bed - I couldn't possibly get so near to the thing. 'Flick'! THUD!!!! The spider lands on the carpet.

"Quick Twiglet!!" I cry.

"Slurp!" and it's gone.

Armin retires back to bed, and I wonder how I'm going to explain what has happened to his non-English-speaking mother, who's paid over £500 for a peaceful two-night stay for herself and her innocent young son.

Not Missing You?
19/10/2017

Why would anyone want to share a house with anybody else 24/7/365 if they didn't have to - unless they were still bringing up their children together?

I have known my best mates from university for 35 years now. They are top of the pile, selected from everybody else I have ever met before or since. Yet a week of their company, sitting in the sun in Cyprus, was absolutely lovely and quite enough for me. I like having time on my own, doing my own routine thing, as well.

I am quite pleased in a way to be back, all alone, in rainy, dismal Dartmoor, where everything stays where I put it, and I can work within my own rather odd (probably), way of life.

So why should Ben, who has appeared so recently simply out of the ether, be more exciting and interesting to be with, even than my bestest mates of all this time?

Yesterday he arrived for tea and cake; followed by hot tub in the garden as the sun set behind my two beloved hunters chomping on their haylage a stone's throw away; smoked salmon canapes in front of the log fire while Faye sang Beyonce and Les Mizz rather well to us; a choice of four main courses and puddings after my trip earlier to Tesco's on our way home from Fraye's school; and then a couple of rounds of Boggle. Which Faye won, as is now becoming par for the course.

This morning none of us bothered to get up until we'd had two cups of coffee in bed; and I made us all brunch, using Sashka's special "AgaBake O

Glide" non-stick parchment paper thing which is good for eggs; after which Ben departed for his Sidmouth home, and I retired back to bed with my laptop. It's been absolutely lovely. I may not see him again, now, for a week, while his son comes home for the Trinity Conservatoire half term break. I'm not sure yet, whether I'm going to mind this long gap, or not...

Hoist by my own Petard
29/10/2017

The floor is entirely concealed beneath chewed bits of Ex's antique oak chair. Apart from a bit of the carpet, which is adorned with a small, circular dog poo.

"Make yourselves at home!" I had gushed in my welcoming note to my latest guests - as I always do when I'm still out at the swimming pool. "Treat the house as your own! Enjoy tea and cake in the kitchen! Play the piano! Jump in the hot tub!"

And unfortunately, unusually, this particular couple has taken me at my word. So that now one of them is playing the piano in my sitting room, while the other boils the kettle on the Aga in the kitchen, and two dachshunds race around all the ground floor rooms of the house (which now smells as a result of their visit) growling and playing with each other under my feet, and begging for scraps.

Faye and I are tired, and wondering where, when and how to eat. We had been so looking forward to a TV supper in front of Netflix on our new tv, as a special half-term treat. Alas, our guests have shut the sitting-room door and don't retire until 10pm, so we have to make do with real time TV (who watches that anymore?) on the tiny tinny telly in the kitchen, as we tuck into our 'cooks in two minutes' plates of bland pasta.

We have three nights of this cuckoo syndrome. I am going to have to re-word my policies.

At least the stupid dog didn't tuck into the legs of Ex's £3000 card table!

Life Enhancement
30/10/2017

I advertised myself online as a 'life enhancer'. Well it would seem that Ben and I do, indeed, enhance each other's lives.

As it turned out, my brother, who lives on the other side of the country in Suffolk, was visiting Mum, and decided to bring her over to Hexworthy for lunch, so I suggested this might prove the perfect opportunity for Ben and him to meet. Which they did; and they got on well. They are both very decent, kind, gentlemen.

Next, Faye and I decided to see Kingsman 2.

'What an ideal afternoon on which to meet Ben's son!" I thought.

So that's what happened. Ben took us to The Old Firehouse in Exeter for lunch - the perfect quirky venue for our potentially awkward teenager meeting. Followed by a very jolly film.

It would seem that a week apart for Ben and me would definitely be too long!

Ponies and a Swimming Costume
6/11/2017

F*** SH** BU****!!!!!!!!! I scream, and leap out of the hot tub in my swimming costume, in the pitch darkness, illuminated only by the jacuzzi's orange, purple and lime green flashing disco lights, to the horror of my guests, who were quietly walking down the drive on their way for supper at our local pub, with just a head torch to guide them.

I can see the murky moving shadowy forms of wild Dartmoor ponies already through my garden gate, making their way towards the smooth, now dusky grey square of pristine 'lawn' that I have spent so many hours lovingly nurturing throughout the summer months.

I fling a 'fluffy 200 thread-count' white guests' towel around my fat, soaking form, race dripping water on the thick pile carpets through the house, pull some wellies onto my wet feet, and, wielding a 2000+ lumens super-torch, charge out again to grab the automatic gate-opening gadget from inside the car; and on down the drive towards the bewildered guests; Twiglet barking his head off.

I shine my bright beam around the garden, in the sudden silence, and there is a closed gate, Ben with nothing on except his sopping swimming trunks, repairing the new fence that the ponies have broken through, Twiglet our wonder horse-dog who has driven them out, wagging his tail and smiling with pride, and the guests standing blinking by the gate, having closed it after the fleeing ponies.

"When you get to the pub you can tell them that you just saw Mad Mary in the freezing cold dark dead of night, wearing only a wet swimming costume, towel and wellies, rounding up ponies, if you like," I said.

Teenage Coms
6/11/2017

My children enjoy talking to their Dad and to me (I think). Whereas all around me I am seeing other teenagers actively avoiding their parents, let alone communicating with them.

My explanation is this.

When children in functional families are naughty they get told off by both parents together - two big people united in confrontation, looming over one little person.

Whereas single parents and their children have to discuss and negotiate their way through disagreements, equal parties, one to one, avoiding confrontation at all costs, as they have no back-up. And they end up friends.

Project Mary
6/11/2017

It would appear that Ben has been operating 'Project Mary' now, for five months. We met while he was taking a sabbatical after the end of his marriage, and re-appraising his life. So he has decided to use this time to concentrate on me, organising his life around mine. That is a really long time! It feels much shorter! It has been fab! It is *so* absolutely wonderful finally to have somebody to do things with - walk, talk, hot tub, sunbathe, swim, go on holidays, watch X-Factor, eat in, eat out, go to parties, go to school things, go to films and plays etc etc etc...

I really have been so very lonely living all on my own in the back of beyond, without companionship, over all these years.

But.

Now I think that it's time he found a complementary interest. It is hard work being central to somebody else's existence.

I am beginning to feel a bit claustrophobic actually. I really hadn't realised how much I enjoy being on my own at Wydemeet, without feeling responsible for someone else's happiness. Especially when they don't seem to have anything much other than me going on in their lives, and are seemingly available and wanting to be with me wherever, and whenever I click my fingers, everything always being on my terms.

I think I'm needing a bit more excitement, intellectual stimulation (moi? Did I actually write that??!), new adventures, originality, wit, new ideas, disagreements ..... Disagreements??? Ooo-errr. What's going on here?

Stimulation
12/11/2017

"I have got to end this relationship, I'm so sorry," I say. "I just feel it's become too one-sided."

I have finished giving breakfast and saying goodbye to one set of B&Bers, the second couple are out riding my horses, and Faye is still asleep upstairs.

Well. He's not only hurt. He's astonished. He hasn't been expecting this at all. It has come winging its cruel way to him, entirely out of the blue.

"I can feel myself becoming increasingly unpleasant, and I don't like it, and it's only going to get worse," I continue.

"Let's talk about this," he replies, but I can't think of anything more to say, and simply remain sitting at the kitchen table, dumbly gazing at the floor.

So he picks up his suitcase and dogbed, calls his sweet black labrador, and, with a "don't bother to see me off," drives away.
As anticipated, two long emails and a poem arrive at various intervals during the day, but I can't read any of them because my lovely B&B couple is back from riding and stays relaxing with me until teatime, in front of the sitting room fire.

Finally, after they have left for London, I am able to read what he has written properly, and to reply. This time, assuming he is alone to cry if need be, with an opportunity for proper reflection, I tell him the real reason for my decision. That at the end of the day, I simply find our relationship insufficiently stimulating.

Trainers
13/11/2017

"You are one of the least informed people that I have ever met. Just saying something facetious or obnoxious does not make you interesting. Pontificating about stuff is not conversation. Do you have original thought?

You are just completely egocentric.

You are so self obsessed that you don't bother to listen to anyone around you.

I find your obsession with titles rather repulsive.

The only good news for you with B&B is that they probably have not heard all your stories before.

You are often drunk.

I have often thought that I was too good for you.

I was under the assumption that beneath your Ex-obsessed, crusty, cantankerous outer self there lurked a more pleasant and kind person - too many fairy tales read in my youth.

You are 58 and have no obvious muscle definition.

That girl is not particularly fat, but you are. I have never before slept with someone as fat as you.

You are the laziest woman that I have ever slept with.

You seem to think that lying like a sloth is a turn on. It might have been when you were younger and less fat and fitter. But if you lose weight then you will be even more wrinkly.

You are by far the most 'lookist' person I have ever met.

Be careful, because as you lose your looks, you may have nothing left for someone to love about you.

Your hypocrisy is staggering, as is your intolerance.

There is coldness about you that permeates. "

Hmmmm. All I'd said to him was that I wanted to end the relationship because I felt it was too one-sided, and later, in my midnight email, that although I think he has a fine brain, extraordinary memory retention, and is well-informed, I feel he is a lazy thinker (a very polite euphemism for the dreaded, unforgivable 'b'-word). I added that, for me, making love means face to face wrapped up in each other's arms.

I think the underlying problem, though, after all's said and done, is that I simply cannot conduct a serious relationship with someone who wears bright blue trainers for dinner.

Rabbit Rabbit Bunny Rabbit Jabber Jabber
16/11/2017

I waited eight years for him.

And now, after all that, I find I don't want him. Or, I'm beginning to think, actually, anyone.

His actions, after my initial announcement, proved exactly as I predicted - even the timings of them. Three emails on the first day, begging me to reconsider. The immature, idiotic, knee-jerk reaction to my email telling him the real reasons why I wanted to part. An apology the next day at 11am (I'd anticipated it would come before lunch). An 'explanation' the day after that. Coffee yesterday. And an emailed rapprochement this morning. Which said that I am beautiful inside and out. Like my daughter. Well I'm not quite sure about that, but I keep repeating it to myself in my head, and to anybody else who will listen, and I hope we will remain warm, firm friends for the rest of our lives, after such a near-miss.

All served to re-confirm that I have made the right decision. I was finding that I knew what he was going to say before he said it, things which I hadn't said already because I felt they were too obvious and therefore rather dull. So I was becoming increasingly irritable and impatient, and had to knock the thing on the head before I became even nastier. Not really beautiful at all.

I am extraordinarily, surprisingly cheerful, having reached the ultimate conclusion that I am better off manless; and the more middle-aged people I discuss my new epiphany with, the more I find who seem to be rather envious of my situation - single or married. Out hunting yesterday, four of the ladies were discussing their rabbits. Much better than men, they said, although apparently the ears bit tends to snap off with over-vigorous use.

The whole thing has turned out to be a huge eye-opener for me. I believe that lovely Ben is the nicest person I could ever meet through the internet, after my lengthy, endless, dedicated search.

Online dates tend to appear out of the ether, from a totally separate world, and you have to work hard to find things that you have in common with each other. I can often recognise them amongst the couples who come to stay at Wydemeet, as they tend to look a little surprising together. The man is almost always younger than the woman. Less good looking, less well dressed, less charming, less charismatic, less well-spoken, and all-round less interesting. And the woman often pays the bill.

If one's date lives far away, on every occasion that you meet there is immense pressure that your time together should be wonderful, and worth the endless, lengthy, expensive journeys to and fro, as you slowly get to know one another.

In my case, I am lucky enough to live in a pleasure-dome. My home is purpose-built to provide spacious, comfortable, clean, warm, serviced, luxury holiday accommodation, surrounded by stunning romantic moorland and rivers to be explored, horses to ride, hot tub, etc etc. When I have all that, as well as ties such as children and B&B guests, it would have to be something supremely special to tempt me away.

So I am finally, after eight fairly fruitless years, giving up on the whole online dating thing, believing that I'm never going to find anybody for me that way. Boo hoo.

I suppose I could adopt a sheep. But would he/she make me laugh? Otherwise I could invest in a rabbit. But according to my hunting friends, the powerful ones cost fifty quid. And from what they say, it sounds as though I'd break the thing.

So it would seem that I have turned a huge circle, ending back more or less where I started. Enjoy what I have now – what I have spent all these years building up all around me. My lovely, huge, network of local friends. My fabby B&B with it wonderful guests. My great big house where everything finally now works. Our acres of land and beautiful surroundings. No new demanding job; no demanding, distracting bloke tempting me away from it all.

Finally I am poised and ready to properly commit, comfortable in my own skin and in my own company, to truly throw myself 100% into everything that I have built up around myself over the past 22 years, and really make the most of my supremely lucky, privileged, comfortable way of life.

To relax, to 'do it my way'. In my own time. And in my own space.

ADDENDUM

Unpaused
9/12/2017

Oh no! Judy's pressed the unpaused button! I'm back online again!

"I've been missing the funny stories," was her excuse.

"So this is all we're left with" was the strapline of someone living half-an-hour away in Totnes. I laughed and 'favourited' him. Next thing I know his profile has been 'withdrawn' and there is literally nobody left anywhere, on the whole site, that I like the look of. What a waste of £32! I always said no one I'd go for would ever find themselves online.

Ben was there, looking for 'stimulating conversation with an emotionally intelligent woman'. The computer gave us 100% match.

I emailed him to warn him that he'd see my profile popping up, and it was all Judy's fault for pressing the button. "I'll never meet anybody nicer than you through it," I said, "so my heart really isn't in it."

Red rag to a bull. Daily emails back from him, saying 'would this work? would that work?' He was meeting a bio-chemist on Wednesday, but his heart wasn't in it either. He still wanted me.

So I sent him an email expanding on what I'd said last time. "Good bant, in the language of teenage son Will, is what I'm after," I explained. "My gang seek to entertain. We're always looking out for the larfs; for the absurdity, irony, nuance or subtlety of any given situation. Whereas you say it exactly as it is, which is also lovely up to a point. But sometimes we say it as it isn't, for effect," I wrote. "Being 'happy in one's own skin' can lead to complacency," I continued, adding that I am almost certainly the world's best example of that.

Well. OMG. A second tirade of early-hours knee-jerk vitriolic abuse.

"Now I see that I was only ever in lust with you," he rants, forgetting that he has gone on and on about how fat and inert I am in the bedroom department. "Your only redeeming feature is that you appear to have brought up two nice children."

What a shame. I'm not forgiving two of these. He's clearly learned nothing at all, after all that. Five very happy months with me. I am so sad and disappointed to have lost what should have been a very good friend.

AGEING JAMES BOND
12/1/2018

"What are you doing here? Why aren't you at our local?" I blurt, upon walking in on our neighbour who, at last month's carol service, had asked Faye whether Ex's new wife is 'an improvement' on me.

He's lounging on a sofa, right in my path, as I enter 'The Two Bridges' - my venue of choice when meeting blind dates because nobody I know ever goes there.

"I have a seat reserved here at all times," he replies. "Why are you here? Meeting one of your men? Got a room booked upstairs have you?"

I bristle and walk past him to the bar, where a very respectable bloke is waiting, standing tall and straight.

I can't tell you how relieved I am that he isn't some weirdo.

He buys me a Spritzer and himself a pint, and I usher us through to the other room where my neighbour (who, incidentally, refers to the locals as 'peasants') can neither see nor hear us, and explain the situation.

After a couple of hours of excited chat, the waiter brings over some menus, while my date visits the loo.

"Gosh, everything on here looks completely delicious!" I enthuse, my mouth watering at almost every suggestion listed.

"I'm not hungry," he says on his return.

God - that's a first. They're all supposed to love me and to want to stay with me for as long as possible, to wait on me, and to please me! What have I done wrong? Am I too fat? I thought I'd hidden my rolls successfully under my Tesco's voluminous F&F black polo-neck!

He's off 'Giraffe Watching' in Botswana next week. "Not brilliant timing," I mutter.

And he's 68! Blimey - that's nearly 70! But he looks younger than Ben did at 51. He is like an ageing, less flirty, more civilised James Bond - he skis, sails, mountain climbs, motorbikes, reads, visits ruins, listens to Radio 3 etc, and once found himself the boss of a chap he had previously sold a Ferrari to - as a derivatives broker, whatever that is - those ones who earned so much in the 80s.

He has a house in Polzeath next to the new development ('Hurlingham-on-Sea'), where my sister has just bought a time-share. His father was a professional motorbike racer, and he has four cars, including a TR6; but today he's driving his car of choice - a Honda Civic. Hardly James Bond!

This is the first time ever I have felt slightly out of my depth meeting an online date.

When I get home (rather hungry), I email him and tell him so. He still hasn't replied. Oh ho. This bloke, who I would be proud to introduce to anybody, is clearly not going to be pushed around by me. Hurrah! At last! Or else. Eeek! Perhaps he's just not that smitten?

Fingers Crossed!
15/1/2018

"Dear James Bond

I have been wondering and wondering all morning. Would you like to meet up again before you leave for Africa?

I have cancelled my subscription to this stupid site either way.

Love

'M'"

Well eventually he replied saying that he was too busy to do so, 'sadly', but he'd be in touch on his return, the weekend of January 27th.

What am I to make of that, then? I see that he's still logging into Encounters, so I can't be the 'be all and end all', even though I am such good company, so glamorous, woman of substance, ten years younger blah blah blah. How annoying.

Meanwhile I have just been 'favourited' by the Numero Uno of the '20 Most Popular' men on the site! This one is a good-looking army officer and is only 45! How chuffed am I? I 'message' him and tell him so.

Then I change the description of myself on my profile page from 'above average' to 'very attractive'.

I am being taken out for dinner tonight by someone whose username is 'SongWriter'. He has sent me a recording of himself singing along to our school choir's rendition of 'Silent Night' on YouTube, and is threatening to bring along his guitar this evening. Help!